Second Language St[
English-Medium Classrooms

PARENTS' AND TEACHERS' GUIDES

Series Editor: Colin Baker, *Bangor University, UK*

This series provides immediate advice and practical help on topics where parents and teachers frequently seek answers. Each book is written by one or more experts in a style that is highly readable, non-technical and comprehensive. No prior knowledge is assumed: a thorough understanding of a topic is promised after reading the appropriate book.

Full details of all the books in this series and of all our other publications can be found on http://www.multilingual-matters.com, or by writing to Multilingual Matters, St Nicholas House, 31–34 High Street, Bristol BS1 2AW, UK.

PARENTS' AND TEACHERS' GUIDES: 20

Second Language Students in English-Medium Classrooms

A Guide for Teachers in International Schools

Coreen Sears

MULTILINGUAL MATTERS
Bristol • Buffalo • Toronto

Library of Congress Cataloging in Publication Data
Sears, Coreen
Second Language Students in English-Medium Classrooms: A Guide for Teachers in International Schools/Coreen Sears.
Parents' and Teachers' Guides: 20
Includes bibliographical references and index.
1. English language—Study and teaching (Elementary)—Foreign speakers—Handbooks, manuals, etc. 2. Students, Foreign—Handbooks, manuals, etc. 3. Education, Bilingual—Handbooks, manuals, etc. 4. Second language acquisition—Handbooks, manuals, etc. 5. Mainstreaming in education—Handbooks, manuals, etc. I. Title.
PE1128.A2S328 2015
428.0071–dc232014044396

British Library Cataloguing in Publication Data
A catalogue entry for this book is available from the British Library.

ISBN-13: 978-1-78309-328-1 (hbk)
ISBN-13: 978-1-78309-327-4 (pbk)

Multilingual Matters
UK: St Nicholas House, 31–34 High Street, Bristol BS1 2AW, UK.
USA: UTP, 2250 Military Road, Tonawanda, NY 14150, USA.
Canada: UTP, 5201 Dufferin Street, North York, Ontario M3H 5T8, Canada.

Website: www.multilingual-matters.com
Twitter: Multi_Ling_Mat
Facebook: https://www.facebook.com/multilingualmatters
Blog: www.channelviewpublications.wordpress.com

The policy of Multilingual Matters/Channel View Publications is to use papers that are natural, renewable and recyclable products, made from wood grown in sustainable forests. In the manufacturing process of our books, and to further support our policy, preference is given to printers that have FSC and PEFC Chain of Custody certification. The FSC and/or PEFC logos will appear on those books where full certification has been granted to the printer concerned.

Typeset by Techset Composition India (P) Ltd., Bangalore and Chennai, India.
Printed and bound in Great Britain by Short Run Press Ltd.

Contents

Figures and Tables

Figures

Tables

Text Boxes

Acknowledgements

The content of this Handbook is the result of many years of teaching and working within the international school community. During that time I have shared thoughts and ideas with countless colleagues and professional friends about teaching globally mobile students in general and emergent bilingual students in particular. I thank all these people for the wonderfully enriching dialogue that is a feature of life in international schools.

I want also to acknowledge the contribution that the students themselves have made to the ideas set out in this Handbook. Sometimes the voices of the people most concerned in the educational process may be overlooked. In this connection, I owe an enormous debt of gratitude to two people at the University of Bath in the UK. The first is Dr Mary Hayden, Director of the Centre for the Study of Education in an International Context (CEIC). Her support, encouragement and flexible approach enabled me to carry out a substantial research investigation into what emergent bilingual students themselves think about their globally mobile lives and their experiences of international education. The second member of staff at the University of Bath that I wish to thank is Dr Trevor Grimshaw, Director of Studies on the MA TESOL programme. The writing up of my research in the form of three articles published in the *Journal for Research in International Education* was guided and encouraged by Trevor. He himself contributed largely to the co-writing of the first article on the construction and maintenance of identity in globally mobile students and continued to offer much help and support during the writing of the second and third articles which reported on the research itself.

The result of carrying out the larger research enquiry and the later small-scale investigation (described in Appendices A and B of this Handbook) was that I came to feel that my understanding of the reality of the lives of emergent bilingual students and their families was more firmly grounded. I heard from their own mouths about the aspects of the educational experience that they found supportive and effective and the elements that caused unease or anxiety. For these insights I am deeply grateful to the school concerned and to the open-minded and positive response I received from all the students, parents and teachers whom I encountered there.

When it came to the writing of this Handbook, there are further groups of people that I should like to thank. The first group relates to my need to experience at first hand and to keep myself up to date with advances in the use of technology as an integral part of the classroom experience. Among other schemes that allowed this to happen was a visit to the primary school of the International School of Milan where Terry Haywood, the Headmaster of the whole school, made it possible for me to observe the use of embedded technology in action. The visit was a lovely experience with teachers willing to welcome me into their classrooms and eager to discuss their practice in this area. I thank them all and, in particular, Laura Haines who coordinates EAL provision in the school.

A further group that I would wish to mention are the long-standing professional friends and colleagues with whom over the years I have often talked and corresponded and frequently presented and written alongside. I, together with many others in our field, would wish to mention Edna Murphy at the top of this list. Edna has been the instigator of much of the writing that has focused on the education of emergent bilingual students in international schools. As an editor of the *International Schools Journal* and as the editor of and contributor to a number of publications, she has been a consistent voice in advocating a more effective and equitable provision for speakers of other languages in English-medium international schools. Along with Edna I would also like to mention a number of people, many of whom are cited in this book, who have contributed by their work and writing to an understanding of effective practice in the education of emergent bilingual students. These include: Michael Allan, Kevin Bartlett, Frances Beckhechi, Jeffrey Brewster, Maurice Carder, Eithne Gallagher, Ochan Kusuma-Powell, Mary Langford, Patricia Mertin, Richard Pearce, Debra Rader and Caroline Scott, among many, many others.

Lastly, I should mention the role of the publishers and my editor, Colin Baker, in the production of this Handbook. The idea of writing an up-to-date contribution to the and Parents' and Teachers' Guides series came about during a lunch with Tommi Grover, Managing Director of Multilingual Matters. Since then, Colin Baker, a distinguished contributor to the field of bilingualism and bilingual education, has guided me as my editor through the process of writing. Colin wears his expertise and eminence very lightly and is a most tactful and persuasive editor who brings about change for the better by nudging and suggesting rather than diktat. His approach results in a sense for the author of being part of a shared project rather than a lone contributor working in isolation. I truly thank him for his kindness and encouragement. Thanks, too, should go to Sarah and the team at Multilingual Matters for their work on the technical side of publishing and promoting the Handbook.

I cannot finish without mentioning the part played by David Sears in this and all my endeavours. His encouragement, practical common sense and humour have provided the supportive background to my projects through the years. I thank him for his cheerful support and his belief in the value of making a worthwhile contribution in whatever field we are called to work.

Coreen Sears

Introduction

The Overall Aim of This Handbook

This Handbook is for teachers working in international schools. The overall aim is to offer general information and practical suggestions for creating a rich and positive educational experience for emergent bilingual students being educated in an English-medium international school classroom. The reason for producing a Handbook such as this arises from conversations and emails with teachers. On numerous occasions I have been told that teachers in international schools desperately need help and practical support in providing a positive educational experience for all the students in their classrooms. These are teachers of classes where students display the widest possible variety of personal linguistic and cultural diversity, may have had multiple prior educational experiences as a result of their global mobility, and where the classroom contains students at every point on the English-language learning continuum. It is not surprising that teachers in international schools where such classes are the norm have expressed a need for a practical manual that focuses entirely on their particular situation.

The profile of 'emergent bilingual students'

The use of the term 'emergent bilingual' to describe students from a range of linguistic and cultural backgrounds who are being educated in English-medium classrooms is relatively recent. It is part of the move to emphasise the importance to these students of their continuing development in all the languages in their repertoire. Even where teachers only interact with such students in the part of their lives that is spent in an English-medium environment, it is vital to appreciate the necessity and value to these students of achieving their potential in order to become proficient users of two or more languages. When students are described as emergent bilinguals it keeps this fact in mind and influences the teaching and learning decisions that teachers make in their classrooms.

Target readership

The target readership is primarily teachers who are new to international education and international schools. However, judging by the response to my first Handbook (1998), more experienced teachers, curriculum and literacy coordinators, librarians and school leaders as a whole also found it very useful in enhancing their work with emergent bilingual students. A further aim of this Handbook is its potential use as a framework for professional development and in-service training among teacher colleagues. The content overall is designed to make sense as a whole or to be used in small portions, whichever is most useful. Finally, the extensive Resources sections contain numerous links and references that should allow teachers to explore topics further in response to the needs of students in their classrooms and their own interests.

Changes in International Schools and International Education

This Handbook follows upon an earlier publication (1998) which addressed the challenges that were then typically found in international school classrooms. By that date, the international school movement was well established, with some of the earliest schools such as the International School of Geneva and the International School of Yokohama having functioned in various forms since the 1920s. By the 1990s, there were around 1000 schools that called themselves international, with a rapid increase in numbers towards the end of that decade (Hayden, 2006).

The chief reason for another Handbook is that so many aspects of international education and international schools have changed in the last 15 years or so since the first Handbook was published. The numbers of schools describing themselves as international has increased and they now take a wider variety of forms. At the time of writing, according to statistical information provided by the International School Consultancy Group (ISC) (www.iscresearch.com), there are estimated to be around 7000 English-medium schools world-wide that describe themselves as international, along with around 2000 schools that offer International Baccalaureate (IB) programmes (www.ibo. org). A major cause of this increase is the unstoppable trend towards globalisation (and the associated increase in the use of English as an international language). This has meant that many parents are anxious to equip their children for a life that looks rather different from when they themselves went to school.

The increase in numbers of international schools applies both to the schools that serve a globally mobile population of families and to the schools that largely serve local children from the community in which the school is situated. Among the schools that serve local communities there is a trend towards offering programmes of study in both English and the local language(s). Schools of this type offer either a balanced bilingual programme in both languages or extensive language teaching and other studies in the language of the local community. In schools of this type up to 95% of the students may have a home or primary language that is other than English.

Schools that cater for globally mobile students

There remain a large number of international schools that cater almost exclusively for the globally mobile children of parents who move around the world to take up new employment assignments. The group of people who move globally in the course of their employment has grown in number and now it is a common feature in the careers of senior personnel all over the world for them to relocate to new countries and continents. The families who move globally represent the widest possible range of national, cultural and linguistic diversity. This has led to a large increase in the percentage of students in English-medium classrooms in international schools who come from diverse linguistic and cultural backgrounds. In the 1990s it was common to find up to 75% of students in international schools speaking English as a home or primary language. Now, the profile of student bodies in international schools is often quite different. In many schools it is common to find up to 75–80% of students coming from diverse linguistic and cultural backgrounds and with different home or primary languages.

Thus the average classroom displays a much greater diversity than was previously the case in many schools (and certainly since I wrote the first Handbook). It is now no longer possible to think of emergent bilingual students as being in some way unusual or different from the mainstream student body, a view that was prevalent when there were perhaps only 10% or 15% of such students in a class of largely first language English speakers. These students now themselves comprise the mainstream and teachers need to be prepared for the challenges and opportunities of classrooms where students' experiences are so rich and varied.

Three Significant Trends in the World of International Education

Apart from the rapid and continuing increase in the numbers of international schools and the overall rise in the numbers of emergent bilingual students in most classrooms, three further aspects of teaching and learning have become increasingly established features in the world of international education. Each area has a potential impact on the experience of emergent bilinguals in international schools; learning how to engage with these changes in the most effective way is an essential part of a teacher's task in the classroom.

The expansion of programmes and curricula specifically designed for international schools

The continuing spread of programmes of study and curricula created specifically for schools that offer an international education is now an established trend in international education. The International Baccalaureate Organisation (IBO) (www.ibo.

org) is one of the major providers and its Primary Years and Middle Years programmes (www.ibo.org/pyp; www.ibo.org/myp), as well as the universally recognised IB Diploma programme with its recently established Career-related Certificate (www.ibo.org/ibcc) are now offered in many international schools of all types. Curricula such as the International Primary Curriculum (www.greatlearning.com/ipc) and the very recent Middle Years Curriculum are also increasing their spread across the sector. One of my aims in this Handbook is to explain the workings of these programmes and to offer suggestions about ways of including all students in planning and practice.

Wide take-up of embedded educational opportunities offered by technology

International schools of all types have been among the first schools worldwide to take up the embedded use of sophisticated technology in classrooms. Most teachers, whether they come from state or public school systems or from independent schools, will be accustomed to incorporating aspects of technology into their everyday teaching. However, many international schools, perhaps because of their aspiring parent bodies, have chosen to commit huge resource to both hardware and software. This can be an exciting and stimulating new area of professional development for teachers – I shall try to reference and incorporate the new uses of embedded technology throughout this Handbook. (Section 2 of Chapter 7 gives an overall introduction to the embedded use of technology in the classroom.)

Greater commitment to maintaining and developing students' home languages (mother tongues)

A third area where earlier trends have become more deeply embedded, perhaps in response to higher numbers of emergent bilingual students in international schools, is an increased emphasis on the value and potential of maintaining and developing students' home languages (described as the mother tongue in many international school settings). This increased awareness of the need to promote emergent bilingual students' development in their home language and culture as well as in English takes two forms. The first is a marked increase in the provision of systematic school-sponsored in-school or out-of-school teaching in students' mother tongues. A second area associated with the maintenance and development of students' home languages and cultures is the introduction in a planned and consistent manner of the use of these languages in English-medium classrooms. This approach, which is still in a relatively early stage of implementation, is designed to enhance emergent bilingual students' learning in both (or all) their languages with the overall aim of providing an additive educational experience. (Section 2 in Chapter 9 contains information on two such approaches under the headings 'The interlingual classroom' and 'Translanguaging'.)

The Overall Content of this Handbook

This Handbook is divided into five parts. It was planned to be read as whole. However the divisions in the material have been designed to break down the content into manageable chunks and to make it easier for teachers to focus in on a specific topic. Each part deals with critical areas of interest and concern to teachers who work with emergent bilingual students.

Part 1: The World of International Education

Part 1 of this Handbook is devoted to introducing the world of international education. The schools themselves are the focus of Chapter 1. Here, readers will find a description of the typical development of individual international schools as well as the aspects that most international schools have in common. The features of two main types of international schools are discussed as well as an account of the recruitment of the teachers who work in them. Chapter 2 focuses on a feature which is central to many stakeholders in the international school community, that of mobility. The chapter includes discussions on the profile and lifestyle of families who move for the first time and of families who are serial movers. It also introduces the topic of what it means to be a globally mobile student who receives much of her or his education outside the home country. Chapter 3, the final part of Part 1, is devoted to describing the different ways in which globally mobile students, parents and teachers learn to adjust to moving into a new setting. It explains how international schools have evolved to meet the needs of these groups and considers the idea of 'third culture kids' as a means of describing the experiences of globally mobile students.

Part 2: Programmes and Policies in International Schools

Part 2 is made up of one chapter that sets out the programmes and curricula that are offered in international schools and which may be unfamiliar to new teachers. Chapter 4 includes the programmes of the IBO as well as the programmes and curricula which are derived from English-speaking national education systems. The focus of the chapter is on the ways that schools pick and choose among programmes of study in order to answer the needs of the school community, and how teachers can set about the task of including all students in an English-medium classroom in the ongoing teaching and learning.

Part 3: Bilingualism and Language Learning

Part 3 contains two chapters that together offer a discussion of the underlying body of theory that underpins bilingualism and language learning as a whole. The aim is to present the different theoretical aspects in ways that highlight their practical implications for teachers and students in real-life classrooms. Text Boxes are included throughout these chapters to expand on ideas where that seems helpful and to provide examples of how the lived experiences of individual emergent bilingual students relate to the theory.

Chapter 5, the first chapter in Part 3, addresses the topic of what it means to grow up and be educated in two or more languages and cultures. It sets out the importance of ensuring that emergent bilinguals achieve an additive experience in an English-medium classroom and it considers the advantages of being an 'elective' bilingual, the category into which most students in international schools fall. Finally, Chapter 5 looks at how schools embed their provision for the language learning of all students, including their role in the maintenance and development of students' mother tongues, by means of language policies.

Chapter 6 focuses on the language learning process itself. It looks at variations in the way individual students learn a language and the type of language that students need to learn in order to be able to function fully in the academic programme of the school. It sets out the conditions in a classroom that make for successful language learning and it highlights some typical features that may cause concern to teachers as they observe their students' progress along the language learning continuum.

Part 4: Day-to-Day Life in Mainstream Classrooms Containing Emergent Bilingual Students

Part 4 contains three chapters which describe the practical resources in the school and in individual classrooms that serve to promote students' learning of English and their home languages. Thus Chapter 7 contains sections on school-wide features that teachers can bring to bear on working more effectively with emergent bilingual students. In this chapter, such areas as assessment, the embedded use of technology, the use of libraries/media centres and the monitoring and support of students with suspected learning issues are discussed. A further important element addressed in the chapter is the role played by specific English-language teaching specialists in an international school both alongside the teacher in the classroom and via withdrawal classes.

Chapter 8 continues with a discussion with practical examples of the need to explain aspects of the teaching and learning culture in international schools to students and parents. This is followed in Chapter 9 by practical suggestions for enabling emergent bilingual students to access the language of the classroom. The chapter includes sections on creating an effective language learning experience, the role of students' mother tongues in an English-medium classroom, and specific detailed approaches that teachers can use to help emergent bilingual students make sense of what they hear and read.

Part 5: Working with Emergent Bilingual Students in the Mainstream Academic Programme

Finally, Part 5 contains four chapters that address the essentials of daily life in a classroom that contains students from a range of linguistic and cultural backgrounds and who are at different levels of English-language development. The focus is on the overall integration of content area and language learning and includes detailed suggestions relating to each content area about ways of scaffolding the learning of emergent bilingual students in the mainstream curriculum. Other areas related to working effectively with emergent bilingual students in international schools are incorporated into the chapters as appropriate. These include an account of the opportunities for professional development for teachers working in international school classrooms and a whole chapter devoted to the detailed planning of a new unit of instruction to take account of the learning needs of all the students in the class. The approach of Part 5 is specific, practical and realistic.

The Author

The experiences of emergent bilingual students in English-medium international school classrooms has been the focus of my professional life for all the years since I moved away from the UK and entered the extraordinary and fascinating world of international education. When in the 1990s a sabbatical from the International School of Brussels and a Fellowship Award from the European Council of International Schools allowed me to take six months away from frontline teaching, I took the opportunity to investigate and reflect on the nature of effective teaching and learning in these classrooms. The result was the publication of my first Handbook (1998).

Since that time, which has included a return to the UK, I have visited numerous international schools, been involved in accreditations and reviews, continued my writing and spoken at countless conferences. I have also, with the support of Dr Mary Hayden, Director of the Centre for the Study of Education in an International Context (CEIC) at the University of Bath, UK, furthered my understanding of the life experiences of emergent bilingual students by carrying out the extended research investigation which is used as a foundational source for some of the content in this present Handbook (described in Appendix A).

Final Comment

This entirely new Handbook is based on the fresh insights I have gained over the past years and reflects the many changes and developments that have occurred in the sector during that time. However, it remains similar to the first publication in that its prime aim is to reflect the real-life challenges and experiences that face teachers in international school classrooms.

I had thought that the first Handbook would be useful largely to teachers in isolated smaller schools who did not have easy access to professional development. In the event, teachers from all sizes and types of international schools have told me over the years that the usefulness of the Handbook lay in the way that it captured the reality of life in their school and was honest about the challenges that teaching in an international school may present.

Many of these teachers mentioned the Text Boxes as their favourite sections, and perhaps that was because I used the Text Boxes to write out of my own experience. For this reason I have included more Text Boxes in the new publication. In this Handbook they supply extra material to expand on the content of the main text as well as offering many examples of life in individual international schools and accounts of individual students. I hope you will enjoy them and recognise your own school and circumstances in both the Text Boxes and this new Handbook as a whole.

Note: Ensuring continuing access to internet content

There is always difficulty in providing specific website addresses and app links in publications that are used over some years. At the time of going to press, the detail given in this Handbook is accurate and the links still up-and-running. An option in all cases is to search for websites and app information via Google or another search engine, using the key words as given in the text.

References

Hayden, M.C. (2006) *Introduction to International Education*. London: Sage.
Sears, C. (1998) *Second Language Schools in Mainstream Classrooms: A Handbook for Teachers in International Schools*. Clevedon: Multilingual Matters.

Part 1

The World of International Education

1 Introducing International Schools

Chapter 1 is devoted to introducing the world of international schools. It sets out some of the distinctive characteristics of an international school and provides a brief historical overview of the ways in which the international school sector has expanded and developed. It looks at the different groups of families that international schools serve and it describes the process of teacher recruitment. Finally, it briefly considers the elements that make a school truly international.

The sequence of Chapter 1 is as follows:

- Introduction: international schools and international education.
- Introducing international schools.
- What do international schools offer the families they serve?
- International schools that cater for the children of globally mobile families.
- International schools that largely serve the children of local families.
- Teachers in international schools.
- What makes an international school international?

Text Box 1.1 Terms and ideas introduced in this chapter

English-medium school: This is a school where all classes except for foreign language classes are taught in English. In many schools of this type, English is also used for communicating with parents and other stakeholders in the school community.

Language of instruction, medium of instruction: Terms used to describe the language or languages through which the curriculum is delivered.

Bilingual school: Most lay people apply the term 'bilingual' to any school that functions in two or more languages, regardless of the balance between the languages used in the classroom or the make-up of the student body. In the body of literature relating to bilingual education, however, a significant distinction is made between 'strong' forms of bilingual education and 'weak' forms, with 'strong' forms being regarded as essential for effective outcomes. Effective outcomes for bilingual education are viewed as 'bilingualism, biliteracy and biculturalism' (Baker, 2011).

(Continued)

3

Text Box 1.1 Terms and ideas introduced in this chapter (*Continued*)

Emergent bilingual students: A continuing subject of discussion is what to call students in international schools who are not monolingual speakers of English. The term 'second language students' which was used in an earlier Handbook (Sears, 1998) now seems inappropriate in the face of the multilingual repertoires of many students as well as carrying overtones of disempowerment. The term adopted in this Handbook is 'emergent bilingual' since it retains the idea of bilingual students using different languages for different aspects of their lives.

Global mobility: This term describes the lives of the increasing numbers of families worldwide who move around the globe to take up new career assignments and employment opportunities.

Local community, local language(s), local students, local families, local hires: These terms relate to the location in which an international school is situated, also known in the world of international education as the host country. In some cases this location will itself be a multilingual, multicultural environment.

National education system: This term refers to government-sponsored or mandated education systems which are to be found in state schools (or public schools in the US).

'Western-style' education: This is a portmanteau term to describe the sort of education that is generally found in international schools. It relates to the curricula and programmes that derive from English-speaking countries and which are found in many international schools or at least in the English-medium element of a school. It is often characterised by people new to international schools (and who may come from quite different educational backgrounds) as being child-centred, individualistic, encouraging, and 'more informal' than many state education systems.

English-speaking countries, English-speaking students: Describing a group of nations and nationals in these terms is difficult territory since today this terminology is linked with postcolonial theories of dominance and privilege. Nevertheless, this is a term used on many websites relating to international education. What is meant are those countries and peoples who have historically used English as their primary language. It is a fact that many international schools are linked specifically (now if only by name) to those countries, and that many schools still draw on teachers from those countries to teach the English-medium element of their curricula and programmes.

Mother tongue, primary language, first language, home language, etc.: Over the years many terms have emerged to describe the language that seems foundational in an individual's language repertoire. Perhaps the need to define such a thing derives from a monolingual view of language use. The fact is that the majority of people in the world conduct different parts of their lives via different languages rather than through a single language. It is often difficult for a family to single out one language which is their primary language, especially among the families who send their children to international schools. The term 'mother tongue' has remained in use in English-medium international schools to describe the primary language in a child's life outside school.

Note: Students' primary languages are described by the IBO (www.ibo.org) as Language A. This term is often used alongside the other terms in schools that have adopted the IB programmes.

World English, World Englishes: Any discussion relating to the varieties of English that are developing around the world tends to draw upon the historic fact of colonialism. Describing a regionally based variety of English as a World English is an attempt to move away from the view, still prevalent, that standard American or British Englishes are inherently more prestigious. What may change this view is the use of their own variety of English by individuals in fast-developing populous regions such as the Indian subcontinent.

International-mindedness: This term lies at the heart of the IB programmes and has been taken up more widely throughout the international school sector. Its definition has taken different forms over the years. At present, 'international-mindedness' is being characterised as the concept that unites all types of international schools and even some schools in national systems that aim to promote a specific world-view.

Overseas hires: This term denotes teachers and other staff who are hired by the school from overseas. Typically they are trained and experienced in the type of curricula and programmes that are taught in international schools.

Introduction: International Schools and International Education

What does a school that started life in a disused textile factory in Beijing, China, have in common with a purpose-built, fully equipped school situated on a new campus in the Arabian Gulf or with another based in a pink-washed stucco building in a South American capital city? The answer is that all these schools describe themselves as offering an international education to the students they serve.

The diversity of geographical location, the differences in the history and development of each school and the range of facilities on offer to students are typical of international schools as a whole. However, alongside this variety among individual schools, there are also many features which schools that describe themselves as international have in common. The aim of this chapter is to provide a basic understanding of the sector as a whole, introducing some of the general features of an international education while acknowledging the tremendous diversity to be found across the schools themselves.

The content of the chapter

Section 1.1 is devoted to a broad outline of the history and development of international schools and to describing the ways in which international schools may differ from schools in national systems. Section 1.2 is concerned with the special features that are to be found in the majority of international schools and which make them attractive to the families they serve. Sections 1.3 and 1.4 describe two types of international schools: those that serve the children of globally mobile families and those that largely cater for local families. Section 1.5 introduces the topic of teacher recruitment in the international school sector and Section 1.6 asks a question that continues to occupy the minds of international educators: 'What makes an international school international?'.

1.1 Introducing International Schools

International schools are to be found in locations worldwide where there is a sizeable expatriate community or a pool of local families that perceive the benefits of an international education for their children. Increasingly, there are clusters of international schools in certain locations. This is the case with cities such as Geneva, Brussels, London and New York where there are large populations of international civil servants or of expatriate personnel working in corporate headquarters and global finance. It is also true of locations in countries with fast-developing economies such as China and India and in the countries of the Arabian Gulf. Alongside the founding of this type of school, individual international schools spring up in answer to the needs of families in more far-flung situations where parents work for large companies or provide expertise to the local community. The majority of international schools are independent and fee-paying, the financial aspect being one of the reasons for the numbers of smaller and larger schools in any given location.

Note: For an immediate impression of the size and variety of the international school sector, readers might like to search the internet under a heading such as 'international schools in Singapore'. Most major cities have websites setting out the range of schools available to the expatriate population in the location. Such lists give an instant snapshot of the types of schools available, the programmes they offer and the students they serve.

1.1.1 The early days in the life of an international school

Many schools are founded in response to the arrival of a group of expatriate families in locations where there are few or no schools to cater for their children's needs. In this situation, it is common for international schools to start their lives in small, sometimes makeshift premises. Often newly founded schools are situated in large old houses, in empty industrial buildings or in a series of prefabricated huts. There may be very little outside space for play or for sport and they may have few facilities in the way of media centres, technological gadgetry or art and music rooms. In contrast to the rather basic nature of the facilities, newly founded schools of this type frequently have a strong sense of community, with teachers and parents working together to improve the school and its facilities. Stories abound of school communities joining together to fundraise for new sports equipment or to help in the overall refurbishment of the school. Many teachers, parents and students who have experienced the early days of a new school speak with great affection of the communal sense of purpose and cooperative spirit that pervades a school at this stage of its development.

1.1.2 Changes in the make-up of the student population as the school grows

The pattern of student recruitment and the growth of the student population in a newly founded international school generally follow one of two paths. In the first case, a school will open in a location in answer to an immediate need for international, English-speaking education on the part of a small number of recently arrived expatriate families. Where this happens, the student population can comprise a range of ages, with the small numbers leading to mixed-age classes. In the second case, newly founded schools have more time and space to arrange a planned increase in student numbers. This generally happens when a school has sufficient financial or other backing to build up the school by starting with classes for only the very youngest students. In this case, new classes are opened at the bottom of the school as each year group moves upward until the school reaches an optimum size.

1.1.3 The age-group of students served by international schools

The eventual size of the school and the age group of the students it serves depend on the local need for an international school. Some schools are viable only as primary/elementary schools; in other locations, there are sufficient potential students available to sustain a secondary/high school. However, in most locations, the governing bodies of international schools know that they can seldom depend on a consistent enrolment year on year.

Improving or worsening economic conditions, political upheavals, policy changes on the part of major corporations or the sudden opening up of a new factory or plant can lead to a sudden influx of new families or the loss of a number of students. These factors mean that admissions departments in international schools must be continually on their toes in order to reflect the changing circumstances. The result is that it is quite common in an international school for the number of classes at a year level to increase or decrease from year to year. Most long-term teachers in international schools have experienced, at least once, the taking down or putting up of classroom partitions in a school in order to accommodate rapid changes in student numbers.

1.1.4 How an international school evolves and develops

In general, as a school expands and becomes increasingly financially viable, so the owner or governing body finds the means to finance and construct attractive and spacious buildings, often with well-equipped sports and other facilities. Further facilities may continue to be constructed as the school expands in response to an increased population of students. This can be a time when a theatre is added to campus facilities, or a further gymnasium. To teachers and students new to schools of this type, the scale and quality of the provision can sometimes be very striking. There were frequent references to the scale and grandeur of their new international school by the students who participated in one of the research studies used as a foundation for this Handbook (described in Appendix A). Many spoke about the size of the school, about the wonderful play facilities for younger students and about the two huge gymnasiums. One student described how there had been no library in his old school in the Czech Republic and how they had been obliged to share reading books. In the new school he not only had computers and books to hand, but also had his own special cupboard (locker) where he kept his possessions.

1.1.5 Technology in international schools

Another feature that is now common in new and expanding international schools is the high level of commitment to embedded technology in school programmes and curricula. The websites of many international schools make a special feature of their technology provision, many offering separate links which set out the number of workstations, tablets and other technological devices that are available in the school. This commitment to technological innovation arises for two reasons. The first is that international schools view technology as an integral aspect of a globally focused education. The second is that international schools recognise that they compete to some extent with other schools in the same location. They view the provision of the latest technological devices as an effective means of attracting parents to enrol their children in their school.

1.1.6 Brand new purpose-built international schools

Some international schools do not pass through these developmental phases. With various sorts of financial backing, the founders of some new international schools are immediately able to house students in purpose-built, well-equipped facilities with high-quality technological, sporting and artistic provision.

1.1.7 Observable differences between schools in national schooling systems and international schools

In most international schools there are some easily observable obvious differences from schools in national systems. On one level these difference are quite superficial. On another level they give illuminating insights into the ways in which international schools serve the families who choose an international education for their children.

Some readily observable differences
Buildings may be non-standard and clearly temporary.

Many international schools start life in borrowed or makeshift buildings. The Western Academy of Beijing (www.wab.edu/), for example, was first set up in the disused wing of a textile factory. It now has a new purpose-built school campus. One school in a northern European city started life in a large 19th-century house complete with marble staircases and wood panelling. The students had their PE sessions in the local park, guided by a member of the local professional soccer team, and were given woodwork lessons in the former butler's pantry.

School buildings may strongly reflect the local architecture.

The new campus of the British International School of Jakarta, Indonesia (www.bis.or.id/), for example, has a beautiful assembly hall built in the local vernacular style, made of local materials with a hipped roof and high open ventilation spaces. One school in Bangkok is built around a series of rills and pools containing plants and flowers. The students move across bridges to get to their classrooms.

Newly built schools may appear to be large and well-equipped (and sometimes magnificent). They may have state-of-the-art theatres, sophisticated sports facilities and multiple music and art studios.

Newly built schools in the Gulf region, for example, frequently have splendid buildings and facilities, (although often with little outside space because of the great heat). Schools in this region may have separate sports facilities for boys and girls. They invariably have air-conditioning.

Evidence of a major investment in technological hardware and software is apparent.

It is common now to see many students in international schools carrying mobile technological devices around schools along with their books. Many schools have ranges of computers in classrooms and media centres to augment this provision. There is evidence of the integral use of technology in all areas of school life.

The administrative and maintenance personnel are frequently recruited from among the local community.

In most international schools, the teaching staff is largely recruited from English-speaking schooling systems. In many schools only the administrative staff and maintenance personnel come from the host community. The presence of host country personnel is a feature that most experienced teachers speak of as enriching the life of an international school. They provide contact with the culture and language of the local community and prevent the feeling that the school lives in a 'Westernised' bubble separated from the community outside.

The parents of students in international schools tend to look noticeably self-confident and well-groomed.

This is something that new teachers often mention when they first teach in an international school. Later, they become accustomed to working with a parent body of this type. In any case, teachers should try not to feel overwhelmed by the apparent attitude and status of parents.

The most confident and well-heeled parents are deeply concerned about their children and need reassurance from a friendly and competent professional.

Note: *On the other hand, the dress of students in international schools may come as something of a surprise to new teachers. Whereas students in their previous schools and in the schools in the locality surrounding an international school may be carefully turned-out in well-pressed uniforms, students in international schools may appear to be rather informally dressed to some eyes. T-shirts, shorts in the summer and skimpy tops can be seen in many international schools.*

Students in international schools tend to be lively, energetic and noticeably outgoing. Most international schools are not very quiet places.

The friendly and informal atmosphere of many international schools has evolved because of their role in welcoming and including newcomers. There tends to be a more open and sociable relationship between all members of the school community than is usual in national schooling systems.

Displays in school often reflect the art and culture of the locality in which the school is situated.

The potential to engage with the readily accessible elements of a new culture is one of the most exciting and engaging aspects of working in an international school. Experiencing at first hand the art, music, festivals and sports of the host community is among the unique aspects of studying and teaching in an international school. (For more about engaging with a new culture at different levels, see Chapter 3 as a whole.)

The appearance of the school may reflect the linguistic and cultural diversity of the students.

In enlightened English-medium schools, there is evidence of the languages and cultures of all the students being incorporated into the life and work of the school. In bilingual international schools, the school languages are embedded in the life of the school.

The school displays material relating to programmes of study that may be unfamiliar to new families and teachers.

Some schools display material specifically related to programmes of study that are largely found only in international schools. It is common, for instance, for schools to display the 'learner profile' that is an integral feature of all the programmes of the International Baccalaureate Organisation (www.ibo.org). (The 'learner profile' is a list of behaviours and attitudes that are found in the ideal learner.)

Note: Many elements mentioned in this section are the topics of later chapters in this Handbook. What it means to be globally mobile is the focus of Chapter 2, how schools help students to adjust to life in the new school is addressed in Chapter 3, and Chapter 4 is concerned with the programmes of study that have been designed specifically for use in international schools. Other aspects, including the uses of technology in international schools, are included throughout the Handbook.

1.2 What Do International Schools Offer the Families They Serve?

Schools that describe themselves as international serve several different groups of families. These groups include globally mobile families who move from country to country, often for reasons connected to a parent's employment. They also include more settled families who choose an international education because of the specific advantages they feel it offers their children. Schools that contain many local students may also offer a bilingual curriculum, as do some of the schools that cater for a largely mobile population. Families in both these groups are likely to speak a range of home or primary languages and to represent many national and cultural backgrounds.

1.2.1 The use of English in international schools

The mention of language or languages highlights a distinctive aspect of the majority of international schools which is that teaching takes place either wholly or partly in English. The reasons for this use of English in international schools were initially historical. The older international schools, some of them dating from the 1950s, were frequently founded by organisations such as missions and religious orders, embassies or groups of expatriate parents with links to English-speaking countries who could not find a suitable school for their children in the new posting. It was natural for these schools wherever they were situated in the world to use English as the sole language of instruction, or as one of the languages in a bilingual school. More recently, the use of English in international schools is closely tied to the increasing global use of English across sectors such as diplomacy, business and the world wide web. At the same time, the student bodies now include high numbers of students with other home or primary languages. Placing children in a school where the teaching takes place in a language that may be unfamiliar to the family concerned obviously has huge implications for students, parents and teachers. It is the central topic of this Handbook. (The reasons why parents choose to send their children to an English-medium school are spelt out in detail in Section 2.2.)

One organisation serving the international school community (The International School Consultancy Group: www.iscresearch.com) includes the use of English as a defining feature in its description of what comprises an international school: 'A typical international school teaches wholly or partly in English, is independent and is located in a non-English speaking country.' (Even this is not entirely typical, with many international schools being located in English-speaking cities such as New York, London and Sydney.)

1.2.2 Internationally recognised programmes of study: Another reason for parents to choose an international education

A further reason that parents frequently give for choosing an international education is the advantage for their children of gaining universally recognised qualifications. This is true of families who move around the world and of settled families who are local to the school. These parents perceive the value to their children of gaining the type of school-leaving qualification that will give them entrance to universities overseas and to wide employment opportunities. (This viewpoint is typical of parents who 'elect' to send their children to international schools. A discussion of the advantages of being an 'elective' bilingual is included in Section 5.3.)

Early programmes and curricula used in international schools

The first international schools (some founded as early as the 1920s) generally adopted curricula and educational approaches that derived from the founding nationals (generally from English-speaking countries). Schools at this stage were unequivocally English speaking, chiefly because many schools began with a student body that largely comprised children and young people from English-speaking countries. The teachers, apart from local teachers hired to teach the local language or as teaching assistants, were recruited either from the same English-speaking countries or from among expatriate nationals from those countries who were living in the locality. In many international schools today it is still possible to find large elements or traces of the programmes and curricula that were put in place by the early founders of the school. This is also true of the names of schools, where the words 'American' or 'British' may be included alongside the word 'international'.

Programmes designed with international schools in mind

Gradually, as the families whose children attended international schools became more diverse, the international school community felt the need to offer programmes that were more 'international' in character and which were less closely tied to the educational system of one English-speaking country.

One of the chief providers of these programmes of study is the International Baccalaureate Organisation (IBO; www.ibo.org). The first of their programmes to be widely implemented was the IB Diploma programme (www.ibo.org/diploma/). This course of study, designed for the final two years of schooling, leads to a universally recognised school-leaving and university entrance qualification. With its origins in the International School of Geneva in the 1960s (www.ecolint.ch/), the IB Diploma is recognised by universities throughout the world and has also been adopted by national education systems and independent schools worldwide. The introduction of the IB Career-related Certificate (IBCC; www.ibo.org/ibcc/), where students take elements of the Diploma programme alongside courses with specific vocational objectives, has widened the range of students for whom the IBO courses are suitable. At the time of writing, around 2400 schools in some 140 countries according to the IBO website have adopted the Diploma programme, although many of these are national schools rather than international. The diploma is a very attractive qualification for multilingual students since its options allow such students to give evidence of their full linguistic repertoire and life experiences.

Following the establishment of the Diploma programme, the IBO introduced the Primary Years (PYP; www.ibo.org/pyp) and Middle Years (MYP; www.ibo.org/myp) programmes. At the time of writing, over 1000 schools worldwide, national and international, are authorised to teach the PYP and MYP programmes. (These programmes are examined in greater detail in Chapter 4.) Other programmes of study such as the International Primary Curriculum (www.greatlearning.com/ipc) and the recent Middle Years Curriculum have also come into being and are used by schools to offer continuity and consistency in the face of student and teacher mobility.

External accreditation

As the international school sector has matured and expanded, many schools now seek accreditation from an outside agency for the quality of their programmes and other offerings. This is something that parents now expect since it offers some sort of guarantee for the education provided in a school where the school language and programmes it offers may be unfamiliar to prospective parents and students.

A number of agencies now offer accreditation services to international schools, among them the Council of International Schools (CIS; www.cois.org). Schools that still have strong links to the education system of an English-speaking country and continue to attract students from that country often prefer to be accredited by a number of bodies. Thus it is common to see on a school's website that it has been accredited by an organisation such as the US-based New England Association of Schools and Colleges (www. neasc.org) or the UK-based Office for Standards in Education (OFSTED; www.ofsted. gov.uk), alongside the CIS.

1.3 Schools That Cater for the Children of Globally Mobile Families

Some of the first schools that described themselves as international were those that were set up to cater for the children of globally mobile parents. A group of schools continues to fulfil this role by offering an essential service to families who move round the world with their children in order to take up new career assignments. Typically, schools of this type make their appearance in cities which attract large numbers of expatriates who have moved there on short-term assignments.

1.3.1 The founding bodies

The founding bodies have been and remain very diverse. Many of the first schools were established by an embassy or groups of embassies to provide education for the children of their staff. An example of this type of foundation is the International School of Beijing (www.isb.bj.edu.cn), which was founded by the precursor to the US Embassy in the 1970s.

At that date, according to the account on the school's website, eight children were taught in two classes in a hallway in a diplomatic compound. From 1980 onwards, the small schools of the British and Australian embassies joined with that of the US Embassy to be followed by the Canadian and New Zealand Missions. At this point, the school was formally founded as the International School of Beijing with the mission of providing an English-speaking education for the children of the five founding embassies.

As space allowed, children from other embassies and other language backgrounds were accepted. Since 2002, the Beijing Municipal Education Bureau has allowed the school to be restructured as an 'independent school for foreign children'. Around 1800 students from many language and cultural backgrounds now attend the school, which has a new 'purpose-built facility', offers the IB Diploma and is accredited by the Chinese Authority NCCT, by the CIS and the New England Association of Schools and Colleges (www.neasc.org/).

Other schools were and are founded by individual organisations to provide education for the children of their employees in places where an English-speaking education is unavailable. The international schools set up in New York, Geneva and Vienna to educate children of United Nations personnel are typical of this type of foundation. Other schools cater to the needs of expatriate students who are the children of aid workers or where a company brings in a large number of globally mobile expatriate workers. Among these companies are the energy companies who recognise the need to provide schools as part of the remuneration package they offer to personnel who work in difficult and isolated geographical locations. One such oil company has established schools in the desert in Oman and on the Russian island of Sakhalin, among others (www.tes.co.uk/employer/shell-company-schools-1057210).

Schools set up by a single proprietor or by a small group of business people or educators comprise a further large number of international schools that cater for the children of globally mobile families. Individuals or groups of people perceive a gap in the provision for expatriates in a neighbourhood and set up a school in order to meet an acknowledged need. Many of the smaller international schools are included in this group, although there are some very well established chains of large international schools that are privately owned.

1.4 Schools Containing Large Numbers of Local Students

A large group of schools which describe themselves as 'international' differ considerably from the schools that cater for a globally mobile population. These are the schools where the majority of students, sometimes as many as 95% or more, come from local families. These families are generally well-established in the local community and it is not unusual for the parents themselves or members of the extended family to have had overseas higher education or employment experiences. The parents frequently speak several foreign languages themselves and the family as a whole tends to be involved in international business or diplomacy, or at the very least to have travelled widely. It is not uncommon for parents to be of different nationalities and for family life to be conducted in two or more languages. As a whole, such families share a desire for their children's education to equip them to participate in the global workplace. The acquisition of English and the opportunity for their children to gain a universally recognised school-leaving qualification are usually prime reasons for their choice, as mentioned earlier.

Many local parents who choose an international school wish their children to maintain contact with the local schooling system and with the home and community language(s). As a result, schools that serve this group of families tend either to have evolved as bilingual schools or to offer opportunities for students to continue their studies in their home language both in and after school. Frequently these schools also provide specific tuition targeted at examinations which occur at key stages in the local education systems.

Students in these schools tend to stay much longer than is typical of international schools that serve a globally mobile community. There is often a high use of the local language even in schools that use English as the medium of instruction. It is typical, for instance, in schools of this type to hear the local language in the playground or on the sports field. Younger students often communicate with teachers in the local language, only moving over to English when that language is more established. In these schools, typically, there is a sense of a bilingual, bicultural environment, even when English prevails in the classroom.

Text Box 1.2 Being a local student in an English-medium international school

Antonio, aged seven, lives with his Italian parents in a northern Italian city. His father gained a higher degree in the United States and he has an uncle who lives with his family in the UK. The parents decided to send Antonio to the English-speaking kindergarten attached to an English-medium international school 'because English is so important nowadays'. At the age of five he moved into the primary section of the same school. In his class of 20 children, only two students were not Italian speakers.

The school follows the IB PYP (www.ibo.org/pyp) and the mainstream elements of the overall curriculum are delivered in English by teachers described in the school prospectus as 'native English-speakers'. From the start, Antonio received one Italian lesson a day taught by an Italian teacher together with some Italian studies classes. In the first year, the Italian lessons were largely non-academic in approach; in the next year they included literacy teaching. Antonio continued to use Italian in the playground and at first among his friends in the classroom. Older students tended to use English among themselves in the mainstream classrooms.

When he is nine, his parents will probably decide, along with most other parents, to send him to after-school classes in Italian language and curriculum designed

(Continued)

Text Box 1.2 Being a local student in an English-medium
international school *(Continued)*

to prepare him for the end of primary examination which Italian children customarily sit. When he is 11, his parents will decide whether to put him in the Italian
system or keep him in an English-medium environment. A fair number of the other
students at the school go on to attend an Italian middle school and then return to
the international school for their last two years of schooling to take the IB Diploma
with its bilingual options.

1.4.1 Where these schools are to be found

Certain parts of the world contain many schools of this type, among them
Italy, Spain, South America and the Middle East, and increasingly the fast-developing
countries of Asia such as India and China. In some cases, the school is an old foundation
that has evolved to cater for outward-looking entrepreneurial families. Such schools pick
and choose the international programmes that expand and enhance their stated aims
and objectives, as well as offering part or all of the local curriculum.

The history of St Andrews Scots School in Buenos Aires (or Escuela Escocesa San
Andrés in Spanish) (www1.sanandres.esc.edu.ar/) is an example of how a school typically evolves and changes. The school was founded in 1838 by Scottish immigrants to
educate their children, as they said, 'in their language, culture and faith'. Over the
years the school has developed in response to its changing student body. It is now a
bilingual Spanish/English school with 1900 students. It offers a balanced bilingual
programme with the students taking the National Argentine curriculum alongside the
International General Certificate of Secondary Education, a qualification offered by
Cambridge International Examinations at 16+ (www.cie.org.uk/) and the IB Diploma.
This school is one of around 30 full members and many associate members of the
English-Speaking Scholastic Association of the River Plate (www.essarp.org.ar).

Another school, the International College in Beirut (www.ic.edu.lb), educates its
students in three languages, Arabic, English and French, via the IB PYP and prepares
them for four options in the way of school-leaving examinations. In this school students
can opt to take the English-track Lebanese Baccalaureate, the French-track Baccalaureate,
the National French Baccalaureate or the IB Diploma.

Most international schools that serve the local community do not have such long
and illustrious histories, although many offer school programmes tailored in a similar
way to the needs of the local community. Many schools of this type have been recently
established and more are in the pipeline. The success of bilingual schools, whether they
have a long or short history, is a reflection of the current desire of parents to give their
children a globally focused education while maintaining a close connection to the local
language and schooling system.

1.4.2 Globally mobile students in schools that contain large numbers of stable local children

One of the chief challenges that faces administrators and teachers in schools that largely serve the local community is the presence of small numbers of students who speak neither English nor the local language. Often these students have been placed in the school because there is no schooling available in the family's home language, or because parents wish their child to experience an international education. Frequently the family only expects to stay for two or three years.

In these cases, the school is faced with the challenge of including students with this profile in the social and academic life of the school. Students in this position rarely have a foothold in the wider community outside school that local students take for granted. In an English-medium classroom or where classes are taught in the local language, they are faced with the task of making sense of a curriculum or programme of study which is familiar to their longer term classmates but which is new to them. Administrators and teachers have to plan in a proactive way in order for the educational experience of these students to be positive.

1.5 Teachers in International Schools

Teachers in international schools are recruited via a number of recognised paths. A school's recruitment/hiring policy is largely driven by the need for teachers who are fluent speakers of the languages of instruction. A second priority is to recruit teachers who are familiar with the curricula and programmes which the school offers. Thus schools that offer the IBO's programmes search for teachers who are already accustomed to working in those programmes and schools that offer the range of curricula; examination courses that derive from the UK tend to recruit a high number of their teachers from the UK.

A further source of English-speaking teachers is the pool of expatriate spouses who have settled with their working partners in the location. Other excellent users of English may be recruited, although schools are aware that parents have a strong preference for nationals from one of the English-speaking countries. For this reason, high numbers of teachers from Australia, Canada, New Zealand, the UK and the USA are to be found in international schools. Teachers of the local language and curriculum are largely recruited locally and are frequently termed 'local hires'.

Text Box 1.3 Teacher recruitment

Most international schools are permanently in need of well-qualified teachers, both local hires and from overseas. (At the time of writing, according to the ISC database (www.iscresearch.com) there are almost 300,000 teachers working in

(Continued)

Text Box 1.3 Teacher recruitment (*Continued*)

international schools.) As a teacher, contemplating the possibilities of working in an international school, how to do you set about narrowing down the choices that are available? What are schools looking for and what have you to offer? What will you gain from working in an international school and from living in a new location? How do you set about applying to the school(s) of your choice? Here are some thoughts on teacher recruitment:

What do schools hope to gain from overseas hires?

- Schools hope to recruit teachers who are versed in new methodologies and technological innovations.
- They need teachers who have worked in schools that implement similar national and international curricula and programmes to those that they have adopted.
- They wish to employ teachers for whom English is a primary language to teach the English-medium elements of the academic programme – preferably, in the eyes of parents, from a so-called English-speaking country.
- They need teachers with the flexibility to take on new methodologies and teaching approaches.
- They need new teachers to act as mentors and models to existing staff, both long-term resident expatriates and locally hired teachers.
- They look to new teachers to bring fresh ideas and novel approaches and to raise the energy level in the school.
- They need friendly, competent and articulate professionals who will inspire anxious and questioning parents with confidence.

What are the advantages of teaching in an international school?

- International schools offer the opportunity for new career experiences and professional development.
- They offer the chance to experience working in new programmes and curriculum approaches.
- They offer the possibility of enhancing existing skillsets and of developing new areas of expertise.
- They provide the opportunity to acquire new qualifications under the schemes that many schools offer.
- They provide the opportunity for new friendships and cultural experiences within the school environment.

What are the possibilities to be gained from the location?

- You will be able to experience in depth the culture, history and way of life of the new location (but only if you step outside the school community).
- You will be able to acquire a new language in optimum circumstances (but only if you become involved in the local community).

- You will be able to pursue new sporting and leisure activities.
- You will be able use the new location as a jumping-off point for further travel.

What experience/training/qualities do you have that make you attractive to an international school?
- You have the academic qualifications and professional training appropriate to teaching your target age group of student.
- You have experience in teaching the curriculum or programme the school offers.
- You have a level and type of experience that will allow you to adapt to the school curricula or programmes.
- You speak a second or foreign language to a high level.
- You can show yourself to be well-travelled/versed in working in multilingual and multicultural environments/capable of adapting to new situations.
- You have sporting, artistic or other interests that will bring something further to the school.

What are the possible pitfalls?
- Assess the remuneration packages with great care. What are the accommodation arrangements? What are the local taxation arrangements? How would the proposed salary allow you to live in the location? Is paid home leave included in the contract?
- What is the reality of living in a particular location? Climate? Security? Transportation availability? Local attitudes towards women?
- Is the school a supportive environment or are new teachers left to fend for themselves? Find out whether the school offers orientation or support programmes for new teachers. (Schools often mentioned their transition programmes if they exist.)
- Sadly, some schools may not be all that they seem – read between the lines when viewing school websites. Opt for schools that are members or associates of a reputable accreditation and professional organisation.

Helpful websites and links (see the Resources section at the end of this chapter)
- Recruitment organisation websites.
- International school review sites (reviews on these sites are based on individual experiences of schools – they provide broad guidance only).
- Individual school websites.
- Online directories to be found on websites of regional organisations.

1.6 What Makes an International School International?

Whenever a group of international educators meets together at a conference, the conversation seems to turn to the topic of what it really means to call a school 'international'. Some contributors to the discussion argue that the use of English and the provision of globally recognised programmes of study do not in themselves make a school international. Others argue that the international nature of these schools lies in the diverse linguistic and cultural backgrounds of the students to be found in many international schools. There are theoretical underpinnings to both these arguments, some of which are explored in later chapters of this Handbook.

Among teachers it is perhaps a contribution by a long-term contributor to the field of international education who suggests an answer to the 'international' question that matches their experience in these schools. Drawing on research about the attitudes of students in international schools, Jeff Thompson (1998) suggests that it is not the curriculum itself or the language used in a school that makes it international. He argues that the international element comes from the interaction between students from diverse backgrounds in informal settings and in their relations with teachers who can be described as 'internationally minded'. Among the international school community, the idea of 'international-mindedness' has been taken up as a key element in offering an effective international education.

Note: Aspects of the debate about the nature of the international element in international schools are included throughout this Handbook. See Text Box 4.6 'What do we mean by international-mindedness?'; see Section 5.3 'The benefits of being an "elective" bilingual' and Section 5.4 'Elective bilinguals in international schools and their view of English'.

Key Points in This Chapter

- Individual international schools tend to have unique histories and profiles.
- International schools tend to have certain things in common. These include the use of English wholly or partly as a language of instruction and the opportunity for students to gain universally recognised qualifications.
- There are consistent differences that distinguish international schools from schools in national systems.
- A group of international schools caters for the children of globally mobile families.
- A further group largely serves the children of local families.
- The families that international schools serve generally perceive the value for their children of acquiring English and of gaining universally recognised qualifications.
- Large numbers of teachers in international schools are recruited from English-speaking countries.
- Schools focus their recruitment on acquiring teachers who are experienced in delivering the curricula and programmes that are offered in the school.
- Teachers of the local language and culture in English-medium schools and teachers of the local curriculum in bilingual schools are generally hired from among the local community.

- It has been suggested that what makes an international school international are the informal elements in an international school rather than the programme offerings themselves.

Resources

Websites of international schools mentioned in the text
British International School of Jakarta: www.bis.or.id.
International College, Beirut: www.ic.edu.lb.
International School of Beijing: www.isb.bj.edu.cn.
International School of Geneva: www.ecolint.ch/.
St. Andrews Scots School, Buenos Aires: www1.sanandres.esc.edu.ar/.
Western Academy of Beijing: www.wab.edu/.

Programme and examination course providers
Cambridge International Examinations: www.cie.org.uk/.
International Baccalaureate Organisation: www.ibo.org.

Worldwide and regionally based international school organisations (including accrediting bodies)
English-speaking Scholastic Association of the River Plate (ESSARP): www.essarp.org.ar.
Council of International Schools (CIS): www.cois.org.
ISC Research (site offering extensive data related to international schools): www.iscresearch.com.
New England Association of Schools and Colleges: www.neasc.org/.
Office for Standards in Education (OFSTED): www.ofsted.gov.uk.

Some major recruitment organisations targeted at international schools
Council of International Schools (CIS): www.cois.org.
International School Services: www.iss.edu.
Search Associates: www.searchassociates.com.
Teach Anywhere: www.teachanywhere.com.
One of the sites relating to recruitment in Shell Company Schools: www.tes.co.uk/employer/shell-company-schools-1057210.

Review sites relating to international schools
www.expatexchange.com (parents' views of individual schools).
www.internationalschoolsreview.com (teachers' views of individual schools).

References

Baker, C. (2011) *Foundations of Bilingual Education and Bilingualism* (5th edn). Bristol: Multilingual Matters.
Sears, C. (1998) *Second Language Schools in Mainstream Classrooms: A Handbook for Teachers in International Schools.* Clevedon: Multilingual Matters.
Thompson, J.J. (1998) Towards a model for international education. In M.C. Hayden and J.J. Thompson (eds) *International Education: Principles and Practice*. London: Kogan Page.

2 Being Mobile: Parents, Students, Teachers

Chapter 2 is concerned with the 20% of international schools that cater for a globally mobile population. In these schools mobility is a feature shared by most of the parents, students and teachers. Understanding the impact of mobility on people's lives is an essential element of working successfully in this type of school.

The sequence of Chapter 2 is as follows:

- Introduction: living a life of global mobility.
- Globally mobile families whose children attend international schools.
- Understanding the challenges facing families who move for the first time.
- Working with students and parents who are serial movers.
- Being a globally mobile child.
- Settling into the location as a newly arrived teacher.
- How international schools welcome and support families on the move.

Introduction: Living a Life of Global Mobility

Globally mobile families make up one group who send their children to international schools. Indeed most of the longest established international schools were originally founded to serve the children of parents who move around the world to take up employment opportunities. The purpose of this chapter is to describe in detail the nature of a globally mobile lifestyle and to shed light on the experiences that parents, students and teachers encounter in a life of mobility.

Thus Section 2.1 describes the characteristics of families who send their children to international schools, followed in Sections 2.2 and 2.3 by an account of the experiences of families making a first move or the next move in a series of moves.

A description of the lives of globally mobile children follows in Section 2.4, which also includes an introduction to the term 'global nomads' and what such a description signifies. Section 2.5 offers thoughts on the experience of newly arrived teachers and, finally, the role of the school in supplying an immediately accessible social community for globally mobile expatriate families is examined in Section 2.6.

2.1 Globally Mobile Families Whose Children Attend International Schools

The families whose children attend international schools come from every national, cultural and linguistic background. They also include families where the parents themselves are of different national and cultural backgrounds and where several languages are used within the home. Other families derive from historically English-speaking countries and are essentially monolingual. Both groups include single-parent families. In international schools that serve a globally mobile population one experience is shared by the greater part of the community. Many have moved at least once, more have moved several times and all expect to move again.

The degree of mobility that some children accept as normal became very apparent during a recent research enquiry described in Appendix A (Sears, 2011a). This is how one 11-year-old boy from Israel described his moves in a very matter-of-fact manner.

> I was born in Israel, but the first school I went to was in Africa, in the Ivory Coast. I was only three so I don't remember it, but I know I was there and that they talked French. After that I went for two years to Chicago, to an English-speaking Jewish school. Then we went back to Israel and I went to school there. Now we're here [a city in Northern Europe].

He later described the moment when his parents talked to him about his most recent move. They had told him that they were all going to move soon, and that it might be to Australia, or maybe to Belgium. For most adults, the idea of having so little command over their own destiny would be overwhelming. For many students in international schools a series of dislocations and relocations is the life they know and one which is shared by many of their peers in school. It is quite usual to meet children who have moved more frequently than the Israeli student mentioned above. Some students never return to live in what the family might call its home location for the duration of their school years.

2.1.1 Global mobility among families in international schools

For the families whose children attend international schools, global mobility is part of a normal career path in their chosen profession or way of life. Often the move represents a promotion or offers wider experience to the employed parent and is thus viewed as advantageous for the family as a whole. Senior civil servants and diplomats are typical of these groups and most schools in cities such as New York, Geneva and Brussels, where the offices of international organisations are situated, contain large numbers of students from these backgrounds. The families of parents who work in global business and finance represent another group whose children attend international schools. This accounts for the large number of international schools that can be found in established business centres such as Hong Kong and Singapore, as well as in the expanding cities of East Asia and the countries of the Gulf.

A further group of globally mobile workers who may send their children to international schools includes personnel working for aid and non-governmental organisations (NGOs) and journalists. The locations frequented by this group are often more far flung and challenging than is the case with other expatriate workers. However, wherever there are children who require an internationally recognised education in places where numbers of foreign workers are to be found, it is now normal to find international schools of the different types set out in Chapter 1.

2.1.2 The reality of moving globally

The use of the word 'global' in connection with the moves that many families are asked to make is a real indication of the degree of change that they may experience. Many students will have literally crisscrossed the globe while still quite young. The child of an employee in one oil company, for instance, may have spent several years at an international school in the desert in Oman where the company has a large plant. During this time the family must learn to deal with great heat and to take up hobbies and pursuits that are appropriate in that climate and habitat.

The next posting, however, with the same company, may be to the island of Sakhalin off the west coast of Russia where there are only four months in the year when it does not snow and the sea may be frozen for a large part of the time. Here again, the family must learn to adapt its way of life and work to create a viable and enjoyable life for all its members, this time where intense cold is a prevailing factor. Finally, with this particular oil company, there is likely to be a further posting at some point to the European city which is its headquarters. For many employees and their families, this city is home. For a brief period they can re-enter a familiar way of life and their children may be able to attend local schools.

The reality of life for many children is that they move every two to five years throughout their childhood and into young adulthood. Many of these moves involve a change of climate, of language and of lifestyle, not to mention peers and friends, and with each move involving a change of school. Attending an international school where global mobility is accepted and understood may be the sole consistent element in their lives apart from their families.

2.1.3 Changes that impact on the family in the new posting

Chief among the changes that are likely to have an impact on the family is a change in the language of the local community and in the case of children whose first language is not English, the language of the school. Each member of the family may be faced with negotiating a large part of their new lives in an unfamiliar language and culture. This in itself may lead to stressful feelings of isolation, frustration, fatigue and occasional fury. Ideally the family home should be a place where a familiar pattern of life reasserts itself, but this is not always the case if the family is living in temporary accommodation until their permanent home becomes available. (The content of Chapter 3 is devoted to the topics of adjustment and adaptation to new locations.)

2.1.4 Understanding the challenges that face families who move

One of the challenges of being a teacher in an international school is to support newly arrived students as they move through the cycle of adaptation. If it is a first move, the experience takes a different form from that experienced by students who have made multiple moves. It is recognised in international schools that the wellbeing of the family as a whole has an impact on the ways in which children cope with a new move. Maintaining contact with parents and offering support for the family is a vital aspect of teaching in an international school for that reason. The following sections describe some of the different patterns of mobility and the ways in which parents and children may respond.

2.2 First-time Movers

This section is concerned with first-time expatriate families. For this type of family the whole experience of becoming an expatriate is new. They not only have to learn how to live in the new location, but must also deal with the practical and emotional issues of leaving behind family, friends and a familiar way of life. In some cases, the employer may offer guidance and support from the moment the contract is signed. The logistics of the move are organised and families are helped to find a new home, buy a new car and to fulfil any local bureaucratic requirements. Other families may find themselves having to manage independently. In either case there may be hitches in the provision of accommodation or delays in the arrival of goods that have been shipped. It is not unusual for newly arrived families to spend the first few weeks or months either in a hotel or in short-term rental accommodation.

2.2.1 Choosing a school

The first thought in the minds of most parents is the question of schooling for their children. Help in choosing a school, where there is a choice, may be included in the relocation package. It is not unusual, for instance, for employers to provide parents with a paid trip to the new location before the move takes place. This first visit enables parents to view schools and to find accommodation with the journeys to school and work in mind.

A small-scale survey of new parents in one international school described in Appendix B of this book (see also Sears, 2011b), gives some insights into the reasons why families choose an international education for their children. (The parents who completed the survey all had newly arrived young children attending beginner-level classes in English as an Additional Language at the school.) The results of the survey showed that the choice of an English-medium education was made largely for practical reasons. Both parents in each family felt that English was a valuable tool for their children's future education and employment, even from a very young age. Fathers overall placed the learning of English as far and away the most important reason for choosing an English-medium school. The mothers were more nuanced in what they said. Several thought that the school they had finally chosen for their children looked the most 'international'. They felt that their children would 'fit in' better and that their needs would be recognised and addressed. Several parents said that they themselves felt more 'at home' in the school they had chosen – they had been immediately welcomed and made to feel part of a community.

A further reason for choosing an English-medium international school mentioned by many parents was that they expected to move again outside their home country. They recognised the need to place their children in a schooling system that could offer a consistent education wherever they might be posted.

2.2.2 The early days in a new posting

Accommodation and schooling are major features in planning for the move; once in the new setting, however, other more immediate issues have the potential to cause stress. Finding a doctor to treat a suddenly sick child or sourcing trustworthy tradespeople when the sink gets blocked or the boiler fails can present enormous challenges to new arrivals. Crises of this type are all the more stressful when neither parent speaks the local language. Sourcing the necessary residence permits or identity cards can be another source of concern. Conversation about battles with the local bureaucracy at the town hall is common at expatriate coffee mornings.

Non-working spouses and partners

The person who largely copes with these challenges tends to be the non-working spouse or partner (although eventually they may find employment). It is an established fact of life in expatriate postings that the working partner moves immediately into a relatively familiar environment from the moment that they go to their place of work. It is the partner at home who generally experiences the most challenging aspects of settling in the family. The isolation may be compounded by a requirement for new employees to make a tour of their geographical area of responsibility, a trip which can involve days or even weeks away from the family.

In some locations, a supportive network immediately swings into action with offers of practical advice and emotional support for new arrivals. Many established expatriate locations have organisations (mostly aimed at women) which offer targeted support for newcomers and continuing opportunities for socialising and group activities. In other cases, newly arrived parents are left to fend for themselves. Whatever the circumstances, the school has a key role in easing the passage of new parents. Most international schools go out of their way to supply clear and informative documentation and to be overtly welcoming and inclusive in their communications.

Expatriate single parents

Single parents who bring their children with them when they take up expatriate posts face different challenges. A prime need is effective childcare since their new jobs are likely to involve long hours and perhaps travel. Usually new arrivals in this situation have been accustomed to facing up to this challenge in their previous location – some single parents bring long-term carers with them as part of the package that they arrange with their new employers. Others have to hire new staff to take over the role of filling in all the gaps in childcare, including sometimes the task of interacting with the school. Teachers should be aware of the need when this is the case to keep the carer and the parent fully informed. They should also make every effort to include both the parent and carer in all the activities of the school where possible.

2.2.3 Entering school: Keeping parents informed

For parents and children who are not yet proficient users of English, entry into the school community is potentially more stressful. Many schools include specific help for both parents and students and one school, the International School of Brussels, (www.isb.be/), offers checklists on its website setting out necessary information for the first day at school. It also gives details of what children of different ages will need for school and how to obtain the items. This particular school makes this process easy by supplying an attractive pack containing all the necessary stationery items as well as setting out how parents can obtain PE kit from the school shop. The school also provides an extensive list of FAQs for parents, which cover various aspects of school life. The aim is to inspire parents and children with confidence and to limit the level of anxiety as far as possible.

In the case of bilingual schools, or English-medium schools that contain large numbers of local students who speak the community language, these notices are usually given in two or more languages. In some English-medium schools, however, the information tends to be supplied in English only, based on the assumption, often faulty, that both parents are proficient speakers of English.

Many schools do make attempts, often via the Family Association or the Parent Teacher Association, to link up speakers of the same language. In some cases, there are large enough numbers of one national group for consistent provision to be made to support new arrivals to the school. Schools with numbers of Japanese students often have a Japanese parents' group which communicates the essentials to newcomers. It is the case, however, that provision for parents who are not proficient speakers of English tends to be patchy. Sometimes it will become apparent to teachers that parents are not aware of a vital piece of information concerning their child's life in school. When this happens, teachers should try their utmost to find a speaker of the family's language to communicate important information.

Providing a friendly and overtly welcoming interface between the school and the new family is a vital role for teachers. They must be ready to show understanding of the parent's situation and be prepared to offer practical help where there is evident confusion. It is also the responsibility of the teacher to make it clear that the school welcomes parental involvement and is open to dialogue at all times. The first contact that teachers make with new parents is very significant since it can set the tone for all future dealings.

2.2.4 Managing the relationship with those left behind

Managing the relationship with those left behind in the home location is an underlying issue for many first-time movers. By the time a family moves for a second time, all parties have become more accustomed to the situation and recognise that strong relationships can and do continue. It is helpful if some members of the extended family have moved previously, since that enables those left behind to understand that a voluntary move is not a sign of betrayal or rejection. Often it is grandparents who express hurt and sadness at the removal of their grandchildren, feelings which they express in a number of ways. They may ring regularly to check on their grandchildren's continuing use of the home language or they may question them on their pattern of religious observance.

Fortunately, modern technology offers rich possibilities for regular communication and for keeping families living abroad in touch with those who remain behind. Photos and video clips of the location, the new family home and the new school transferred via electronic means are wonderful ways of making friends and relations feel connected. Instant messaging allows children and parents to communicate with friends and family in real time and Skype offers a cheap means of allowing long phone calls to grandparents, cousins and friends.

This level of continuing closeness and involvement is enhanced if there is a realistic hope of family and friends at home being able to visit the expatriate family in their new posting and of expatriate families being able to return home regularly. Fortunately, most globally mobile families have the financial means to make visits home (sometimes included in their expatriate packages) and to act as hosts to visiting family and friends. In any case, other practical reasons lead them to maintain their links with home. Most expatriate families expect to return to their home base at some point. This being the case, they have every incentive to maintain the connection with their home language and culture, their friendship circle and pattern of religious observance. Many also keep continuing contact with the home schooling system, knowing that their children may be called upon to re-enter that system either at school or university level.

2.2.5 Issues relating to the new location

Other aspects of the new posting may present challenges to members of the family in different ways. Among these are concerns about security which may be an issue in some locations. Such concerns include the possibility of kidnapping, the presence of terrorist threats, and general instability in the region where the family has been posted. Where these risks are real, the school and the employer will always give advice about the appropriate ways to keep the family safe. However, until it becomes quite automatic to carry out the recommended security procedures, life in these postings can feel constrained and even threatening. Later in the posting, an awareness of security issues becomes part of life and most families are able to rebuild their sense of security and to take up their normal activities.

Different cultural expectations in new postings

A further issue that families may face for the first time is a difference in expectation about the ways that women and girls and men and boys are expected to behave. This applies both to cultural expectations in the local community and also to school life in general. For some families, the local customs relating to women and girls may appear restrictive and even threatening. This might be the case in settings where women are not allowed to drive or to carry out certain activities independently. In many societies, for instance, women and girls are not expected to be seen in mixed company apart from with family members.

On the other hand, families from different backgrounds may be upset and disapproving of the freedom that is given to women and girls in the new location. They may feel uneasy about the form of dress that seems to be normal. They may be particularly concerned about the type of social life that is customary in most international schools. Managing the impact of differences of this sort is a regular feature of leading a globally mobile existence. For the most part, however, the majority of families learn to adjust their lifestyle and to build up lives that are acceptable to themselves and which are viewed as appropriate within the cultural context.

2.3 Serial Movers

A large number of the families whose children are educated in international schools might be described as serial movers. Their lives are made up of a series of moves lasting between two and five years. These moves may take the form of a series of foreign postings or be interspersed with time in the home setting. Thus children may have moved in and out of school systems and in and out of school languages. Neither do parents always choose an international school in every new posting. When families are posted to an English-speaking country, many opt to place their children in local state or independent schools so that they can gain further experience of an English-medium education.

In other postings, where the local language is regarded as globally prestigious, some parents prefer to place their children in local schools so that they have the opportunity to acquire this language. This is a choice that may be made in countries where French or another world language such as Spanish or Arabic is spoken. A Korean student interviewed in the course of the research enquiry described in Appendix A recounted how his father had been influenced by just these considerations in the choices he made for his son's education in the family's different postings. During the family's first posting to Jakarta in Indonesia his father had placed him in an English-medium international school. When they arrived in Paris, however, his father decided that he should go to a French-speaking school in order to become proficient in a further prestigious language. Since then his family had been posted back to Seoul for three years where he had re-entered the Korean system. Now he was attending an English-medium school once more (Sears, 2011a).

Text Box 2.1 Creating an ongoing language passport

A new practice has come into use in some international schools that involves students setting out their own history of mobility and educational experience with the emphasis on the languages they have encountered and used in each location. Often these accounts are gathered together in a notebook or binder and may be called 'language passports' or 'the story of my life'. Apps that provide frameworks for building narrative and opportunities to download photographs and graphics offer an alternative approach, although a permanent hard copy has many advantages. (*Voice Thread* and *Explain Everything* are two of the possible apps for use in creating language passports or life narratives; see the Resources section at the end of this chapter for links.) The aim is for students to create, with the help of their parents where necessary, an ongoing account of their globally mobile lifestyle which they carry with them from school to school.

Such accounts also offer students a way of validating their educational and linguistic experience. Research (Sears, 2011a) indicates that globally mobile students use narrative as a means of maintaining their sense of self in a life of constant change.

2.3.1 Mid-year arrivals

Other features of a mobile lifestyle have an impact on class teachers as well as students. Many employers aim to move employees with children only in the school holidays. Sometimes, circumstances intervene which make this impossible. This may be for internal organisational reasons or can sometimes be the result of the family moving from one hemisphere to another. (Schools in the Southern Hemisphere have their long summer break around Christmas and the school year starts at the end of January. In the Northern Hemisphere the school year starts in September.) As a result, new children may enter a class in the middle of the school year and indeed a degree of coming and going throughout the school year is the norm in international schools.

Experienced teachers are accustomed to offering the same level of introductory support to these new arrivals as they do to the whole class at the beginning of the school year. They are also accustomed to the seemingly limitless permutations of postings, schooling and languages that some children will have experienced. For new teachers, especially those who have experienced a previously stable way of life, this degree of mobility can be challenging. Soon, however, they will recognise that this lifestyle is the norm for most families and is the experience that unites the whole community in international schools that serve a mobile population.

2.3.2 Becoming a 'seasoned' mover

Families for whom mobility is a way of life become 'seasoned' movers. This description can be true of the families of diplomats, of international civil servants and of highly mobile business personnel. Such families follow an established pattern for making decisions about key aspects of living in the new setting and are accustomed to the process of rapidly adapting to and settling into a new location. The quicker the practical issues are arranged and contacts with the local network are made, the sooner something like a normal life can resume. Since many postings last for three years or fewer, there is clearly an advantage in getting through these early stages as fast as possible. (This is especially the case, as experienced movers know, since what is believed to be a two- or three-year stay can sometimes be terminated at short notice.)

2.3.3 The challenges of being a serial mover

A life of global mobility does not always follow this positive pattern for some families. New circumstances may make the idea of yet another move less attractive. Sometimes these circumstances relate to family members back at home. The illness of grandparents and parents is the most typical of these and may present great challenges to families living abroad. Individuals who have been expatriates recognise this pattern of events and understand that there is no satisfactory way of coping with the need and desire to be in two places at once. The result is usually a series of rushed flights home and tense phone calls with relatives, frequently accompanied by unresolvable guilt and sadness.

Other factors present challenges in a life of mobility. A life of constant uprooting and dislocation is only manageable when there is a strong partnership at the heart of the family. Reasons for difficulties in a relationship caused by a global lifestyle are not hard to find. Stress can be placed on the partnership when the individual who customarily takes on the role of carer and facilitator for the family as a whole finds a new posting difficult. This situation is recognised by people who move frequently. Individuals who view themselves as a competent human beings and who generally enjoy the challenge of moving may find themselves unable to engage positively with the next move. It is as if they have used up all the energy they customarily bring to bear on managing the entry to a new location. The thought of the next move is overwhelming.

This can be true of working partners, but most often it is the 'trailing' partner who begins to feel that a life of constant mobility is unrewarding and unsatisfactory, particularly if constant moves prevent them from building up a substantial working life. A life of ease and freedom to choose what you do with your time might appear very attractive to fully engaged and hard-working teachers in international schools. In some locations, however, non-working partners in the family appear to lead a life that we might recognise from a novel set in the 1930s. They concern themselves with the children (with extensive help), attend coffee mornings, run fundraising activities, support their partners at social events and go shopping. This may be very enjoyable for a short time but for many 'trailing' spouses and partners this way of life has little long-term appeal.

It is understandable that those who have given up their own careers in order to accompany their partner on a move may at times feel frustrated and resentful, whatever the attractions of the new lifestyle.

Finding a meaningful occupation as a 'trailing' spouse or partner

Often the first time that new teachers appreciate some of the issues relating to non-working partners is at the first parent conference. It is common to find that a parent who has previously appeared as a rather anxious and concerned individual is in fact a lawyer or a journalist or a teacher. In making the move they have left behind a large part of what defined themselves in order to become the full-time manager of the family. Often it is the mothers for whom this is a major problem, but increasingly it is fathers who have opted to place their working life on hold so that their partners can take up an advantageous career opportunity.

In more stable circumstances both partners would pursue their careers and sometimes, if the local visa regulations allow it, it is possible for so-called 'trailing' spouses and partners to find appropriate work in the new location. (Locally hired teachers are an example of this.) Some employers of expatriates are in a position to offer work to the partners of their employees. Israeli Embassies around the world are known to adopt this policy wherever possible. They see this as a means of enhancing the wellbeing and effectiveness of the family as a whole and of retaining links with the home country and culture. Unfortunately, such opportunities are not available to everyone. Visa restrictions and the non-transferability of qualifications in many locations tend to limit the possibility of employment for the 'trailing' partners of expatriates.

The possibilities presented by the growth of digital technology offer a positive option for the non-employed partner in this situation. By this means, some trailing partners are enabled to continue in their former area of work on an online basis to the benefit of the whole family.

Where is home for a globally mobile family?

Topics such as the nature of home and where a family belongs are part of the basic currency of life in international schools even if not expressed in those terms. Parents and children may say they are from India, for instance, or Japan, or the United States, even if they have not lived in these places for several years and in fact rarely visit them. For families who move, home may be a concept that provides a sense of security rather than a place that they communicate with or visit regularly. It is common, for instance, for individual members of a family to think of a different place as home.

Children making their first move usually feel a continuing affinity with the country that is their birthplace and may express this feeling very strongly. Children who have experienced a series of moves more commonly accept that home is the place where they live at the present time and where their family is.

Text Box 2.2 Where is home for a globally mobile family? A parent's view

The concept of home in a globally mobile family was discussed in a semi-structured interview carried out in the course of the research enquiry described in Appendix A. The participant was Gunilla, a Swedish mother of three boys married to a

German-speaking American/Argentinian husband (his family had moved to Germany to further his father's career). The interview was interesting because it offered an insight into the way in which individuals in globally mobile families may each view home as being a different place. The family in question had experienced numerous moves which involved a number of schooling systems and exposure to several languages. Neither parent felt strong ties to their birth countries.

A key point of interest that emerged was that the parents had made a decision to call one location in their series of moves 'the family home'. The country involved was not the place of birth of either of the parents and the local language was not a primary language of any member of the family. The reason given for the choice was that all the members of the family had been very happy in the posting and it had lasted for six years instead of the standard three. The mother, Gunilla, describes how the choice came about:

Researcher: And where do think the boys will choose to go to college?

Gunilla: Well, Stephan wants to go to the States.

Researcher: I suppose that is because your husband has an American background.

Gunilla: My husband is American – they're all American. My children have American passports. But going back to your question about family roots – it's an interesting one. I mean I've lived in Boston, Los Angeles, Paris, Montevideo, Atlanta and now Amsterdam. Paris, Boston and Los Angeles I don't count because it was my professional time – and you know, us with our children in Paris, Atlanta and now Amsterdam, we have the feeling we're living as expats.

Researcher: But you say you don't feel that about Montevideo? You didn't have any family connection there, did you?

Gunilla: No. It's because we had loads of friends. It's home for us now, our emotional home. When we left Uruguay, we were there from 1996 to 2002, we made a few decisions and one was to keep the house so we would always have a place to go back to. And we said this will be our emotional home. Whatever happens this is our base. This also means we invest in time and in finances to go back every 6–12 months and the children always go to school there and see their old friends and pick up their Spanish.

2.3.4 Globally mobile parents: A well-educated and articulate group

New teachers will find that mobile families are clear sighted about their life of constant relocation. Most recognise the benefits that come with being sponsored expatriates and most understand the challenges. Because many parents whose children attend international schools are themselves well-educated, they tend to be articulate and considered in their assessment of the pluses and minuses of mobility. It is not unusual to find parents who have read widely on the issues of bringing up a family in these circumstances, and most schools expect a good attendance at the courses they offer in 'managing a mobile lifestyle'.

2.4 The Reality of Being a Globally Mobile Child

A mobile lifestyle of the sort described in the previous sections raises many questions about the impact of constant relocations on families as a whole and on children in particular. At first, it might seem that children live a privileged and cosseted existence and it is true that many students in international schools are rich in a material sense. Sponsored expatriate families tend to live in comfortable, sometimes luxurious accommodation, may have live-in staff and most enjoy frequent and glamorous-sounding holidays. Listening to the talk of young globetrotters, it is clear that many are familiar with a lifestyle beyond the reach of most children and also of most teachers.

After a period of working with these students, however, it becomes apparent that their lives contain inbuilt challenges that their more stable peers do not face. Each time they move, they must learn to reframe their notion of home and of where they belong. Every move requires them to adapt to the new school and a new location and to create once more a circle of friends. All this takes place in the knowledge and understanding that they will probably be asked to move again. For these reasons, the experience of globally mobile students in international schools is quite different from children who stay in one place.

Text Box 2.3 Where do I belong? A student's view

The topic of belonging came up during a semi-structured interview with Omar, aged 12, from Malaysia, carried out in the course of the research enquiry described in Appendix A. His account is interesting because it illustrates the shifts in schooling and exposure to diverse cultures that globally mobile students like Omar experience. It is also interesting because Omar himself recognises that he 'misses' the place he has just moved from rather than the place he might be expected to 'miss', which his original home in Malaysia.

Researcher: Right, let's just do a quick trip through your life. Your father is a diplomat, isn't he? Can I ask you what languages you speak at home?

Omar: My father Malay and my mother sometimes English.

Researcher: What age were you when you went to Ghana?

Omar:	I was in proper school. I was about four. I was there till I was seven.
Researcher:	And where did you go next?
Omar:	We went back to Malaysia for about six months though we weren't in our home town. My father's job was in another place.
Researcher:	Did you go to school there?
Omar:	I went to a sort of international school and we spoke English.
Researcher:	After six months in Malaysia, where did you go next?
Omar:	We went to Cuba. I went to the International School of Havana.
Researcher:	Did you go into ESL there?
Omar:	No, I didn't because I had to take Spanish. They said my English was good enough.
Researcher:	How long were you in Cuba before you came here?
Omar:	Three years
Researcher:	Could I ask this question – it's a difficult one for people who move a lot. Which of these places do you feel is home? Do you still have friends in Malaysia, for instance?
Omar:	No. I only knew my cousins in Malaysia. Right now, Cuba is the place I miss a lot.
Researcher:	When you came here is that where you missed?
Omar:	Yes. Because when I went to Cuba I missed Malaysia.
Researcher:	I see – you miss the place you lived in before, don't you?
Omar:	Yes. I realise now, if I stay here longer, I will get used to this place.

2.4.1 The importance of the family unit

The role of the family is critical in the lives of children who are constantly moving. Children in international schools tend to spend more time with their immediate family members, and to look to their parents to initiate their social and recreational activity. Friendship has different dimensions when you move every few years and thus children may not readily build up a network of friends outside school. In some cases, where it is feasible for expatriate children take part in locally organised activities such as sports or scouting or guiding, they may acquire friends from within the local community. Sometimes, however, it is not customary in the locality for children to mix with non-family members and in these cases many expatriate children spend time outside school only with other young people whose families are globally mobile and who are friendly with their parents.

2.4.2 Patterns of attachment in different postings

Children who move build up patterns of attachment in each posting which are different from children who have never moved or who stay in touch with a familiar way of life. It is common when new arrivals are asked about their previous posting for students (particularly young children) to talk about a carer who was very dear to them. In some cases, the time spent with the maid or nanny results in children having acquired her language. It can happen that newly arrived young children may know more Tagalog (the language of their Filipina nanny) than their parents' language.

Older children also express great sadness at leaving a special person behind; remaining in touch can be difficult, either because carers lack access to technology or because they now care for another expatriate child. Other objects of attachment associated with a previous posting may be dearly loved pets. Sadly, owing to quarantine regulations, these pets must often be left behind and for many children this is a traumatic separation. It is quite common for newly arrived students to mention the loss of a pet as the reason for their sense of loss at leaving their former home.

Children assessing the pluses and minuses of a life of mobility

In line with their parents' clear-sighted view of what it means to be globally mobile, children who move are very perceptive observers of their mobile lifestyle. Perhaps this is a way of managing the constant cycle of transition and adaptation that is part of this way of life. The very youngest children can give an account of the reasons for enjoying a mobile lifestyle and also the challenges it presents. Until they are teenagers, most children 'go along' with their parents and appear to accept and even embrace most aspects of their family's mobile existence. As they become older, they are more vocal in their objections to being moved, although older students will continue to express a balance between the advantages and disadvantages. Most accept that they have become 'people who move'.

2.4.3 Introducing the term 'global nomad'

The term 'global nomad' has been coined to describe children and young people who have moved globally from place to place throughout much or all of their childhood (Schaetti, 2000). Individuals who are described as global nomads are held to share certain behavioural characteristics which distinguish them from young people who have stable childhoods. Websites abound that offer support to global nomads who find it difficult to settle in one place or to relate long term to people they meet in young adulthood. An illuminating account of one person's experience as a global nomad is given on the website of http://www.worldweave.com/procon.htm, under the heading of 'The pros and cons of being a global nomad'.

Table 2.1 displays some of the characteristics that have come to be associated with global nomads. It should be treated with caution because, of course, individuals react in different ways to similar experiences.

Note: A further term, 'third culture kids' (TCKs), is also in current use to describe the same group of individuals. This term draws on the idea of globally mobile students occupying a third cultural space that differentiates them from their stable peers. The theory and descriptions associated with the term 'third culture kids' are addressed in Section 3.6.

Table 2.1 Some characteristics associated with global nomads

Global nomads . . .	Why might they feel like this?
May suffer a sense of rootlessness.	They have never developed a feeling of attachment to one place for any period of time. Where do they belong?
May feel a continuing sense of restlessness – they find it difficult to stay long in one place even in adulthood.	Throughout their childhood they were expected to move every few years. They get bored, or want to resolve everyday problems by moving on.
May have difficulty in committing to long-term relationships.	They have probably become expert in making friends rapidly and letting those friendships go equally rapidly. They may shrink from a total commitment to any one relationship.
May suffer from feelings of unexplainable loss and grief.	Their moves happened repeatedly and were out of their control. They didn't have time to process their feelings of sadness and loss at continuously leaving behind people and places.
May feel a sense of kinship and connection to many parts of the world. This may not be shared by their more stable peers who may seem narrow-minded and parochial.	They have been exposed to a wide range of experiences of different lifestyles, cultures, political regimes and viewpoints. They may find it difficult to engage in the seemingly small-town concerns of stable residents.
Will probably have an outsider's view of their own country. This is sometimes painful and separates them from their home-country peers.	Living away for periods of time from the home country and being exposed to other ways living and different viewpoints gives global nomads an objective view of their home country. They may become aware that their home country (particularly if it is economically powerful or has a colonial history) is viewed differently by other nationals from the way it is perceived from within.
Are adept at being openly friendly and engaging with new people. They can always find something to talk about with new acquaintances and will quickly enter into social arrangements.	When they arrived at a new posting, they developed the ability to create new friendships and social networks quickly. They knew they would move on – there was no time to waste in getting to know people slowly.
Have probably developed cross-cultural skills. This may be in relation to a host country culture or because of the multinational nature of their international school.	They are accustomed to difference and enjoy it. They may be alienated and feel isolated by any anti-immigrant and anti-foreigner viewpoints expressed by their more stable peers.
Probably speak more than one language and think that is quite normal.	They find it difficult to adjust in countries where one language is seen as overwhelmingly most useful and powerful (such as English!).

2.5 Newly Arrived Teachers

Most of the literature concerned with mobility and international schools focuses on students and their parents. But mobility is a fact of life for teachers too, and first-time movers will generally experience many of the same challenges as new students and parents.

Most schools address the needs of new teachers by offering an orientation prior to the opening of the school term. Some have adopted a more wide-ranging approach to welcoming new teachers. Under this type of provision, a volunteer from among the established teaching staff takes on the role of 'buddy' or mentor. These teachers meet new arrivals at the airport and ferry them to their initial accommodation. Later they may help them to find appropriate accommodation and chauffeur them to appointments to sign contracts and on shopping trips. In some geographical locations, it is customary for accommodation to be included in the remuneration 'package'. This may be an attractive option in the early days. It takes some of the uncertainty out of the process of settling in and provides possibilities for making rapid social contacts.

It is also true that some schools largely leave newly arrived teachers to make their own way. This can be the case with small schools, and schools containing large numbers of local students where mobility is not a shared experience. If this appears to be the case with a new school, it is good policy to research the new location thoroughly online before arrival. It is always easier to have some prior understanding of the pattern and costs of accommodation and of things such as transport, security and way of life.

2.5.1 Choosing how to live in the new location

International schools are places where moving is a shared experience and where welcoming new arrivals and discussion about settling in are part of the way of life. Established colleagues are generally happy to share their knowledge and expertise, not only about school-related matters but also about building a life in the host country. In most schools this type of assistance is given as a matter of course and many newly arrived teachers find a long-lasting friendship group from among their peers at the school. Other new arrivals opt from the start to live somewhat outside the school community, preferring to create a different sort of lifestyle. In any school, there are teachers who are content to remain within the English-speaking community and to spend their leisure time with colleagues taking part in largely expatriate-sponsored activities. Others prefer to try to learn the local language, live in areas unfrequented by expatriates and generally embed themselves in local life.

2.6 The School's Role as a Centre of Community

A visitor to the campus of a large international school on a typical Saturday in the school year will find a hive of activity. Regular sporting fixtures will be taking place on the pitches and courts, and other school facilities will be occupied either by school-organised groups or by members of the wider expatriate community. On many campuses it is usual to see children practising 'Little League' baseball and expatriate theatre groups rehearsing in the school's auditorium. This type of sponsorship is viewed by the school as part of its role in fostering a sense of community within and around the school.

At all these events, groups of parents and children gather round in various active or supportive roles. These activities may include preparing and serving food, participating in fundraising efforts and manning information booths. The overall impression is of individuals and groups gathering together to socialise and to support ongoing community events.

2.6.1 Contributing to the wellbeing of the whole family

Most international schools willingly take on the role of providing a ready-made community for globally mobile families. They view this provision as an essential part of offering a positive and effective learning environment to students. Where parents (chiefly the 'trailing' partner) are happy, then their children are likely to settle in more quickly and to engage more fully. As a result, schools expend much effort in including parents on an ongoing basis. One large international school in East Asia makes clear its commitment to this philosophy by offering opportunities for parents to find 'meaningful and varied ways to engage in their child's learning and life at our school'. These include the activities customary in many schools such as serving on the governing body, volunteering as a class representative and participating in the Parent Teacher Association, but also include volunteering and supportive activities across a wide range of events.

2.6.2 The international school: A 'one-stop' shop?

For mobile families and teachers, the ability to move immediately into a community which understands their lifestyle and offers opportunities for rapid inclusion in a social group is attractive. One website describes this type of provision at an international school as a 'One-stop Shop – a place where families can find everything they need'. It may be this sense of an all-encompassing community, however, that leads outsiders sometimes to view international schools as privileged enclaves existing inside an exclusive 'English-speaking bubble'.

The reality of the life that families build for themselves is more nuanced. In the population of any school, numbers of parents and teachers interact with the local community out of necessity or make conscious efforts to move outside the context of the school and to embrace accessible aspects of the local culture. In any location also, there are families and teachers who stay longer or who make real friends among residents in the local population, sometime finding new partners. Among this group, the experience of living in the locations understandably takes a different form from that of short-term expatriates.

Key Points in This Chapter

- A life of global mobility is the norm for some emergent bilingual children and their families.
- Parents place their children in international schools to learn English and to ensure consistency of educational provision in a life of mobility.
- There are built-in challenges to being globally mobile.
- The experiences of first-time movers and serial movers tend to take different forms.
- Globally mobile children tend to share certain characteristics.
- The term 'global nomad' has been coined to describe children and young people who experience a globally mobile lifestyle.
- Teachers new to international schools also experience the challenges of transition.
- Newly arrived teachers receive different levels of support from their employing schools.
- A recognised role of international schools is to serve as a hub for school families and the wider expatriate community.

Resources

Websites of international schools mentioned in this chapter
International School of Brussels: www.isb.be.

Websites offering resources on the topics mentioned in this chapter
For creating an interactive narrative – *Explain Everything*: http://www.newschooltechnology.org/2013/02/explain-everything/.

For creating an oral interactive narrative, check out *VoiceThread* via the Educause Initiative site: http://net.educause.edu/ir/library/pdf/EL17050.pdf .

Global nomads: http://www.worldweave.com/procon.htm.

References

Schaetti, B.F. (2000) Global nomad identity: Hypothesizing a developmental model. Unpublished PhD dissertation, The Union Institute, Cincinnati, OH.

Sears, C. (2011a) Integrating multiple identities: Narrative in the formation and maintenance of the self in international school students. *Journal of Research in International Education* 10 (1), 71–86.

Sears, C. (2011b) Listening to parents: Acknowledging the range of linguistic and cultural diversity in an early childhood classroom. In E. Murphy (ed.) *Welcoming Linguistic Diversity in Early Childhood Classrooms*. Bristol: Multilingual Matters.

3 Adjusting to a Life of Change

Chapter 3 is concerned with change and adaptation. It sets out the phases of adjustment that globally mobile individuals tend to move through when they meet new cultures during their lives of mobility. It describes the ways in which international schools have evolved into places where mobile students from different cultural and linguistic backgrounds can feel at home. Finally, it examines the experience of growing up as the sort of individual who may be described as a 'third culture kid' (TCK).

The sequence of Chapter 3 is as follows:

- Introduction: adjusting to mobility.
- Culture shock: phases of adjustment.
- Adjusting to a new culture: the ice-berg theory.
- Adjusting to a life of transition.
- Students talking about their lives of global mobility.
- Supporting students in transition.
- International schools: supportive spaces for children who move.
- Living between cultures: being a TCK.

Introduction: Adjusting to Mobility

A major aspect of a globally mobile lifestyle is the need constantly to adjust, sometimes in a three-yearly cycle. When individuals move, they inevitably face a period of adjustment to the new setting, whether the move is made as part of a family or unaccompanied, perhaps as a teacher. The process of coming to terms with a new location takes several forms, including adaptation to living in a new cultural setting and adjusting to the fact of the move itself. Globally mobile individuals may vary in their response to the new surroundings but the need to adjust at some level is inescapable.

Phases of adjustment

The process of adjusting to a life of mobility has been described as a series of phases. This approach has been applied to the way individuals adapt to a new cultural setting and to a life in transition. Talking about change in terms of phases is common currency on the international school circuit and schools usually accept that it is part of their role to support students and parents during the adjustment period.

Sections 3.1 and 3.2 of this chapter are concerned with adjusting to a new cultural setting. Section 3.1 contains a description of the generally recognised phases that people experience, including the impact of what is often called 'culture shock'. The second section examines a further facet of cultural adaptation by using the image of the 'ice-berg' to account for the experiences of new arrivals.

Further sections discuss aspects of the transitioning process. They include a description of the recognisable phases, how students talk about their experience of transition and what schools do practically to support students through the process. Finally, Section 3.5 describes the ways in which international schools have evolved in order to provide supportive spaces for globally mobile students and Section 3.6 introduces the concept of TCKs.

Text Box 3.1 Ideas and terms associated with talking about culture

Ice-berg theory of culture: The image of an ice-berg is used to convey the idea that much of what we view as belonging to a particular culture is very superficial. It is easy to think of Japan, for instance, as a land of samurai, kimonos, cherry blossom and (nowadays) of technology and gaming. According to the ice-berg theory (Ruhly, 1976), those features only represent about 10% of what comprises the culture of Japan. The core beliefs, expectations and values of a culture make up a hidden 90%. New expatriates in a location may initially only perceive the 'top 10%'. Life becomes potentially more complicated when they become aware of the deep differences that are hidden beneath the surface. These differences include ideas about the ways to raise children, the nature of friendship, the concept of fairness, body language, and so on. Expatriates who move beyond the 'tourist' phase (see Section 3.2) of the new culture are likely to have to engage with these underlying elements.

Culture (as in 'belonging to a culture'): Culture used in this sense is generally taken to be the defining values, customs and habits which are shared by a social group. Membership of these groups can be the result of an accident of birth, as in the case of belonging to one nation or tribe, or it can be the result of life choices or events which happen at a later date. Used in its widest sense, this view of culture can include the cultures of gender, of particular professions, of sports and of artistic communities. The understanding of culture that underpins this book is that cultures do not have precise boundaries. Most individuals are members of multiple cultural groups, each having its own values and customs. Many individuals learn to operate in different ways in the different cultural settings they inhabit. A French-speaking woman doctor from Canada, married to a Japanese businessman and the mother of two trilingual children would not be an unusual person within the community of an international school. She is an example of an individual who moves in multiple cultural spheres.

Culture (as in 'languages and cultures'): This phrase is frequently heard in the world of international education. It is a shorthand means of talking about the many different ways of being and thinking that comprise the school community. Often culture in this sense stands in place of the word 'nationality'. It is this notion of culture which is being celebrated at the international festivals that are a feature of international schools and which showcase food and drink and national dress. Viewing culture in this way can lead to more general stereotyping such as in assuming that: 'all Korean students are good at mathematics' or 'all Japanese students find it difficult to learn English'. Increasingly, schools are becoming aware of the more profound elements of their students' cultural backgrounds, including the need to take account of students' and parents' expectations about teaching and learning. In any case, globally mobile families have been exposed to multiple experiences because of their travels and it would be foolish to assume that they continue to represent only one cultural background.

School culture (as in 'international schools have their own culture'): This use of the word culture refers to the distinctive ethos that evolves in organisations and institutions as a result of their unique history and mission. In many international schools, particularly those that serve globally mobile families, a distinct culture has evolved in answer to the needs of their target student population. They tend to be overtly welcoming and inclusive and have developed programmes and pedagogic approaches that enable mobile students to experience a relatively seamless education.

Culture shock: This term is used as a shorthand means of describing the moment when recently arrived individuals begin to find things difficult in the new posting. For many people the first few weeks or months are full of interest and excitement. Culture shock may occur when the excitement wears off and the reality of making a life in the new location breaks through the euphoria.

Transitions, transitions programmes: In recent years this term has emerged as a means to describe the experience of being an individual who moves frequently. The experience of moving is broken up into phases with recognised characteristics. In the school setting, transitions programmes help stakeholders in the school community process their feelings about their mobile lifestyle. Most programmes offer practical approaches and activities to ease the transition experience, ideally for students, parents and staff.

Third culture kid (TCK): A term used to describe young adults who have experienced a globally mobile childhood and who have more in common with the community of individuals who have moved constantly than with a single stable cultural setting. TCKs have turned to the internet to share their feelings and to keep in touch with their peers. (See Section 3.6 'Living between cultures: Third culture kids', for a detailed discussion of this topic.)

(Continued)

Text Box 3.1 Ideas and terms associated with talking about culture (*Continued*)

Cross-cultural, intercultural: Both these terms refer to the ways in which two or more cultures interact. Many employers of multinational workforces see the value of teaching cross-cultural awareness or intercultural communication to their employees in order to create a more effective team approach.

Bi-cultural, hybrid, multicultural: These terms refer to individuals who appear to reflect the values, attitudes and customs of two or more cultures. Often they are also bilingual or speak a number of languages. This can happen as a result of having parents from two or more cultural backgrounds, or from living the whole of one's childhood years in a country outside the passport country. Like bilinguals, bi-cultural individuals often present only the aspect of themselves which fits in best in a given social setting.

Cultural, linguistic and social capital: The idea of languages, cultures and social standing attracting capital derives from Bourdieu's (1991) work. His notion of capital encompasses the idea that these elements carry different levels of kudos or status according to the setting that is being described. In Bourdieu's case, he was referring to schools containing students whose first language was not French and who did not have access to the way in which people learnt and behaved in French-speaking schools. The idea is frequently used now to describe the capital that English carries and which can overwhelm and disempower speakers of other languages and from other ethnic backgrounds in English-medium schools.

3.1 Culture Shock: Phases of Adjustment

This section is concerned with one way of describing the experiences of individuals as they come to terms with living in a new cultural setting. The term 'culture shock' is often used when talking about adjustment in this way.

The subject of adjusting to a new culture is a frequent topic in the expatriate magazines that are often published in locations where there is a large community of temporary foreign residents. Many of these articles include the term 'culture shock' in the heading and describe the process of adjustment to a new cultural setting in terms of recognisable phases. For many first-time expatriates it is helpful to realise that they are not alone in feeling the range of emotions that crowd in upon them as they come to terms with living in the new location. To this end, some enlightened international schools lay on well-attended courses for new arrivals that explain the likely phases of adaptation and provide a supportive meeting place for participants in the early days.

Talking about adjusting to a new culture in this way is undoubtedly a helpful way of breaking down and reflecting upon the experience. Many expatriates would recognise the validity of the aspects of adjustment that are described. Cultural commentators,

Table 3.1 Phases in adjusting to a new culture

Phases in adjusting to a new culture and way of living	*Implications*
Honeymoon period – an entry phase	For some people, the excitement and novelty of the new location and a new way of life carries them forward on a wave of euphoria. They enjoy the differences and embrace all the new experiences. They go on trips to explore the new location and try out all sorts of new food and drink. The thrill of the move helps to overcome any initial difficulties. They think they will settle in easily to the new way of life.
Living in an expatriate 'bubble' as A permanent tourist: one of the ways of adjusting to a new cultural setting	Some families tend to live their lives effectively as tourists for the duration of their stay. This tends to be more likely if they have a limited-term contract, or are serial movers. It seems less unsettling for the family to stay within the familiar orbit of the school and the expatriate community. They seldom engage deeply with difficult aspects of the local culture such as language and they rarely move outside the expatriate community for their social activity.
Reality breaks through: Culture shock	For many families, at some point, the realities of their new life break through the euphoria of living in a new, exciting place. Many of the regular chores and activities involved in running a family seem complicated and take longer to do. The differences that seemed so compelling at the beginning of the posting now seem much less attractive. Finding real friendship seems very hard work after the initial phase. Above all, it is all different and that is very tiring. Possibly relationships within the family are fretful and strained as a result of a seemingly imposed move.
Learning to adapt	Eventually, in most cases, individual family members begin to understand how things function in the workplace, at school and in daily interaction with the local community. Doing things doesn't take so much effort. They begin to appreciate in a deeper sense some of the underlying values in the new culture. They may commit to the new location and sign up for language classes. They may move outside the expatriate community and find their social life in a wider circle that includes people from the local community. This may happen when both partners work in a two-parent household and when their children join local scouts or guides and sports clubs.
Re-entering the home culture	Returning home, particularly after a number of years abroad, may involve a similar process of adjustment. Families feel that their home country ought to be completely familiar and that they will just slot back into their previous pattern of living. They may experience the same initial euphoria at being near family and friends once more, at speaking their own language and being able, apparently, to take up where they left off. In fact, after the initial phase, they will become aware that things have moved on at home and that their family and friends are used to them being away. Suddenly everything may seem very predictable and dull and, above all, few people want to hear their tales of living abroad. In effect, they must build up their contacts and create a new way of life as if their home location were a new place.

Note: This table comes with the caveat that the phases it spells out are useful ways of talking about adjustment issues. They are helpful theorisations rather than matters of fact.

however, might wish to point out that it is misleading to describe culture as an entity with fixed boundaries. Cultures have 'fuzzy' edges and individuals react to new cultures in line with their prior experiences and existing cultural expectations. Table 3.1 sets out what are viewed as the standard phases in adjusting to a new culture.

3.2 Experiencing Life in a Different Cultural Setting

Looking at what happens in practice when individuals make their homes in different cultural settings suggests further ways of reflecting on the process of adaptation. One influential contribution to the discussion about the nature of cross-cultural adjustment is offered by the 'ice-berg theory' of culture. In the light of this theory, some of the experiences of newly arrived residents as set out in the 'culture shock' cycle become easier to understand. When culture is viewed as an ice-berg, where a significant part of the structure is invisible, then the reasons for misunderstandings and frustration become clearer.

3.2.1 The 'ice-berg' theory of culture

The 'ice-berg' theory of culture (Ruhly, 1976), as described in Text Box 3.1 'Terms and ideas discussed in this chapter', uses the concept of an ice-berg, where a large percentage of the mass of ice lies hidden under the surface of the sea, to suggest the nature of culture. In this theorisation, the concept of culture is held to mean the defining values, customs and habits which are shared by a social group.

When expatriates first arrive in a new location, it is the immediately obvious cultural differences in the new community that strike them first. These represent the top 10% of the cultural ice-berg, according to the theory. These aspects include language, food, dress, styles of building, national celebrations, the ways men and women act outside their homes, tourist sites, and so on. It takes much longer, if ever, for new arrivals to perceive the 90% of culture that lies beneath the surface of the ocean. These hidden elements include the nature of friendship in the new location, how relationships between men and women work, ideas about courtesy, attitudes toward age, views on raising children, the impact of religious observance on everyday life, and many, many more.

3.2.2 The reality for short-term expatriates

Realistically, short-term expatriates who may stay in a posting for only three years are fortunate to gain access to the inner workings of local society. A real experience of closeness to individuals and participation in local community events tends only to happen in many locations when newcomers are experts in the language or have previous personal contacts. In many settings, the family is central to social life and it may not be customary for outsiders to be invited into the family home. In these locations, such contact as takes place tends to occur in restaurants or other neutral spaces and to involve an international elite among the local population.

In some locations there may be a greater chance of meaningful social contact. In societies where friends as well as family occupy a central place in social life it may be possible to strike up friendships. Often it is neighbours who may bring newcomers into contact with local people by inviting them to parties or barbecues or events associated with local festivals. On other occasions, as in any location in the world, children on the street become friendly and introduce their families to one another.

On the whole, rather limited opportunities for meaningful contacts between expatriate families and the local community are explained by two features recognisable to any family that has experienced expatriate living. The local population, particularly the families who live near a house that is constantly let to expatriates, become wary of

Text Box 3.2 Viewing culture as an ice-berg

The top 10% are the easily observable aspects of the new cultural setting. The bottom 90% are the structural underpinnings of the new society, invisible at first to outsiders. This understanding of culture in terms of multiple layers helps explain the real-life experiences for expatriates.

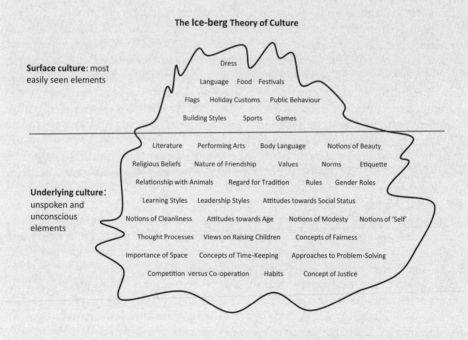

The Ice-berg Theory of Culture

Surface culture: most easily seen elements

Dress
Language   Food   Festivals
Flags   Holiday Customs   Public Behaviour
Building Styles   Sports   Games

Underlying culture: unspoken and unconscious elements

Literature   Performing Arts   Body Language   Notions of Beauty
Religious Beliefs   Nature of Friendship   Values   Norms   Etiquette
Relationship with Animals   Regard for Tradition   Rules   Gender Roles
Learning Styles   Leadership Styles   Attitudes towards Social Status
Notions of Cleanliness   Attitudes towards Age   Notions of Modesty   Notions of 'Self'
Thought Processes   Views on Raising Children   Concepts of Fairness
Importance of Space   Concepts of Time-Keeping   Approaches to Problem-Solving
Competition versus Co-operation   Habits   Concept of Justice

Source: Modified from image sourced via opengecko (www.opengecko.com).

investing too much time in welcoming people who will move on in a very short time. For expatriates themselves, the number of moves and the effort needed to engage deeply with members of the local community mean that often they choose to remain within the immediately accessible expatriate circle.

Text Box 3.3 Dress as an example of how the ice-berg theory works in practice

Dress is an example of the ways in which expatriates experience aspects of a new culture, especially when clothing in the new setting is laden with cultural, social and religious meaning. Any arriving expatriate to a country in the Arabian Gulf who is new to the culture of this part of the world will be struck immediately by the dress of the local population. The men in their headdresses and white thobes and the women dressed in enveloping black robes are thrilling signs of difference. Perhaps some newcomers will notice equal numbers of people who are dressed quite differently, but for most expatriates it is the glamour of local costume and the promise it offers of an exciting and exotic experience which is most striking.

As the early days and weeks pass, the implication of the differences in dress becomes apparent to newcomers. First, the magnificent dress is largely confined to nationals of the Gulf States: groups dressed differently tend to be professional or manual personnel who provide services for the host community as office workers, tradespeople, construction workers and providers of transport. It is obvious that these differences in dress reflect differences in status between the various groups, but most newcomers recognise that they have little real insight into how this new society functions. Secondly, the dress worn by men and women in the Gulf countries clearly represents a range of societal values about the status of the sexes, about the relations between men and women and about family life. However, as most expatriates would admit, it is not easy for outsiders to perceive the true nature of the personal and private way of life that lies behind what they see in public spaces.

Many expatriates in these settings settle for a package of commonly held views about what is going on behind the scenes, often gained from articles in expatriate magazines. This is one way of managing the situation and of moving on in their own lives. Other newcomers enjoy the process of making contact where possible with aspects of the host society and of trying to deepen their understanding of what they see and experience. Both groups are likely to confess, when asked, that they only have an observer's knowledge of the guiding principles that underpin life for the different groups in their new home. They are experiencing in their lives the reality of the invisible section of the ice-berg.

3.3 Adjusting to a Life of Transition

3.3.1 Adapting to the move itself

Alongside the need to adapt to a new culture, another process of adjustment is experienced by families who move. Within expatriate communities and the world of international schools this cycle of adjustment is referred to in terms of transition. In a similar manner to the way in which adjusting to a new culture has been described as a broadly recognisable sequence of experiences, so adjusting to a new move is described as a series of phases.

Broadly, the phases cover the time when family members first hear about a move (the first, or one in a series of moves) and how they experience the process of leaving. Later phases describe how individuals typically cope with entering a new environment, and how they become involved in the new setting and settle down. Finally, and very importantly, the transition cycle is completed by acknowledging the issues involved in hearing about the next move and in breaking away and starting again. It is accepted that the time-frame and nature of the overall experience may vary in line with an individual's personality and previous experiences, but in general there is broad agreement over the pattern and sequence of the phases.

New teachers in international schools have two reasons for trying to understand the nature of transience. As new entrants themselves, they may find it helpful to understand their own feelings and reactions in the new environment. And from the first day in the new classroom, they will find that perhaps a third of the students in the class are newly arrived (as are their parents) and likely to be passing through the experiences typical of transitioning individuals.

3.3.2 Recognised transition phases

- *Phase 1: Belonging somewhere.* Children have a sense of belonging in a familiar place. They feel secure in the social setting, understand how it works and have an established place within it.
- *Phase 2: Hearing about leaving.* On hearing of the move, they feel both apprehensive and excited. They begin to disengage themselves from the social setting and may distance themselves from friends. To begin with, others are interested; gradually they too may disengage from friends who they know are about to move.
- *Phase 3: Transition.* Potentially a time of insecurity – a period that may be occupied with visits to the home base before the new move if the family is already living in another location. Children focus on themselves and on what is happening to them. They may experience an acute sense of loss, disruption and grief.
- *Phase 4: Entering a new social setting.* Children go through the process of introducing themselves to the new community and learning how it works. They may experience waves of extreme homesickness for their previous home. Seasoned movers will adopt strategic approaches to making friends and joining a social circle.

- *Phase 5: Involvement (or re-involvement if the move is one in a series of moves).* Children enter a period of engagement and involvement in the life of the community. They have established a friendship network. For the time being, this is their world. Then they hear of the next move and the cycle begins again.
- *Further phase: Re-entry to wherever the child calls home.* Children may find that their ideas of home, probably received from parents and during short trips, do not match the reality. They cease attending international schools where mobility is the norm and attend local schools. They find that the locals are not interested in their stories of mobility.

Note: The headings for these descriptions of the transition process are derived from an article first written in 1996 by Barbara Schaetti, entitled 'Transition programming in international schools: An emergent mandate'. The website for this article is given in the Resources section below.

3.4 The Reality of a Life in Transition: What Students Say

It is clear that students in international schools are used to considering and evaluating their mobile lifestyles. Discussion about the process of moving seems to be a feature of most mobile families, as was revealed in the research enquiry described in Appendix A (Grimshaw & Sears, 2008; Sears, 2011a, 2012). As a result of this practice, students are ready to talk about the process of moving and to make analytical remarks, even if sometimes there is a suspicion that they are repeating what they have heard from the adults around them. The views of students reflect to a great extent the transitional phases set out in the list above.

3.4.1 Hearing about leaving

Memories of the times when they knew they were leaving figure powerfully in students' life stories. From their remarks it appears that they remember the exact moments when they heard about the next move and how they felt at the time. They recognise that when they know they are moving they withdraw from social networks and lose interest in the ongoing happenings of their present school. They know that they may become distanced from their friends. They begin to tot up the advantages and disadvantages of the next posting.

3.4.2 The need to make friends quickly

Students who have made several moves typically recognise that there is no time to waste in making friends and becoming part of a social network. Young children know they must ask to join in playground games and appear friendly and relaxed. As one eight-year-old boy from The Netherlands put it: 'I sometimes feel worried and shy, but

I know you can't be shy. You must ask to join in the football at playtime.' Older students understand that they must strike up conversation with anyone willing to talk to them. At the beginning of their stay, they may find their friends entirely among co-speakers of their own language. Later they may recognise the need to broaden their friendship base if they are to become 'better at English' and part of life in school. One 14-year-old Japanese girl, recognising that she spent all her time with other Japanese students, made the strategic decision to leave the group and sign up for field hockey. In this way she gained acceptance in the mainstream of school life and better access to proficient English speakers who seemed to her to represent the heart of the school community.

3.4.3 Feeling different because 'we are people who move'

In the same reflective manner, students recognise that their relationships with friends in their home country or in their former school are changing. As they become more engaged and absorbed by life in the new school they understand that they have moved on. Gradually it is only friendships associated with people whom they see regularly on visits back home and the occasional deeply felt relationship from previous postings that are sustained, even with the ready availability of technological means of communication.

Many older students recognise that their view of the home country itself has changed. Since meeting and becoming friendly with students from so many different backgrounds they have developed a deep understanding that people have different value systems and view the world through different lenses and from different perspectives. They see a gap opening up between the life they felt was normal at home and the way they live as globally mobile individuals. They recognise, as one 15-year-old girl from Argentina expressed it: 'We are different because we are people who move.'

3.4.4 Becoming involved

The involvement phase may continue for one or several years, according to the length of the posting. During that period, students of all ages experience the loss of close friends whose families are moving on. These changes may cause real sadness and a sense of being left behind. Gradually, though, the sense of loss loses its ability to hurt, perhaps after a summer break in their home country. When school starts again, a fresh social dynamic is created within the new class and students can engage once more in the process of building a supportive social network. The ability to move on from both people and places may seem callous to outsiders who are not familiar with a globally mobile lifestyle. It is a recognised part of the normal cycle for expatriate communities.

3.4.5 Reactions to news of the next move

Response to news of a move varies according to its place in a student's history of moves. For one 11-year-old Danish boy who had lived back in Denmark for three years after a previous expatriate posting, the news of the move was 'a very great shock. I must leave all my friends in Copenhagen behind again'. On the other hand, a 10-year-old boy from Poland, who described himself as moving for the first time from a 'poor school in Warsaw' was thrilled at the chance to learn English and welcomed all the opportunities that the international school could offer.

In general, the research findings indicate that young children come to accept the fact of a new move more readily than their older brothers and sisters. For teenagers and their parents news of a further move can be the start of a period of upheaval and friction within the family. Young people of this age tend to be deeply engaged with their peers and to look for much of their recreational activity outside the family (although in the case of international school students, this activity is frequently focused on school-related activities and involves chauffeuring by parents). It is understandable that older students resent their lack of input into such a major decision. The resultant fierce debates can be very stressful for parents, who may themselves be overwhelmed by what lies ahead.

3.4.6 The upbeat atmosphere of international schools

In emphasising the challenging aspects of a life in transition, it might be thought that the atmosphere in international schools is full of sadness and stress. Any visitor to an international school of this type is in a position to confirm that this is not the case. Very largely, the ambiance of schools that serve a globally mobile community is positive, energetic and cheerful. Mobility is a societal norm in this type of international school and many schools respond to that fact by being proactive in supporting students as they move through the phases of transition.

3.5 Strategic Approaches That Support Transition

3.5.1 In-school support for transitioning students

A number of international schools that serve a globally mobile population have policies in place that provide support for students as they move through the phases of transition. There is a variety in the level of awareness of the issue and in the consistency and type of practice. Some schools have policies in place at every year level; in other schools, support for students in transition is largely left up to individual teachers. Where this is the case, students may experience widely differing levels of support.

As Debra Rader (2011) sets out, the most effective transition policies result in practice that is integrated into the curriculum and is an ongoing element in the classroom throughout the school year. She describes classrooms that are supportive of globally mobile students and which include collections of books in which issues of transition are addressed. These texts are used to raise difficult subjects such as, 'Where is home for people who move?' and 'Where do I belong?' She suggests that effective teachers are willing to engage in discussion with members of the class and to share their own feelings about moving. She emphasises the importance of acknowledging and validating students' feelings and experiences.

Many of the suggestions made in the following example of an induction programme for students who have arrived mid-year would be followed in many classrooms. In schools where a comprehensive, strategic and institutionalised transition programme is in place, students can be sure of receiving support consistently.

3.5.2 Supporting new mid-year arrivals: An example of an induction programme in action

Preparing the classroom

- Include their names on any lists and labels in the classroom: birthday charts, pegs for sports kit, locker doors, etc.
- Ensure that their names are included in any specialist classes or sets that members of the class attend (and that the teacher of those classes is forewarned): for example, specialist English teaching classes and mathematics sets.

Preparing the students in the receiving class

- Find out how to pronounce the new student's name and share this with the class.
- Brainstorm about how existing students can welcome the newcomer and make her or him feel at home.
- Arrange peer buddies in advance (can be a shared role), and ensure they support the new student throughout the school day and at playtime/recess.

Welcoming the new student

- In the case of young students, arrange for a teaching assistant to monitor and guide the newcomer during the first weeks. Make sure the new student knows that this person is there to support them and to answer any questions.
- Make a point of introducing new students to classroom routines by showing them what to do and what are the rules: for example, where the toilets are, when computers are used and by whom, where to find stationery items, how to access the school's virtual learning environment (VLE), etc.
- Engage the new student in creating a 'personal passport' either in hard copy or online. The student uses this document to keep a record of her or his previous moves, language exposure and other significant experiences. The idea is that students keep their passports up to date and take them with them when they move on again. Working with the student on a passport enables teachers to learn something about a student's prior language and learning experiences – invaluable in working with the student in class. (See Text Box 2.1 for more on student passports.)

Communicating with parents (vital in supporting the new student effectively)

- Ensure that parents can understand significant communications from the school. Enlist translators and interpreters from among the school community to help out if necessary.

- Explain the use of the school's VLE (if one exists) and show where parents can find information about school and class events and details of their child's homework.
- Ensure that parents new to international schools understand that concerns about their children are of key interest to teachers.
- Make sure that new parents are invited to all appropriate class and school events.

Note: Some of the suggestions in this section are derived from material provided by Caroline Scott, a former international school administrator: www.communication-acrosscultures.com.

3.6 International Schools: Supportive Spaces for Students Who Move

This section looks in more detail at the reasons why many international schools are largely successful in offering an inclusive welcoming space for students from many linguistic and cultural backgrounds. The first of these reasons is the friendly and accepting social environment, which was commented on by many of the students in the research enquiry described in Appendix A (Grimshaw & Sears, 2008; Sears, 2011a, 2012).

3.6.1 A welcoming social environment

Visits to international schools that serve globally mobile students offer revealing insights into the ways they have evolved to meet the needs of their target population. The first is that they tend to be colourful, lively spaces, frequently including visual images and other references to the culture of the host country. Often several languages are in evidence on notice boards and display boards, and communications reflect the range of groups and communities that is served by the school rather than a uniquely educational focus. It is common, for instance, for the front hall to contain a large notice board given over to extracurricular and community-based activities as well as notices relating to the PTA or Family Association. Often there is a video loop running, or a display of photographs relating to a school or community-based event.

Personnel in the reception areas are noticeably friendly and there is no sense of a barrier between school and parents. In fact, parents tend to be greatly in evidence in international schools, particularly in the parts of the school that serve younger children. In general, international schools do not have an air of hushed calm. Younger children appear lively and chatty and older students are noticeably sociable and relaxed.

3.6.2 The relationship between students and teachers

A longer time spent in a school of this type will reveal other potential differences from many schools in national systems. The relationship between the teachers and the students tends to be informal and relaxed and there seems to be a genuine friendship and liking between the two groups. Where students need to be addressed about challenging behaviour, they are invariably taken to one side rather than brought to book in front of the whole class. Teachers react in a friendly way with each other and there is a greater sense than in many schools of a shared life outside school among all groups.

Above all, teachers in international schools are accustomed to working with newly arrived students who may enter mid-year as well as at the beginning of a new school year. Many use specific strategies to aid students in the various phases of transitioning, and experienced teachers are adept at helping new students of every language and cultural background to integrate into the social life of the class. This process is greatly aided by an understanding among students as well as teachers of what it means to live a life on the move.

3.6.3 What students say about their entry into an international school

Evidence collected during the course of the research study showed that students of all ages appreciate the ways in which international schools make it easy for new students to feel at home. Two 11-year-old boys interviewed together described their first experiences at the school and explained why they thought the school was so good at welcoming new students:

Researcher: How did it strike you when you first arrived?
Aaron: When I first came I thought my only friends would be Israeli, but then I saw all these friendly and nice children and teachers.
Jean-Luc: It's like when new people arrive you welcome them, because, I don't know, you felt welcome so you want other people to join you.
Aaron: People are kind to you when you come so you want to be kind to them.

The two boys, Aaron and Jean-Luc, felt that the school was a place where new arrivals were met with friendly faces. They both ascribed this welcoming attitude to a shared understanding of what it was like to be new. The school was a place where it was customary to welcome newcomers and to include them immediately.

Another student, 13-year-old Luca, described what it was like to come from a rather tough school into an international school.

Luca: The mentality of this school is different. Here, people try to include everybody, and the staff is very nice, teachers and headmaster.
Researcher: Why do you think people here want to be like this?
Luca: Like including everybody – I don't know. It's international, so everybody is not from the same country. So all of them have to be included at some point. Everybody. Because they want to be included, they include everybody.

Luca gives a similar explanation for the welcome that he received, which is that everybody in the school has had a similar experience of mobility and wants newcomers to feel equally welcome. He also mentions the fact that the school is international. For him that makes it all the more essential that the school should offer an inclusive environment. Clearly the atmosphere of the school encourages students to behave in this inclusive way with the lead given by the attitude of the teachers and the school's noticeable welcome for all family members.

3.6.4 Living with different cultures: Fostering openness to cultural difference

The second reason why international schools have evolved into inclusive and welcoming spaces for all students is the way in which they offer cultural 'safe places'. This is most clearly the case in schools that serve a globally mobile community where there may be 60 nationalities represented in the student population. With the presence of such diversity of culture and language, most schools have evolved into settings where students from all backgrounds can feel included from the time of their arrival. They become 'safe places' where difference is the norm and where intercultural learning is fostered.

Students learning about living with different cultures in one international school

Students in the research study described in Appendix A gave examples of experiencing many of the features of learning to live with difference. It is also evident that the school itself offers an ethos where difference is not a divisive issue. In her account, 11-year-old Chiara from Italy describes how she rapidly became part of a group of girls whom she met on the school bus. For her the fact of friendship is initially more important than the cultural backgrounds of the girls. It is interesting to see, however, that when she is describing how she feels in the interview she sets out her awareness that 'everyone has their own way of seeing'. She has come to understand the nature of difference and feels comfortable with her new understanding.

Researcher:	And who is in this group? Where do they come from?
Chiara:	We have one American, and one girl born in Africa and one's that half Norwegian, half Italian, one that's from Thailand. It's just a lot of different nationalities.
Researcher:	What is that like?
Chiara:	It's like good because you get to know everyone else. You get to know how people feel and how the nationalities feel and stuff.
Researcher:	Tell me more about that.
Chiara:	Everyone has their own way of seeing how things are, but I think when you stay a lot of time here, you kind of get accustomed to everything and you can change. But you can see that people, in some ways their culture makes them, like, believe different things.

Fifteen-year-old Leticia describes further aspects of becoming an intercultural person. She realises that she lived a more narrow life before making her first move. She knows that other people think and live differently and has learnt to enjoy this. Later on in the interview she says that she would find living in only one culture 'quite boring'.

Leticia: I was really shy when I moved. And I was really quiet. And I think I was childish and selfish.

Researcher: So, how do you think you have changed?

Leticia: I think I've grown up a lot. I think in Argentina, I was, like, in a bubble. I didn't really care about the outside world.

Researcher: So, when you move abroad, what makes you have to think about other people more, I wonder?

Leticia: Well, you feel different, so you start looking at other people and saying how are we different? And then you start seeing that there are some similarities. . . . I like it. I think it's much better than being with people who are all the same.

3.6.5 Cross-cultural/intercultural learning

Cross-cultural learning, with individual variations, is a feature of life in most international schools although it takes different forms in different types of school. In schools that largely contain local students, whether solely English medium or bilingual, the population tends to be more stable. In international schools of this type, it is common to hear students using the local language in the shared spaces and to watch them switch to English in the classroom and in conversations with English-speaking teachers. Such schools convey a strong sense of the local culture and language alongside the use of English and the evident presence of programmes of study imported from non-local sources. Arguably, students in schools of this type are experiencing life as effective intercultural learners.

Culture learning in international schools that serve a globally mobile diverse population

Commentators have noticed a complex pattern of cultural adjustment in schools that cater for a globally mobile population of students who come from different linguistic and cultural backgrounds (Langford, 1998; Pollock & Van Reken, 2009). Because of the general mobility and multicultural nature of the population they argue that schools of this type have evolved into examples of what has been termed a 'third space'. Within this space, cultural and linguistic diversity is the norm and cultural dissonance is minimised.

This third space is sometimes described as existing 'between cultures'. Students experience a lifestyle together that is distinct from their existence outside school. The culture of the school and its understanding and support for global mobility supplies a cultural safe place which answers their needs. Arguably, a school culture of this type is effective only because it smoothes out and even ignores cultural differences. Some commentators (Kubota & Lin, 2009; Luke, 2009; Pennycook, 1994, 1998) also point out that that the world of culture is not an equal playing field in an English-medium international school. They suggest that the capital of English and English-speaking cultures carries so much prestige in the setting that it may overwhelm students' attachment to their own languages and cultures. It is the students with diverse backgrounds who are in effect making the adjustment, by 'falling into line' with the mainstream English-speaking environment.

Embedding the celebration of cultural and linguistic diversity

Many international school educators would prefer that schools were seen to celebrate cultural difference in a positive way rather than creating a third space where students live 'between cultures'. In line with this thinking, one of the newer trends in international education is for curriculum approaches that systematically embed students' primary languages and cultural knowledge in the day-to-day work of the classroom (see Section 9.2).

3.7 Living Between Cultures: Third Culture Kids

The term 'third culture kid' (TCK), originally coined in 1976 (Useem, 1993), is used to describe individuals with many of the same characteristics as global nomads (see Section 2.4). However, as the name indicates, the aspect that defines TCKs is their experience of having lived in third cultural spaces which is one of the focuses of this chapter. David Pollock's description spells out clearly the nature of TCKs:

> A Third Culture Kid (TCK) is a person who has spent a significant part of his or her developmental years outside the parents' culture. The TCK frequently builds relationships to all of the cultures [he or she encounters], while not having full ownership in any. Although elements from each culture may be assimilated into the TCK's life experience, the sense of belonging is in relationship to others of a similar background. (Pollock & Van Reken, 2009: 13)

3.7.1 The realisation of their difference in young adulthood

TCKs typically come to realise that their childhood experiences in globally mobile families moving around the world because of a parent's work or occupation have made them different from their peers. This is often the case when they return as young adults to the place they think of as home and which may coincide with the time when they go to college or university. Most TCKs in this situation say that they find it difficult to explain who they are to students who have always lived within the same national boundaries. As a result, the question that many TCKs hate to be asked is: 'Where are you from?'

Young adulthood is customarily the time when TCKs question their identities and there are a number of websites where TCKs and global nomads can share their thoughts and concerns. Most set out the definition of what it means to be a TCK, including Ruth Van Reken's own site, described as 'A home for third culture kids' (www.tckworld. com/). The realisation that there are numbers of people who share the same feelings of disconnection is consoling to many adults who have experienced a globally mobile childhood. This understanding helps them to make sense of their own lives.

Note: The book, *Third Culture Kids: The Experience of Growing up Among Worlds* by David Pollock and Ruth Van Reken, first published in 1999 but frequently reprinted and updated, remains the standard text on the impact of a globally mobile childhood on children and young people, and therefore of a life of transience.

3.7.2 Third culture kids share a common understanding and experience

The chief element that binds TCKs together is that most find more in common with people who have moved around the world, almost regardless of the nature of the experience, than they do with their stable peers. They immediately have an innate shared understanding of what it means to have experienced this lifestyle and most share certain characteristics because of that experience. These include being able to speak more than one language, or bits of several languages, and being highly accepting of other cultures. They may find their peers who have never moved narrow minded and unaware, and recognise that people they meet may find it difficult to place them. They learn only to give out information about themselves that their opposite number can understand and empathise with. In the presence of non-TCKs they feel they are withholding many essential truths. Some TCKs yearn to settle in their adult life, while others continue a life of constant mobility. Many adult TCKs recognise that they feel the urge to move after three years in a new place in line with their childhood pattern of moves.

This definition of a mobile childhood does not go completely unchallenged. Some commentators question whether educated people in today's world ever feel part of only one culture. They point out that nowadays people move in and out of cultural groups and that their identities are multiple and complex. It is typical of many individuals that they move away from home to pursue higher education and may then move to another city or country in pursuit of employment. They may never return to their former home and perhaps never feel part of only one social and cultural group ever again. The fact remains that TCKs feel themselves to be different because many of their formative years were spent on the move. They have no experience of what it is like to grow up in a stable setting and, for many, that awareness shapes their adult lives in significant ways.

Key Points in This Chapter

- Globally mobile families live a life of constant change that involves adaptation and adjustment.
- Adjusting to a new culture involves a process of adjustment often described in phases.

- The ice-berg theory of culture suggests another model for the way newcomers experience a new cultural setting.
- A life of transition generally involves a further cycle of adjustment.
- A number of international schools offer programmes and strategic approaches that support families in transition.
- International schools have evolved into spaces that support globally mobile students.
- International schools offer cultural 'safe spaces' where cultural diversity is the norm and cultural dissonance is minimised.
- The cultural experience of students in international schools is sometimes referred to as living in a third culture.
- TCKs are young adults who have moved globally throughout their childhoods.
- They find they have more in common with their peers who have experienced a similar level of global mobility than with individuals who have lived stable childhoods.

Resources

Websites cited in this chapter

Schaetti, B. (1996) Transition programming in international schools: An emergent mandate. See www. transition-dynamics.com/transprogram.html.

Schaetti, B. and Ramsey, S.J. (1999) Transition dynamics (global nomads). See www.transition-dynamics.com.

Rader, C. (2011) Developing transition programmes in your school. Presentation handout. See www. sgischools.com/pdf/conference2011/Handout%20Developing%20Transition%20Programmes%20 for%20Your%20School.pdf.

The transition support link on the website of the International School of Bangkok. See www.isb.ac.th/ Transition_Your_Child/default.aspx.

Two sites designed to support TCKs. See www.tckworld.com/ and www.tckid.com.

Note: Some of the suggestions in this section are derived from material provided by Caroline Scott, a former international school administrator: www.communicationacrosscultures.com.

References

Bourdieu, P. (1991) *Language and Symbolic Power* (trans. G. Raymond and M. Adamson). Cambridge, MA: Harvard University Press.

Grimshaw, T. and Sears, C. (2008) 'Where am I from?' 'Where do I belong?': The negotiation of identity by international school students. *Journal of Research in International Education* 7 (3), 259–278.

Kubota, R. and Lin. A. (eds) (2009) *Race, Culture, and Identities in Second Language Education: Exploring Critically Engaged Practice*. London: Routledge.

Langford, M.E. (1998) Global nomads, third culture kids and international schools. In M. Hayden and J. Thompson (eds) *International Education: Principles and Practice* (pp. 28–43). London: Kogan Page.

Luke, A. (2009) Race and language as capital in school: A sociological template for language-education reform. In R. Kubota and A. Lin (eds) *Race, Culture, and Identities in Second Language Education*. London: Routledge.

Pennycook, A. (1994) *The Cultural Politics of English as an International Language*. London: Longman.

Pennycook, A. (1998) *English and the Discourses of Colonialism*. London: Routledge.

Pollock, D.C. and Van Reken, R.E. (2009) *Third Culture Kids: The Experience of Growing Up Among Worlds.* London: Nicholas Brealey.

Rader, D. (2011) Addressing transition and mobility issues with English language learners in the early childhood years. In E. Murphy (ed.) *Welcoming Linguistic Diversity in Early Childhood Classrooms.* Bristol: Multilingual Matters.

Ruhly, S. (1976) *Orientations and Intercultural Communication.* Palo Alto, CA: Science Research Associates.

Sears, C. (2011a) Integrating multiple identities: Narrative in the formation and maintenance of the self in international school students. *Journal of Research in International Education* 10 (1), 71–86.

Sears, C. (2012) Negotiating identity in English-medium settings: Agency, resistance and appropriation among speakers of other languages in an international school. *Journal of Research in International Education* 11 (2), 117–136.

Useem, R.H. (1993) Third culture kids: Focus of major study. *Newslinks* 12 (3), 1–29.

Part 2

Programmes and Policies in International Schools

4 Introducing Programmes of Study to be Found in International Schools

The aim of Chapter 4 is to introduce curricula and programmes of study that are found in international schools. Some programmes of study were originally targeted at international students, although they may now have been taken up by national schooling systems. Other curricula derive wholly or in part from English-speaking education systems. Aspects of both types of provision may be unfamiliar to many teachers newly arrived in an international school.

The sequence of Chapter 4 is as follows:

- Introduction: highlighting the programmes and curricula to be found in international schools.
- Programmes offered by the International Baccalaureate Organisation.
- The Primary Years Programme of the International Baccalaureate Organisation: an enquiry-based programme.
- Thoughts on teaching in the International Baccalaureate Primary and Middle Years Programmes.
- Introducing the International Primary and Middle Years Curricula.
- Curricula that derive wholly or in part from English-speaking national schooling systems.
- Bilingual international schools.

Introduction: Programmes and Curricula to be Found in International Schools

Since the methods of recruiting teachers to work in international schools have become more consistent and finely tuned, the majority of teachers in international schools are well-trained professionals, skilled in delivering the programmes and curricula that were offered by their former schools. In some cases, teachers have come directly from another international school and have been employed precisely because of their expertise in a particular curriculum or programme of study. Other teachers, whether recruited from their home countries or hired locally, may find the programmes and curricula offered by the new school unfamiliar. One of the aims of this chapter is to introduce and explain the history and rationale behind these programmes and curricula, so that new teachers may have a secure foundation of knowledge and understanding on which to build.

The programmes of study described in the chapter are those which are found in large numbers of international schools. The descriptions and comments refer to the main elements of these programmes. As is often the case with international education, many schools offer additional features in their programmes that arise from the unique nature of their student body and the cultural and geographical setting. This variety is one of the reasons why teaching in international schools is stimulating and absorbing.

A further aim is to draw attention to aspects of these programmes and curricula that may present challenges to emergent bilingual students. The process of highlighting these areas and offering suggestions to teachers about ways of ensuring that emergent bilingual students flourish in these programmes begins in this chapter and continues throughout the Handbook.

The sequence of the chapter

The first four sections of the chapter are devoted to the programmes offered by the International Baccalaureate Organisation (IBO) (www.ibo.org). The reason for giving so much space to this topic is that these programmes are likely to present a degree of challenge to teachers coming from other educational systems. The IB programmes are typified by certain educational approaches and underlying concepts which are explained in their documents using a terminology that may need clarification for teachers who are new to the IB programmes. Sections 4.1–4.4 seek to clarify the approaches and pedagogy for teachers working in these programmes for the first time, focusing in particular on the enquiry-based aspect of the Primary Years Programme (PYP).

The Primary and Middle Years curricula

Section 4.5 introduces two other programmes which were initially created for use with international students and are now also offered in national schools. These are the Primary and Middle Years Curricula (IPC and MYC), which provide structured programmes of study for primary and middle years students. These curricula are to be found in international schools across the world and may be used within an overall curriculum framework that is drawn from a national schooling system, most frequently in this case from the UK. They are typified by a holistic view of learning in general and include specific resources and activities that reflect their overall international focus.

Programmes derived from national schooling systems

The final two sections are devoted to courses of study in international and bilingual schools that derive from national systems. In the case of English-medium schools, programmes can be taken entirely from one English-speaking system or from a mix of sources including the programmes of the IBO. In the case of bilingual schools where one of the languages is the local language, teaching generally reflects the programme used in the local schooling system. Most of these schools also offer students the opportunity to take the local school-leaving examination alongside an international option. A short list of schools that adopt programmes of this type is provided to give an insight into the complex profile of the academic offerings in some international schools.

4.1 The Programmes Offered by the International Baccalaureate Organisation (IBO)

The programmes discussed in this section are offered by the IBO and were originally designed primarily for international schools (www.ibo.org). The IBO's main programmes include the Primary Years Programme (PYP), the Middle Years Programme (MYP), the Career-related Certificate (IBCC) and the Diploma Programme.

A chief motivation in creating these programmes was to provide educational consistency to students as they move around the world by offering a seamless learning experience from the early years through to university entrance. They also offer the means of embedding international-mindedness (a defining and informing characteristic of international education) in the mainstream curriculum. (See Text Box 4.6 below, as well as Text Box 1.1 'List of terms', for more on international-mindedness.)

Table 4.1 sets out the main elements of the programmes of the IBO.

4.2 An Introduction to Enquiry-based Programmes

One of the programmes that teachers new to international education may meet for the first time is the IB PYP. This programme is offered in around 1000 schools, both national and international, across the world at the time of writing. The key elements of the programme are given in the following description to be found on the 'IB Primary Years Programme at a glance' website: (www.ibo.org/pyp/index.cfm).

> The IB Primary Years Programme (PYP) is a curriculum framework designed for students aged 3 to 12. It focuses on the development of the whole child as an inquirer, both in the classroom and in the world outside. It is defined by six transdisciplinary themes of global significance, explored using knowledge and skills derived from six subject areas, with a powerful emphasis on inquiry-based learning.

Several areas of this programme may be unfamiliar to newly appointed teachers, the chief of which is likely to be the commitment in the programme to an overall approach known as enquiry-based learning. With the aim of enabling teachers to feel better prepared when faced with teaching in the PYP, a brief outline of the basic precepts of this approach to learning are included here.

Table 4.1 Main elements of IB programmes

Name	Developed by	Brief history	Spread across schools and language policy	Features that may be unfamiliar to new teachers
Primary Years Programme (PYP) Designed for students aged 3–12 years www.ibo.org/pyp/index.cfm 'IB Primary Years Programme at a glance'	International Baccalaureate Organisation (IBO)	Developed first by the International Schools' Curriculum Project – adopted by the IBO in 1997.	Offered by over 1000 schools across the world, both international and in national school systems. Within the PYP, languages are described as languages of instruction or additional languages. Additional languages include the teaching of the language of instruction in the school to emergent bilingual students in ESL or EAL classes.	• An enquiry-based programme taught through six 'Units of Inquiry' per year. • 'Units of Inquiry' designed, organised and resourced by individual schools (except Primary Inquirer kits – see below). • Transdisciplinary: i.e. the Units of Inquiry are designed to incorporate elements of a number of different curriculum areas. • Common planning format. • IB 'Learner profile' a key element in planning. • Teacher and student led assessment. No external assessment, except validation of the programme as a whole by the IBO. • Final year 'Exhibition' undertaken by each student.
Middle Years Programme (MYP) Designed for students aged 11–16 years www.ibo.org/myp/ 'IB Middle Years Programme at a glance'	IBO	First developed in 1994, with the intention of providing a 'continuum of education' across the IB programmes. Sometimes taught side by side with state and national externally assessed examination courses.	Offered by over 1000 schools across the world. Within the MYP, languages are divided into A and B categories. Language A is the student's best language or the language of instruction. Language B is either a second modern foreign language for speakers of English or the language of instruction for emergent bilinguals.	• Eight subject groups integrated through five 'interactive areas' providing 'global contexts for learning'. • IB 'Learner profile' a key element in planning. • Criterion-based assessment at years 1, 3 and 5 with optional externally modified e-assessment in the pipeline. • Final year 'Personal project'

| IB Diploma Programme
Designed for students aged 16–19
www.ibi.org/diploma/ 'Diploma Programme at a glance' | IBO | Two-year academically challenging programme with final examinations targeted at university entrance. Accepted globally as a university entrance qualification. | Offered by 4523 schools across the world. Within the Diploma Programme, Language A is the language in which the student opts to sit the Diploma. Language B is the student's next best language. Students can gain a bilingual Diploma by following two Language A courses among other options. | • Students must study one subject from each of five groups plus one more.
• At least three subjects to be taken at higher level and three others at standard level.
• Theory of Knowledge (TOK) component designed to foster critical thinking.
• Extended essay.
• Creativity, action, service (CAS) compulsory component. |
| IB Career-related Certificate
Designed for students aged 16–19
www.ibo.org/ibcc/ | IBO | A recently established programme designed 'to incorporate the vision and educational principles of the IB into a programme specifically tailored for students who wish to engage in career-related learning'. | At the time of writing, 82 schools have adopted the IBCC.
As part of the IBCC's core, students are required to begin or continue the learning of an appropriate additional language. | The IBCC comprises a three-part framework of study:
(1) Students take at least two Diploma Programme courses allied to their career-related studies.
(2) Students pursue approved career-related studies leading to higher education, an internship, apprenticeship or employment.
(3) Students participate in IBCC core elements: these include approaches to learning, community and service, language development and a reflective project. |

Note: The details in this table are correct at the time of publication, but readers should check the IBO websites to be sure that the information is up to date.

4.2.1 What is enquiry-based learning?

The following elements are considered integral to enquiry-based learning. The list draws on material provided on the Canadian Galileo Educational Network link headed 'What is Inquiry?' (http://galileo.org/teachers/designing-learning/articles/what-is-inquiry/).

Enquiry-based learning involves learners in:

- Inductive as opposed to deductive learning:
  - *Inductive learning.* The teacher presents students with learning opportunities to engage with a topic via real-life examples and experiences: the students then construct their own investigations in order to reveal the concepts and underlying structures that relate to the topic area.
  - *Deductive learning.* The teacher introduces and explains concepts to the students: the students then complete tasks that illuminate and exemplify those concepts.
- Discovering answers for themselves rather than being instructed in a topic by a teacher:
  - *Discovery learning* takes place when learners explore, investigate and carry out experiments to test out theories or to solve problems. This is the approach that underlies science investigations.
- Tackling real-world questions, issues and controversies.
- Developing questioning, research and communication skills.
- Solving problems or creating solutions.
- Collaborating within and beyond the classroom.
- Developing a deep understanding of content knowledge.

4.2.2 What does strong enquiry-based practice involve?

Strong enquiry-based practice involves:

- **Authenticity**. The enquiry study reflects a question, problem or exploration that has meaning for the student.
  - *Example: Communities need water.*
- **Deep understanding**. The enquiry study involves the student in formulating searching questions during the process of the study.
  - *Example: 'What factors contribute to water shortages?' 'What effect does shortage of water have on the relations between communities?'*
- **Performance of understanding**. The study requires students to communicate what they are learning to a variety of audiences through presentation, exhibition, website, wiki, blog, etc.
  - *Example: Creation of an interactive poster using imported graphs and images to indicate the contributory causes of water shortage in a given area.*
- **Assessment**. Ongoing assessment is woven into the design of the enquiry and utilises a range of methods including student reflection and self-assessment.

- *Example: Student- and teacher-generated descriptors are used as the benchmarks against which students' learning activities are measured.*
- **Appropriate uses of technology**. Technology is used in a purposeful manner that demonstrates an appreciation of new ways of thinking and doing. The technology is essential to the accomplishment of the task.
  - *Example: High-quality online material is used as a source for students' personal research. The formats chosen to display student learning and understandings may incorporate interactive apps and programs, audio and visual material and online presentations.*
- **Active exploration**. The study requires students to spend significant amounts of time doing fieldwork, design work, interviews, construction, etc.
  - *Example: Students draw upon the resources in the local environment to carry out real-life and virtual evidence gathering.*
- **Ethical citizenship**. The study requires students to view their investigation in the light of its impact on the wider world.
  - *Example: Water shortages will arguably become the source of conflicts between communities in the future. What actions on their part can students take to design a better use of water in their homes and in their schools?*

Text Box 4.1 A brief history of enquiry-based learning

The discussion surrounding inquiry-based learning (also known as discovery learning, project-based learning or problem-based learning) has a long history, from John Locke's *Some Thoughts Concerning Education and the Conduct of Understanding* (1996 [1693]) and Jean-Jacques Rousseau's *Emile, or On Education* (1979 [1762]), onwards to Friedrich Froebel (1792–1852) and Maria Montessori (see *The Montessori Method*, published in translation, 2008 [1912]). More recently, inquiry-based learning owes its evolution to the constructivist theories of Dewey (1916) and, among others, Lev Vygotsky, Jean Piaget (see deVries, 2000) and Jerome Bruner (1960, 1966). (See the Resources section at the end of this chapter for a list of titles.)

4.2.3 Some established concerns about enquiry-based learning

Over the years, theorists and teacher practitioners have raised well-documented concerns about the use of the enquiry-based approach as the sole framework for teaching and learning in schools. See Kirschner *et al.* (2006) for a fuller critique of constructivist (enquiry-based) approaches to learning. Their comments include the following:

- Enquiry-based programmes require well-trained highly proficient teachers in order for the students to receive a rich and meaningful educational experience.
- In the real world, most schools have to 'cover' mandated or exam-related curriculum content. Where enquiry-based programmes lay down the content to be covered in

the Units of Inquiry, some would argue that this is not true student-initiated enquiry-based learning.
- Enquiry-based learning succeeds with motivated students who are able to work independently of the teacher. It may be less well suited to students who have behaviour issues or who are less motivated to engage in classroom activity.
- To be effective, an enquiry-based approach needs considerable time and resources. Where there is curriculum content to be covered, traditional (deductive) teaching methods may be considered more time and cost effective than enquiry-based (inductive) approaches.

4.3 The IB Primary Years Programme (PYP): An Enquiry-based Programme

In schools that are authorised to offer the IB PYP, learning of both content and skills is incorporated into a number of Units of Inquiry. These units are broadly designed to offer students an educational experience that is based on enquiry-based learning and to provide the framework for much of the classroom activity throughout the year. Schools make different choices about the degree to which they include the teaching of English/language, arts and mathematics into the Unit of Inquiry framework. Many schools choose to offer separated-out classes in these subjects, although it is common for schools to link elements of their literacy programme to the theme of the ongoing Unit of Inquiry where appropriate. The IBO's Learner Profile, setting out the qualities that are desirable in learners, underpins the planning of a Unit of Inquiry (www.ibo.org/programmes/profile/).

Text Box 4.2 Terminology in the IB programmes

As a new teacher, entering a school that offers the PYP and MYP can sometimes seem daunting. The IBO has evolved a language of its own with a vocabulary that is full of meaning for teachers who are accustomed to working within its programmes, but which may present barriers to understanding in newcomers. At first sight, PYP and MYP schools can look unfamiliar to new teachers. This is because the terminology associated with these programmes is often displayed on noticeboards around the corridors and halls. Full information about the IBO's terminology can be found on the IBO website: www.ibo.org/programmes/profile/.

Six units in the school year are the norm, with the number of hours devoted to the units varying from around 30 to 90 in different schools. The online Planner for each Unit of Inquiry includes sections that help teachers follow a consistent sequence in their planning. The headings in the Planner include aspects of a Unit of Inquiry such as: the transdisciplinary theme (www.ibo.org/pyp/curriculum/index.cfm), the central idea, a list of summative tasks (for final assessment), and the cross-curricular learning targets that the Unit will address.

The mode of assessment used in the PYP and MYP takes the form of sets of criteria, often created by both students and teacher. The final pieces of work are assessed against these criteria and students are expected to reflect and comment on the overall effectiveness of their own work.

Text Box 4.3 Observing enquiry-based learning in the classroom

In a Grade 4 classroom in an international school in Italy, all 20 students appeared to be Italian speakers, with the class being conducted in English, the school's language of instruction. The focus of the class was the front-loading phase (providing learning opportunities that introduce students to the core elements of the topic) of a new Unit of Inquiry with the Central Idea being described as: *'Energy exists in different forms; it is stored, changed and used in different ways.'* The work of the class was driven by the teacher's guided questions, which included: What is energy? How is energy stored and changed? What are renewable and non-renewable energy sources? The overall aim of this phase of the unit was to equip the students to think up good key questions to drive later research enquiry.

A core approach to managing this phase of the enquiry was the embedded use of iPads. Each student had an iPad and in fact these were the only items on their tables. The students were divided into groups with each group given the task of going round different parts of the school and photographing on their iPads the ways in which electricity was being used in the school. They were told to differentiate between energy sources: i.e. mains electricity supply versus battery driven, and plugs versus sockets.

On their return, each group used the photos to share its ideas and conclusions about the ways in which electricity contributes to the life of the school. They were aided in this process by a SmartBoard (interactive whiteboard) to which the teacher had streamed a set of graphics within the Popplet format (blog.popplet.com/category/popplets-in-education). They used the graphics to group together functions and appliances that made use of electricity in different ways. Finally, they were asked to use the Popplets app on their iPads to construct an account with graphics of how electricity is used in all the processes involved in the creation of a cup of coffee.

The teacher was a skilled practitioner and the teaching and learning was going forward on a number of different levels. At all times she articulated very clearly the sorts of learning behaviours she expected from the class. They should be sensible and focused and listen to other people's ideas. They should take turns and respect other people's contributions. She also drew attention to and made lists on the SmartBoard of vocabulary items in English that might be new to the students. Finally, she constantly asked students to refer to their own experience when offering suggestions and ideas – there was a real sense that the students were exploring and discovering for themselves rather than being the recipients of pre-packaged information.

4.4 Some Thoughts About Teaching in the IB Primary Years and Middle Years Programmes (PYP and MYP)

Most schools offering the PYP prefer to recruit teachers already trained in delivering the programme. However, this is not always possible, so there are usually a number of teachers in a PYP school who are new to the programme and require training. This is true also of new teachers entering a school that offers the MYP, although the requirements of the programme are not immediately so challenging or so unfamiliar.

For teachers new to the programmes, the most effective way forward is to build a good relationship with the PYP and MYP coordinators, who are appointed in every IB school to oversee the programmes and to support teachers. The coordinators' role is to suggest the most useful introductory documents, to offer training options and to give new teachers guidance in filling in the online planners which are the drivers of much of the teaching and learning in PYP and MYP schools.

4.4.1 Including emergent bilingual students in the PYP and MYP

A key role for teachers in PYP and MYP schools is to understand the degree of support that they must supply to emergent bilingual students in their classes. The method of learning within the programmes may be unfamiliar to new students, and teachers will need to articulate and model the sorts of learning behaviours that enable students to engage in the work of the classroom. Much of the learning in the PYP and MYP programmes takes place via focused discussion between teachers and students. To be successful learners within these programmes, students need to be able to contribute to these discussions by questioning, speculating, making suggestions and drawing conclusions. (See Section 12.1 for suggestions about including emergent bilingual students in class talk.) All the professionals who work with emergent bilingual students should be aware of the need to model this type of language explicitly and also to contribute during the front-loading phase of a Unit by supplying key word outlines.

Note: Chapter 11 is devoted to planning for the inclusion of emergent bilingual students in a new area of study or Unit of Inquiry. Readers will find detailed suggestions on teaching the language skills required by the area of study and how to introduce the vocabulary of a new topic with key word visuals.

4.4.2 Explaining enquiry-based programmes to parents

One of the challenges for teachers in international schools that have adopted enquiry-based programmes such as the IB PYP may be the need to discuss the philosophy behind the practice of enquiry-based learning. This goes hand in hand with the need to familiarise parents with the meaning of the terminology used in programmes of this type. Parents who have been used to different schooling systems may have many questions about what goes on in their children's classrooms and about the terminology that is in general use.

Teachers find it easier if the school has opted to separate out the teaching of mathematics and English/language arts from the enquiry-based aspects of the curriculum. When this is the case, the learning activities and assessment regimes tend to be more recognisable and familiar to parents from different backgrounds.

The mode of assessment used in the programmes is one of the chief areas that tends to attract queries, since it can seem very unfamiliar to both students and parents who are used to marking and grading as the means of assessing student work. Two aspects tend to need constant explanation. These are the element of student choice over the form of the piece of work to be assessed at the end of the unit, and the way in which students are encouraged to contribute to the discussion about assessment criteria.

Overall, the best way of putting across the value of unfamiliar classroom practice is to invite parents to sessions where students illustrate their depth of learning and understanding about important issues. It is rare to meet parents who are not impressed when they see their son or daughter demonstrate their learning by means of a multimedia presentation, especially when speaking in a new language.

Text Box 4.4 Emergent bilingual students celebrate their learning in front of an audience of parents and visitors

Many schools arrange daytime or evening sessions for students to display their learning to parents and friends. The aim is to illustrate students' achievements by presenting the results of enquiry-based learning carried out during a Unit of Inquiry. The presentations include a demonstration of students' grasp of the investigative process as well as their mastery of core aspects of a major topic.

In line with the overall philosophy of enquiry-based learning, the class in question had focused on the real-life issues surrounding the giving of aid to less-developed countries. The students in the class had been divided into small groups and one group included Yukiko and Keiji, two Japanese students who had entered the school at the beginning of the year as early learners of English. The third member of the group was Arnaud, a French-Canadian student who was also new that year, and whose English was not yet fully developed. A teacher was assigned to work with this group and together they began by searching on their iPads for development agencies and aid charities. The students were adept at following the links and Keiji quickly realised that some agencies were primarily fundraisers while others set up development projects. It was decided that the key questions would include: What are the outcomes of giving cash donations? What are the outcomes of offering support and expertise for development projects? How can we find out what people who receive the aid think? What can we do ourselves to bring about change if change is needed?

The students spent much time together working on this project and the ESL teacher in the school provided extra back-up in the way of vocabulary and skills teaching to enable the students to create their presentations. A great deal of language

(Continued)

Text Box 4.4 Emergent bilingual students celebrate their learning in front of an audience of parents and visitors (*Continued*)

was generated in the course of preparing a PowerPoint presentation that related to a real-life development project run by Action Aid. The students made one external visit to interview an Oxfam employee, but the inspiration for their substantive piece of work was a visit to the school by the founder of a charity set up to provide livestock for families in South Sudan. After her visit, with the help of the teacher, the students designed a very large flowchart showing how the acquisition of a cow and her calf changes the life chances of a family in South Sudan. This was illustrated with downloaded photos and their own drawings. Each student practised making a spoken presentation of the information on the chart and this was displayed side by side with the PowerPoint presentation and other written material that specifically showed the research basis for answering the questions.

The final stage was the evening meeting at which students presented their work to parents. Arnaud began by talking about the way they had arrived at the key questions. Keiji commented on the PowerPoint presentation and then Yukiko talked through the information on the flowchart. She had experienced difficulty in settling and in making friends and her parents felt that she had not become 'fluent' in English, to their disappointment. On the evening itself, wearing a new dress, she made her presentation. She stumbled at first, but increasingly gained confidence and never lost her drift or determination to put the material across. Her parents, as can be imagined, were overwhelmed by what their daughter had accomplished, but perhaps the most interesting exchange was when Keiji's father talked to the class teacher. He had, he said, never understood the point of enquiry – why not just learn from a book? – but having seen what the students had produced he realised that this type of learning was preparing them for the modern world.

4.5 Teaching in International Primary and Middle Years Curriculum Schools (IPC and MYC)

Two further curricula designed for use in international schools which are also offered in some national educational systems are the International Primary Curriculum (IPC) and the International Middle Years Curriculum (IMYC). Sometimes described as 'off-the-shelf' curricula, they offer a framework for integrating the areas of the curriculum. Literacy can be taught within these curricula or separately as a discrete subject. Mathematics is treated as a separate subject, but applied mathematics can be incorporated into the thematic units as appropriate. The IPC and the IMYC take students up to the age of 14, when generally they go on to follow a two-year course leading the Cambridge International General Certificate of Education (IGCSE), taken at age 16+. After that, many students move into the IB Diploma Programme.

The curricula do not specify a particular pedagogy, although the emphasis is on active and participatory learning. Each unit includes Learning Goals, an Assessment for Learning component and 'international' activities. The units are comprehensively planned and include suggestions about resources to support activities. The following websites offer further information on the IPC and IMYC Units of Work: www.greatlearning.com/ipc/the-ipc/units-of-work and www.greatlearning.com/imyc/the-imyc/units-of-work.

Experienced international educators recognise the benefits of a curriculum structured in this manner. Many schools, particularly those in far flung and challenging geographical environments such as the Shell Company Schools, may experience a rapid turnover of teaching and administrative staff. Such schools appreciate the benefit of a consistent highly resourced curriculum that maintains the quality of the school's offering in these circumstances. The professional development opportunities, offered not only during the school year but during the long summer break, enable new teachers to 'hit the ground running' immediately they enter the school.

Text Box 4.5 Supplying a secure curriculum framework in the desert

The IPC supplies the framework for the teaching and learning in a school situated in the desert in the south of Oman. This school was set up to provide schooling for the children of personnel working in the nearby Liquefied Natural Gas plant. The school exists in the harshest of environments and is one of the main focuses of community activity among the expatriate families of all nationalities that live in an adjacent purpose-built compound.

It is surprising for visitors, therefore, to enter the school building and to find an instantly recognisable child-centred learning environment full of energy and colour. The diversity of the children is matched by the diversity of the teachers, whose reasons for wishing to teach in Oman are wide ranging. One or two are the partners or spouses of LNG workers; others have ongoing connections with the country and are prepared to make the seven-hour journey to Muscat every weekend to hook up with old friends. One teacher made this sometimes hazardous trip (the road is liable to flash floods) in order to attend church in Muscat and to be part of a Christian community. Other teachers were excellent English speakers from various backgrounds. In view of the diversity among the teaching staff, using the International Primary Curriculum (IPC) with its in-built curriculum framework and content seemed to make excellent sense in this school.

Visiting the classrooms confirmed this view. The school used the UK national curriculum outline to teach mathematics and literacy, with the IPC used alongside to provide a cross-disciplinary framework that incorporated the other subjects of the curriculum. A noticeable feature was the way that the learning activities within the IPC had been used to include the students' prior living and learning experiences. Walking

(Continued)

Text Box 4.5 Supplying a secure curriculum framework in the desert (*Continued*)

around the classrooms, there was clear evidence of teaching and learning that drew on life in Oman and the Gulf region as well as providing links to students' languages and cultures. The bases for much of this activity were the international elements in the IPC which served as a means of incorporating the experiences of all the students into classroom activity in this isolated school. One Dutch parent described the school as a haven of interest and activity for her children – it was the sole reason why her family could remain in the posting.

4.6 International Schools That Import Part or All of Their Programmes From National Education Systems

A large number of schools derive part or all of their programmes of study from the national, state and provincial education systems of countries such as Australia, Canada, New Zealand, the UK and the USA. This practice is generally the result of connections with one of these countries arising out of the history of the foundation of the school. The choice of these programmes may also reflect the kudos that attaches to them in the location where the school is situated. In many areas of the world, groups of parents perceive a Western-style education conducted largely in English as the means to give their children access to wider higher education and employment opportunities.

4.6.1 The use of curricula derived from the UK

There are numerous international schools throughout the world that derive their programmes from the National Curriculum of England, although as always with international schools, the school may vary the content of their programme to reflect the nature of the local environment and the parent body. Many of these schools are to be found in the Gulf region. Generally, in these schools at the age of 16, students take the Cambridge IGCSE followed at 18 by either English Advanced Level examinations or the IB Diploma. Students use these university entrance qualifications to apply to universities in their home location or overseas.

4.6.2 Schools offering programmes of studies from multiple sources

While many schools still derive almost their entire curriculum from one English-speaking country, it is now quite common to find schools that offer an array of programmes from multiple sources. The IB programmes are probably the most frequent new introductions, but schools also pick and choose individual items from other English-speaking educational systems. Teachers become accustomed to using a mathematics text-book series from the USA and to teaching literacy via the Australian First Steps Literacy

Table 4.2 Examples of three international schools that draw their curricula and programmes largely from one English-speaking country

Name	Curriculum offerings	Profile and numbers of students	Language facts	Comments
School with an American-derived programme of study				
American International School, Hong Kong Founded 1986 www.ais.edu.hk 'Global citizens; effective communicators; empowered thinkers'	All-through American curriculum, based on US Common Core State Standards. US Advanced Placement courses offered in HS. Around 48% go to US universities; 23% go to university in Hong Kong.	Around 830 students, 37 nationalities (of whom 19% with American passports)	Applicants for Grade 2 and upwards are tested to see that they are 'proficient users of English appropriate to age and in line with language requirements for grade level'. Mandarin is compulsory from Early Childhood through Grade 8.	A school that draws its ethos and programmes entirely from the USA with two-thirds of the students going on to either US or Hong Kong universities. The teaching of Mandarin answers the needs of students from the region (although Cantonese is the form of Chinese spoken in Hong Kong).
School with an Australian-derived programme of study				
Australian International School, Singapore Founded 1993 www.ais.com.sg 'Globally focused, distinctly Australian'	Pre-school to Year 5 PYP. Years 6–8 benchmarked against Australian National Curriculum. Years 9–10 Cambridge IGCSE. Years 11 and 12 IB Diploma or New South Wales High School Certificate.	2600 students in 2012: 66% Australian (37% dual-nationality parents)	Teaching in English, extensive EAL support. Commitment to mother tongue maintenance. In-school MT classes at present in Mandarin, Korean, Japanese and Bahasa Indonesian.	A school drawing on its Australian ethos to offer a mix of international and Australian programmes to its students. Around two-thirds of families have strong Australian connections.

(Continued)

Table 4.2 (*Continued*)

Name	Curriculum offerings	Profile and numbers of students	Language facts	Comments
School with a Canadian-derived programme of study				
Canadian International School (CIS), Tokyo Founded 1999 http://cisjapan.net 'The experience of excellence; the honour of achievement'	Canadian K-12 programme (alongside IB PYP in elementary section). Graduation Certificate and Advanced Placement courses in HS section. Canadian elements derived from and accredited by the Province of Prince Edward Island, Canada	No precise numbers given on website	Student acceptance as set out on Admissions link indicates that entrants must exhibit 'English-language level relative to age, as determined by school test and interview. Outside support for English if necessary. ESL support in school possible. Beginners rarely accepted after start of MS. Students study Japanese from Grades 1 to 10.	The school derived its entire curriculum from Canada until 2009, when it gained authorisation to offer the IB PYP. Its mathematics and English curriculum in the elementary section continue to be sourced primarily from the Prince Edward Island school system. As the result of being an authorised PYP school, CIS commits itself to fostering the development of students' first language. Teachers plan and implement opportunities for students to use their home languages during PYP Units of Inquiry.'

Note: The information which is drawn from the schools' websites is correct at the time of writing.

programme (http://det.wa.edu.au/stepsresources/) which is a favourite in international schools. All this may be within the overall framework of another curriculum.

Table 4.2 gives examples of three international schools that draw their curricula and programmes largely from one English-speaking country, but with additions from other sources in the case of two of the schools. All three schools contain students who are nationals from those countries but all their student bodies are diverse. Two of the schools make it clear that they operate largely in English and expect new students to be 'grade-level' proficient. All three schools offer in-school mother tongue tuition in the languages of the students.

4.6.3 Diverse students in schools that derive their programmes from national systems

A key area of interest and concern for this Handbook is the nature of the educational experience for emergent bilingual students who attend English-medium international schools that offer curricula which largely derive from national schooling systems in English-speaking countries. International schools of this type invariably contain large numbers of students from diverse linguistic and cultural backgrounds, a circumstance that gives many committed international educators pause for thought. What is the nature of the experience of an emergent bilingual student who is being educated in a system that embodies potentially different beliefs about teaching and learning?

4.6.4 The role of the teacher

The role of a teacher working in one of these schools is complex. In order for emergent bilinguals to succeed in the school, teachers must train and tutor them in the content and ways of learning that these programmes require. On the other hand, a vital part of their work is to foster students' development in their home languages and promote their continuing sense of esteem for their home cultures. Many experienced educators would suggest that the presence or absence of 'international-mindedness' is key to the quality of emergent bilingual students' experience.

Text Box 4.6 What do we mean by international-mindedness?

International-mindedness is a concept that has come to be used to identify what it is that separates international schools from national schools (although some national schools are internationally minded). It lies at the heart of the IB programmes and is mentioned by name, or implied, in the documentation put out by the large accreditation organisations.

But what does an internationally minded school look like and what does being an internationally minded teacher entail? Perhaps it is easier to describe schools and

(Continued)

Text Box 4.6 What do we mean by international-mindedness? (*Continued*)

teaching which do not share this quality. Frequent visitors to international schools know that it is possible to enter schools where the mission statement, literature and programmes include the word 'international' and yet feel very uncertain whether the school is truly international in any meaningful way. This can sometimes be the case when the national ethos of one English-speaking country seems to overwhelm the evidently international nature of the student body. The feeling can also occur in schools where there is little or no recognition of the locality and culture outside the school's front door.

Classrooms, too, can appear quite sterile with overwhelmingly Anglophone references, often displayed on bought-in pre-made banners. Sometimes connectivity via technology seems to be more highly celebrated than the international connectivity of the students within the school (although technology has the capacity to enhance international-mindedness in remarkable ways).

Other schools give a very different impression. In these schools there are signs that the school celebrates its diverse population and there is a strong sense of place. The display boards in the corridors reflect the international outlook of the students and teachers by the inclusion of a wide frame of reference in the graphic and written content. There are practical signs of an inclusive approach to art, culture and sport. The classrooms contain multiple global references, and technology is used to bring the outside world into the classroom in all its richness. It may take longer in a school to assess the degree to which teachers are genuinely incorporating multi-perspectival references and viewpoints into their teaching, although a lively, colourful classroom with multicultural artefacts and images and evidence of the multilingual nature of the students in the class supplies valuable evidence.

There is much more to be said about international-mindedness: perhaps the chief point is that internationally minded teachers contribute to positive outcomes for all the students in a school. *Not* celebrating the richness and diversity in most international schools diminishes the quality of the experience of each member of the school community.

4.7 International Schools That Offer Bilingual Programmes

There are numbers of international schools that offer bilingual programmes, some of them with historic foundations. There is a substantial literature relating to schooling in two or more languages in which the programmes tend to be described in terms of the balance in curriculum time given to each language. 'Strong' programmes offer roughly 50% of curriculum time to each language and are considered more effective in delivering

Table 4.3 Examples of two schools which offer teaching in two or more languages

Name	Curriculum offerings	Profile and number of students	Language facts	Comments
School offering bilingual programmes in three languages with English				
Atlanta International School, Georgia, US Founded in 1984 www.aischool.org. 'Prepare your child to succeed in a globally connected world'	An all-through IB school offering the PYP, MYP and Diploma programmes. The majority of students attend US universities.	Primary years programme taught in 50% English, with either 50% German, French or Spanish. MS students study chosen language to advanced level and use it for social studies. Extensive teaching offered to new MS students in the school's languages. Option of IB Bilingual Diploma in school's languages or students' mother tongues via extensive self-taught 'Language A' programme.	Around 1100 students: 50% with American connections, 50% international. 96 nationalities, 50 languages represented.	A school where the aim is for students to emerge as balanced bilinguals in English and one of the school's languages or with their mother tongue. Advice given about mother tongue learning opportunities outside school.

(Continued)

Table 4.3 (*Continued*)

Name	Curriculum offerings	Profile and number of students	Language facts	Comments
Dual-language school designed to equip students with international qualifications				
Chinese International School, Hong Kong Founded in 1983 www.cis.edu.hk	Primary years: school-originated programme taught equally in both Mandarin and English. Year 6: 65% English, 35% Chinese. Integration of concepts such as empathy/kindness, wisdom/right judgement across primary curriculum. Middle Years: IB MYP. Chinese teaching reduced but central place remains. Final two years IB Diploma. High percentage of students qualify for IB Bilingual Diploma. 40% of students attend US universities; 30% UK universities; 10% Hong Kong universities.	1400 students: 63% born in Hong Kong. 31 nationalities in all. (Faculty derives from US, Australia, New Zealand, Canada, UK and from Hong Kong, Taiwan, Philippines.)	Traditional full form characters are used in the teaching of Mandarin, except Chinese as Second Language students in the MS and HS who use simplified forms. French and Spanish are offered as foreign languages. *Note*: the school has opted to teach Mandarin as opposed to Cantonese, the form of Chinese used in Hong Kong and Macau.	This school's aim is to equip students to be fully proficient in Mandarin and English with an internationally recognised qualification in the IB Diploma. The school has recently opened a new campus in Hangzhou, where Year 10 students will experience a year of immersion in Chinese culture and language while continuing their education in English.

Note: The information which is drawn from the schools' websites is correct at the time of writing.

successful outcomes (see Baker, 2011). 'Weak' programmes that offer greater curriculum time to one language, often the more dominant language in the setting, are viewed as being less effective in producing bilingual and bi-literate students.

International schools that describe themselves as bilingual offer a wide variation in the type of programme that is offered, although English, unsurprisingly, is almost invariably included as one of the languages. Some schools divide the curriculum so that different subjects are taught in different languages. Other schools teach the whole curriculum in both languages. In schools where the local language is one of the languages offered, the hours given over to its teaching generally reflect the desire of parents for their children to keep in touch with the local school system and to keep the option open of attending local universities. Many bilingual schools offer the possibility of students taking the local university examination alongside the IB Diploma.

Table 4.3 gives examples of programmes in two schools which offer teaching in two or more languages.

Key Points in This Chapter

- Programmes and curricula in international schools are derived from a number of sources.
- The IBO provides three programmes that are in use in international schools: the PYP, the MYP and the Diploma Programme.
- They serve to give globally mobile students a consistent educational experience from the early years to university entrance.
- The IB PYP uses an enquiry-based learning approach.
- The aim of enquiry-based learning is for students to frame questions about a topic and to initiate and carry out an evidence-based investigation which indicates learning and understanding.
- The MYP integrates the teaching of individual subjects by means of 'areas of interaction' (changes in the pipeline).
- The IB Diploma is a globally recognised university entrance qualification.
- The IB Careers-related Certificate has been recently introduced to serve students engaged in career-related studies.
- The IPC and the IMYC offer an integrated approach to the teaching of all subjects except English and mathematics via thematic units.
- Many international schools derive their programmes of study partly or wholly from national educational systems.
- Bilingual international schools offer a range of bilingual programmes. The balance between the languages varies, with English usually being one of the languages.
- Observers and researchers in the world of international education cite the concept of international-mindedness as the distinctive quality that defines and unites international schools and international education.

Resources

International schools mentioned in this chapter
American International School, Hong Kong: www.ais.edu.hkk.
Atlanta International School, GA: www.aischool.org.
Australian International School, Singapore: www.ais.com.sg.
Canadian International School, Tokyo: http://cisjapan.net.
Chinese International School, Hong Kong: www.cis.edu.hk.

International school organisations
IBO website: www.ibo.org.

Sites related to enquiry-based learning
Galileo Educational Network (a Canadian-based site): www.galileo.org.

Primary Years Programme of the IBO
'IB Primary Years Programme at a glance': www.ibo.org/pyp/index.cfm.
IBO site introducing the 'learner profile': www.ibo.org/programmes/profile/.
IBO site setting out the concept of transdisciplinary themes: www.ibo.org/pyp/curriculum/index.cfm.
IBO site giving sample Units of Inquiry: http://ibpublishing.ibo.org/live-exist.
IBO site giving full account of PYP final year Exhibition requirements: www.ibo.org/ibap/conference/
    documents/Exhibition.
Ways to Learn Through Inquiry: Guiding Children to Deeper Understanding. Available from online IB Store:
    https://store.ibo.org/ways-to-learn-through-inquiry.
Primary Inquirer: offering a range of flexible resources that can be used as part of PYP or enquiry teach-
    ing. The resources include enquiry-based theme kits and PYP Readers and Companions. See http://
    www.pearsonschoolsandfecolleges.co.uk/Primary/Literacy/AllLiteracyresources/PrimaryInquirer/
    PrimaryInquirer.aspx.

Middle Years Programme of the IBO
'IB Middle Years Programme at a glance': www.ibo.org/myp/.

Diploma Programme of the IBO
'Diploma Programme at a glance': www.ibi.org/diploma/

Careers-related Certificate of the IBO
'The IB Career-related Certificate (IBCC): preparing students to follow their chosen pathways in life':
    www.ibo.org/ibcc/.

International Primary and Middle Years Curricula
International Primary Curriculum website: www.greatlearning.com/ipc/.
Website giving links to Shell Company Schools (group of schools for whom the IPC was first created):
    www.wclgroup.com/school-management/shell.
Website giving information about IPC Units of Work: www.greatlearning.com/ipc/the-ipc/
    units-of-work.
International Middle Years Curriculum website: www.greatlearning.com/imyc/.
Website giving information about IMYC Units of Work: www.greatlearning.com/imyc/the-imyc/
    units-of-work.

Further curricula and programmes
Australian First Steps Literacy programme: http://det.wa.edu.au/stepsresources/.

Further resources mentioned in this chapter
Popplet site – useful for supplying scaffolding and writing frames: http://blog.popplet.com/category/popplets-in-education.

References

Baker, C. (2011) *Foundations of Bilingual Education and Bilingualism* (5th edn). Bristol: Multilingual Matters.

Bruner, J.S. (1960) *The Process of Education*. Cambridge, MA: Harvard University Press.

Bruner, J.S. (1966) *Towards a Theory of Instruction*. Cambridge, MA: Harvard University Press.

DeVries, R. (2000) Vygotsky, Piaget and education: A reciprocal assimilation of theories and educational practices. *New Ideas in Psychology* 18 (2–3), 187–213.

Dewey, J. (1916) *Democracy and Education: An Introduction to the Philosophy of Education*. New York: Macmillan.

Kirschner, P.A., Sweller, J. and Clark, R.E. (2006) Why minimal guidance during instruction does not work: An analysis of the failure of constructivist, discovery, problem-based, experiential, and inquiry-based teaching. *Educational Psychologist* 41 (2), 75–86.

Locke, J. (1996 [1693]) *Some Thoughts Concerning Education and of the Conduct of Understanding* (ed. R. Grant and N. Tarcov). Indianapolis, IN: Hacket.

Montessori, M. (2008 [1912]) *Scientific Pedagogy as Applied to Child Education in 'The Children's Houses'* (trans. A.E. George). New York: B.N. Publishing.

Rousseau, J.-J. (1979 [1762]) *Emile, or On Education* (trans. with introduction by A. Bloom). New York: Basic Books.

Part 3

Bilingualism and Language Learning

The two chapters of Part 3 cover different aspects of bilingualism and language learning. Each chapter is designed to offer teachers in international schools insights and information that will make them more effective in their work with emergent bilinguals.

This is a practical Handbook rather than an academic textbook and the approach adopted in Part 3 reflects the aim of making theoretical concepts applicable and relevant to the situation of teachers in international schools. A list of internet links and texts is provided in the Resources section at the end of each chapter to allow readers to investigate the topics more fully.

5 Bilingualism in the International School Context

Chapter 5 is concerned with the theory that seeks to explain the phenomenon of bilingualism and the use of multiple languages in one individual. The aim of the chapter is to present this theoretical content in a way that leads to a greater understanding among teachers of emergent bilingual students of the issues relating to their bilingualism (or multilingualism).

The sequence of Chapter 5 is as follows:

- Introduction: bilingualism (and multilingualism) among students in international schools.
- What do we mean by bilingualism?
- Ensuring an additive experience for emergent bilinguals.
- The importance of mother tongue maintenance and development.
- The profile of elective bilinguals.
- How the families of elective bilinguals view English.
- Promoting mother tongue maintenance and development in international school students.
- Language policies in international schools.

Introduction: Bilingualism and Multilingualism Among Students in International Schools

Bilingualism (and multilingualism) is a way of life for many of the students who attend international schools. The pattern of language usage varies according to the type of international school they attend. In schools where English is the sole medium of instruction, students who speak another language (or languages) outside school experience bilingualism across the different aspects of their lives. In bilingual schools they experience bilingualism as an integral part of their education.

Bilinguals are culture learners

Being a bilingual generally goes hand in hand with being someone who is used to living in a bicultural or multicultural context. Often bilingual students in international schools become skilled culture learners with experience in adapting to the different cultural environments presented by different aspects of their lives. Sometimes this skill at cultural adaptation begins at home, where students may be surrounded by a variety of cultural influences from their birth because of the make-up of their family. For globally mobile students, a need to adapt culturally may begin with their first move when they are faced with the need to adapt to local cultural expectations and to a new school culture. For bilingual students, living with and between multiple cultures is part of everyday life. (The topic of adaptation to new cultural settings is the subject of Chapter 3.)

Diversity in international schools

The first evidence of the diversity to be found in international schools is often the information such schools include in their promotional material. On most websites, it is common for schools to set out the number of nationalities represented in the student body as an indication of the breadth of their student intake. (Nationality is often used as a shorthand means of indicating the degree of diversity in the school.) The current website of the International School of Tanganyika (www.istafrica.com), for example, states that its enrolment of around 1000 students includes 50 nationalities, with 80% of the student body speaking more than one language. It is not unusual for large schools catering for globally mobile students to contain as many as 60 different passport holders. As experienced international school teachers recognise, however, knowing which passports students hold is rarely an adequate guide to their linguistic and cultural profiles.

Text Box 5.1 The reality behind the description on the passport

The life story of Amin, aged 14, illustrates the diversity that lies behind the fact of his passport nationality. Amin has a Kuwaiti father and a Japanese mother. He holds a Kuwaiti passport. He was born in the UK where his older siblings went to local English-speaking schools. When his father had to return to Kuwait for business reasons, the children moved with their mother to Japan. Here Amin went to a local Japanese school and reached an age-appropriate level of proficiency in the curriculum. When Amin's father's business took him to The Netherlands, the whole family joined him there and Amin and his three siblings went to the international section of a Dutch state school. Recently the family have moved to Paris, where all four siblings attend an English-medium international school. They appear to have immediately felt at home because, as Amin said, 'they are used to people like us'. However, he added, the Japanese students did not feel he was a 'real Japanese'. This was despite the fact that Amin speaks excellent Japanese and was continuing his Japanese studies at the local expatriate Japanese school. Perhaps in response to the wariness of the Japanese students towards him, Amin had decided to spend his time with non-Japanese students. His English is now developing rapidly and he also understands Arabic. The family speaks a mixture of Japanese, Arabic and English at home.

From an account gathered during the course of the research enquiry described in Appendix A.

Teachers new to international schools and diversity

The degree of diversity in an English-medium international school may not at first be obvious to new teachers, even those who are accustomed to working in diverse classrooms in national systems. Many mainstream classrooms in international schools give the impression of being monolingual English-speaking environments, so that the many languages and cultures represented in the class may not immediately be apparent. In this type of classroom, teachers only 'see' one half of a student's life – the side that presents itself in school. Only later do they understand the linguistic complexity of many students' lives. Some teachers may be unfamiliar, not only with the bilingual or multilingual reality, but also with the concepts of multilingualism and bilingualism themselves.

Text Box 5.2 Bilingualism and multilingualism are the norm

The use of multiple languages by individuals is the norm over large parts of the world and in many different settings. This is true of individual countries, whole continents, and polyglot cities such as Hong Kong and Singapore where a multilingual existence is part of daily life. In India, for example, individuals customarily use the language of their state or locality, while at the same time having a knowledge of one of the Indian national languages which are used in the wider context. In other settings such as North and South America, where large numbers of the established population were originally incomers, many individuals retain links with their family's language and cultures. And lastly, in most countries of the world, both developed and less developed, there are recently arrived populations who learn to live and work in the language of their new home while continuing to use their primary languages.

New teachers who are familiar with diversity by reason of their personal histories

A significant group of teachers in international schools have a different profile. They choose to live and work in a multicultural and multilingual environment because of their own experience as bilinguals, multilinguals and/or of global mobility. They have opted to work in international schools because they feel at home with the atmosphere and enjoy the challenge of working with students from different backgrounds. This group includes competent second language users of English or another language of instruction in the school. They constitute a valuable resource in an international school since they are familiar with so much of the experience of the students they teach.

The value of understanding more about bilingualism and the pattern of language use

Teachers in international schools will find that understanding more about bilingualism, multilingualism and the pattern of language use in their students will help them to:

- Support students more effectively as they move through the phases of language learning.
- Understand what may lie behind hitches and delays in students' language-learning progress.
- Understand the length of time it takes to become proficient in both languages.
- Be aware of the variety of language usage that may exist in students' homes and social lives outside school.
- Listen with more sympathy and understanding to parents' concerns.
- Offer practical advice and support to parents with a fuller understanding of the issues involved.
- Have knowledge-based discussions with specialist English language teacher colleagues about the progress of students' learning.
- Be able to communicate effectively with the school's administration about such areas as:
  - *entry and exit criteria for specialist English language teaching provision;*
  - *appropriate assessment instruments for use with emergent bilinguals (addressed in Section 7.1);*
  - *the availability of mother tongue classes;*
  - *the effective use of students' mother tongues in the mainstream classroom.*

The content of Chapter 5

The first section of Chapter 5 considers the nature of bilingualism, the different pathways that lead to bilingualism, how global mobility impacts on language usage and the potential advantages of being a bilingual (or a user of multiple languages).

Section 5.2 addresses the importance of mother tongue maintenance and development in achieving an overall additive outcome for emergent bilingual students in an English-medium environment. This is followed by a discussion of what may lead to a less favourable outcome, where students fail to maintain their home language and come to feel a reduced level of esteem for their home culture.

The next section, in contrast, looks at the situation of so-called 'elective bilinguals' and why they tend to experience more favourable outcomes in their overall language and culture learning. A discussion of the ways that families whose children may be described as elective bilinguals view English follows in Section 5.4.

Finally, Sections 5.5 and 5.6 investigate the ways in which some international schools promote an additive outcome for their emergent bilingual students by means of school language policies and mother tongue provision.

5.1 What Do We Mean by Bilingualism?

5.1.1 Trying to define bilingualism

It is a difficult task to define bilingualism in a few words. Perhaps this is because bilingualism is a way of living rather than a single definable concept. What is generally accepted is that bilingualism refers to the ways that an individual uses two or more languages in everyday life. Bilingualism has often been expressed as a continuum of language use. At one end of the spectrum are bilinguals whose command of all aspects of their two languages is relatively balanced and at the other end are individuals who perhaps only use the spoken element of one language and to a limited degree. Balanced bilinguals are recognised as being rare – perhaps the nearest familiar example of a balanced bilingual is someone who works as a simultaneous interpreter, at least in terms of bilingual competence but not necessarily in all different contexts (domains).

The majority of bilingual speakers show different levels of proficiency in their use of language in the different aspects of their lives. In one of their languages they may have a high degree of mastery in the written forms of the language, whereas they may use the other language largely in spoken communication. In many cases bilinguals use different vocabularies for different aspects of their lives. In some cases, the two

---

Text Box 5.3 Bilinguals using their two languages separately

Some students in English-medium schools appear to use their two languages quite separately. A Korean student who was interviewed during the course of the research enquiry described in Appendix A is an example of someone whose use of his languages seemed to overlap very rarely. Jong-Kyu was an assiduous student in school and his use of English had developed very quickly. He knew that he had to move from speaking social English to learning the higher level use of language needed for success in his school work. (And he was committed to success!) In the cause of improving his English, he confined his school friendships to non-Koreans.

His description of life outside school, however, implied a pattern of activity that took place entirely in Korean. His father was a diplomat and much of the weekend was spent playing golf with his father at the sports centre frequented by the expatriate Korean community. Jong-Kyu recognised that his two lives and languages did not cross over. He saw himself as essentially Korean, but needed the tool of highly proficient English to be successful in school and later to find high-level employment – like his father.

languages are used almost exclusively in separate spheres of activity. This can be the case in English-medium international schools where students use English almost exclusively in school and their home language for all family and social activity outside school.

5.1.2 Paths to bilingualism

A recognised way of describing the developing use of two languages in an individual is to make the distinction between simultaneous acquisition and sequential learning. The two terms 'acquisition' and 'learning' are significant in themselves in this context. 'Acquisition' tends to be used when a language is absorbed rather than formally taught, as happens with the very young infant at home. 'Learning' tends to be used when a language is learnt more formally at a later date, either as a student in school or purposefully as an adult.

Simultaneous acquisition

The term 'simultaneous acquisition' is generally used to describe the situation where infants from birth are immersed in two languages at the same time. This may happen when the two parents speak different languages or when the infant spends a large amount of its time in the care of someone who speaks a language other than the parents'. The use of these languages may continue throughout childhood if children lead stable lives and are educated in one of the languages.

Sequential acquisition

The term 'sequential' bilingualism is used when an individual learns a second language after the acquisition of the first language. This can happen when the growing infant goes to nursery or playgroup and then on to a school where the language or languages are different from the one she or he has used as a very young child. It can also happen in adolescence or adulthood when people move voluntarily into another language environment or when they are forced to move due to economic or social pressures. Students who speak other languages outside school are experiencing sequential acquisition when they enter an English-medium international school. However, an individual only becomes bilingual if the first language is developed and maintained.

Text Box 5.4 Acquiring bilingualism sequentially

The story of Aleksander, aged 11 from the Czech Republic, illustrates an experience of sequential bilingual acquisition. It also displays the reality for students as they come to terms with life as bilingual and bicultural people. Both Aleksander's parents were Czech and he had lived and gone to school in the Czech Republic all his life before the family moved to Amsterdam and he entered an American curriculum English-medium international school as a beginning speaker of English. He embraced

English ('I think English is cool') and made rapid progress in both the written and spoken forms. At first both his parents wanted him to focus on English; after his first year his mother began reintroducing Czech reading material ('she kept making me read Czech books'). The family continued to make frequent visits to the Czech Republic where Aleksander moved back into an exclusively Czech-speaking and Czech cultural environment.

Aleksander is at the crossroads in his journey towards balanced bilingualism. His mother wants him to go back to the Czech Republic for his higher education, but Aleksander and his father want him to go to university in the United States ('that's where I will get the best education'). Aleksander's feelings are in a state of flux. Despite his present passion for English and all things American he still retains a strong attachment to his home language and culture. When asked about his feeling for home he says: 'I am proud to be a Czech person.' Probably, the balance between Aleksander's languages will depend on whether his father obtains, as he wishes, a move to the USA. At present the family are due to move back to the Czech Republic after three years away from home.

From an account gathered in the course of the research enquiry described in Appendix A.

Other patterns of bilingual acquisition

The real-life experiences of children who use two or more languages indicate that there are many variables affecting their exposure and use of languages. The concepts of simultaneous and sequential bilingualism just do not provide an apt or full enough description in the case of many individuals, including students who attend international schools. Multiple and changing language use is the norm for many children and young people arising out of changes at home as a result of their parents' choice of school or as the outcome of a global move or change in lifestyle.

Variety of language use in the home

Everyday language use in the families of many students involves two or more languages as a matter of course. It is not uncommon for parents to hold different passports and to speak a range of languages. Sometimes both parents' languages are used in the home; in other cases only one of the languages is used or a third shared language. For the children, none of these languages may be the language or languages of the international school they ultimately attend.

Some language usage reflects the origins of the grandparents or the parents' history of higher education or childhood mobility. Carers and domestic staff may bring different languages into the home along with different cultural patterns.

Within the home it is not unusual for the use of language to change. This can happen to children when their parents divorce or are separated. At this time, one of the established languages in the child's life may be removed or replaced by another language if a new relationship is formed.

Many children are accustomed to situations like these where they hear several languages on a daily basis. In many homes this variety among the languages in use is ongoing experience for children and parents, a fact that is sometimes quite difficult for international school teachers to remember when they work with such students in monolingual classrooms.

Text Box 5.5 Language use may not be as straightforward as it seems

A brother and sister from Brazil, interviewed separately, both said initially that their first language was Portuguese. This turned out to be an incomplete account of their language exposure and usage. Later in the interviews they described how both sets of grandparents were of German origin. Their parents were eager for their children to continue the family's acquaintance with the German language and culture and as a result they had been sent to a Portuguese/German bilingual school in their home city. The school also offered extensive tuition in English. At the same time the family spent their holidays in the USA since both parents had pursued their higher education at American universities and they had many friends there. It was also seen as a chance for the children to gain experience in an English-speaking country. So a family that described itself as Portuguese speaking was in fact at ease with the use of three languages in different settings.

From accounts gathered in the course of the research enquiry described in Appendix A.

5.1.3 The impact of global mobility on the pattern of bilingual acquisition

A single move or multiple moves may have the effect of altering the pattern of children's language use. Globally mobile children and young people do not consistently attend schools with the same language of instruction across their moves. Some students have a pattern of returning home between moves, while others are placed in local schools in new postings, especially if the language of the local community is considered to have a high level of prestige and usefulness. This can be the case, for instance, in French-speaking locations where expatriate parents place their very young children in Francophone playgroups and nurseries before sending them to an English-medium international school.

As a result of their varying patterns of educational experience, it is not uncommon for siblings in the same family to speak a different range of languages. In the case of one family, as emerged during the course of the research enquiry described in Appendix A, a mother described the way that each of her three children had 'chosen' a different language as their preferred language. The eldest child, a teenage boy, had opted for English since 'this is what my friends speak', while the daughter who was the middle child clung to Italian. She had lived the longest in Italy and during her time there had attended an

Italian-speaking nursery and infant school. The youngest child, a boy, spoke Dutch, 'because that is what mama speaks'.

5.1.4 The potential benefits of bilingualism

Research indicates that bilingualism brings advantages beyond the obvious benefits of being able to function in two languages and in different settings. In most studies bilinguals are shown to outperform their monolingual peers consistently in the areas of cognitive development and metalinguistic awareness (that is, being able to think about language as a whole). The work has recently focused on what happens to the brain when an individual regularly uses two or more languages.

Note 1: Readers interested in this subject should search further in the following texts: Baker (2014), Bialystok (1991), Carder (2007), Cummins (2000a), Diaz and Klinger (1991).

Note 2: To view the summary of a report on a study into the benefits of bilingualism, go to The Cambridge Bilingualism Network site. The write-up is headed: 'Cambridge University researchers are spreading the message that bilingualism is good for learning, rather than the hindrance as sometimes perceived'. The sentiment behind this heading reflects a continuing need felt by researchers in the field and bilinguals themselves to defend bilingualism in the face of negative comparisons with monolingualism. A quote in a text box at the side of the first page sets out the positive case for bilingualism: 'The mental gymnastics needed to constantly manage two or more linguistic systems increases cognitive flexibility and makes learning easier.' See: www.cam.ac.uk/research/news/bilingualism-is-good-for-learning.

The potential benefits of bilingualism include the following

Bilinguals tend to have certain *cognitive advantages*, i.e. in the ways they think:

- They show more elasticity in their thinking – they are able to multitask effectively.
- They are able to think more divergently, which allows them to come up with rapid solutions to problems.
- They are able to apply a range of perspectives to new ideas and issues.
- They are adept at thinking through the details and implications of a new idea or course of action.
- They are able to focus on essential information and exclude irrelevant details.

They tend to show advanced *metalinguistic abilities* (particularly in the way language as a whole is processed):

- They understand the similarities and differences between languages.
- They are able to learn new languages more quickly because they know how languages work in general. What they know in one language transfers to new languages. They tend to have more confidence as language learners.

- They are able to adapt rapidly to changes in the linguistic and cultural environment.
- They show more communicative sensitivity and more awareness of the needs of the listener.
- They may be more open to the perspectives and ways of viewing the world found in other groups.

5.2 Ensuring an Additive Outcome for Emergent Bilingual Students

5.2.1 What is meant by an additive outcome for emergent bilingual students?

Additive bilingualism is the desired outcome for emergent bilinguals being educated in a language which is not their home or primary language. Bilinguals achieve additive bilingualism when they acquire the spoken and written forms of another language without loss to the maintenance and development of their home language. The term 'additive' may also be used in relation to culture and biliteracy. In this case, an additive outcome occurs when students continue to participate in the life of their own culture at the same time as they engage with new cultural experiences in school. In other words, an additive experience means that emergent bilingual students gain new skills and understandings from their experience at school without losing their proficiency in their families' language or ease with their communities' culture.

5.2.2 Maintaining and developing the home or primary language to promote an additive outcome in emergent bilingual students

Research indicates that maintaining and developing the home or primary language is an essential element in achieving an additive outcome for emergent bilingual students being educated in a language that is not one of their home languages. This is true of students in national schooling systems and in English-medium international schools. Where students do not continue to develop their home languages, they are in danger of experiencing what is known as a subtractive outcome. This is the outcome that occurs when students focus on the school language at the expense of their home language, which may result in their home language remaining underdeveloped and underused.

The following quotation which appears on a link on the International Baccalaureate Organisation (IBO) website underlines the importance of the mother tongue for emergent bilingual students: 'The importance of mother tongue to identity, self esteem, cognitive ability, and ultimately academic success is well established' (see www.ibo.org/ibworld/jan09/languageisthelearning.cfm).

Note: The term 'mother tongue' has come to be used in the world of international education to describe the home, first or primary languages of emergent bilingual students, although it has largely fallen out of use in other circles.

Reasons for maintaining and developing the mother tongue for emergent bilinguals in international schools

It preserves their sense of self and place in their home society:

Maintaining the mother tongue is critical to students' identity – it is part of their own and their family's shared history. It keeps them in touch with family, friends, their home culture and schooling.

It contributes to their overall learning:

Maintaining the home language while they are learning English or another school language of instruction ensures that students continue their cognitive development. If students' home languages are allowed to lapse they may not develop sufficient proficiency in either of their languages to engage in higher level thinking tasks.

Skills that are established in the home language transfer readily to the new language. Students such as Aleksander from the Czech Republic (mentioned earlier in Text Box 5.4) arrive in international schools with oracy and literacy well established in their home language. They can use their existing knowledge and skills very effectively to support their learning of English.

The next move for globally mobile students may involve a return to their home base where they need to be able to slot back into their home schooling system.

5.2.3 Circumstances that may lead to subtractive bilingualism

Ethnic minority students in majority language schooling systems

The situation of students from minority ethnic backgrounds who are educated in majority language national schooling systems is a key area of focus in the discussion about the causes of subtractive bilingual experiences. Groups that fall within this description and which are frequently cited are the less advantaged Spanish speakers in the US, or French-speaking students in schools in the Anglophone provinces of Canada (see Cummins, 2000a).

The term 'minority' in this context indicates that students belong to a community whose language and culture are different from the majority population in the province or country concerned. The term 'minority' also reflects the contrast with the situation of 'majority' language speakers in the country who have access to high-status employment and are part of empowering social networks. In other words, the description 'minority' refers to a difference in power and perceived prestige between the language communities. It does not refer to the numbers of speakers involved.

Contrasting 'circumstantial bilinguals' with 'elective bilinguals'

In most situations, education through the medium of the majority language is the path that enables students from minority ethnic backgrounds to gain access to good jobs and empowering mainstream social networks. The force of this circumstance has led to these groups being described as 'circumstantial bilinguals'.

The term 'circumstantial bilingual' stands in contrast to that of 'elective bilingual', which is a description that applies to most students in international schools. Students who are described as elective bilinguals tend to enjoy built-in advantages which make an additive outcome more likely. Section 5.3 discusses this issue in detail.

Potential subtractive outcomes for ethnic minority students

There are a number of established reasons why minority students being educated in majority language schools may experience a subtractive outcome. Focusing on achieving success within the school through the school language may diminish the value of their home language and culture in some students' eyes. Time spent on learning to read and write in the home language may seem a 'waste of time' (a thought expressed by a father in the course of the research enquiry described in Appendix A). The outcome for students when their home language and culture appear to count for very little may be a loss of commitment to the home language and a failure to maintain and develop it. In turn, the failure to develop oracy and literacy in this language to a high level undermines students' effectiveness in learning the school language.

The culture of the school itself may be new to students from ethnic minority backgrounds, especially those who are newly arrived in the host country. They may be disadvantaged by being unfamiliar with the learning styles and behaviours that lead to success in the school system. They may find the values and social activity of the school different and at times unacceptable. They may feel their sense of self has been compromised. They have been separated from the communities and cultures where they are accepted and in which they have an established identity, and placed in environments where their out-of-school experiences may carry little social capital (Bourdieu, 1991; see Text Box 3.1 'List of terms and ideas discussed in this chapter'). When all these elements are present, it is clear why some students experience subtractive outcomes.

Note: The role of English and its prevailing influence and domination in some settings are complex, wide-ranging and controversial topics. Readers who are interested in this subject may wish to consult the following texts, among others: Kubota and Lin, 2009; Luke, 2009; Pennycook, 1994, 1998; Phillipson, 1992.

Subtractive experiences can happen in international schools too

Subtractive experiences also occur in international schools. Generally the reasons behind the lack of progress towards bilingualism are complex and multifaceted. Some of the most common reasons are given below:

- The school places little emphasis and value on students' home languages and cultures.
- Students' home languages and cultures are rarely referenced in the classroom (for a discussion of this topic, see Section 9.2).
- The school is a bilingual school with a 'weak' bilingual programme in which less teaching time is scheduled for the language which is not English and where the

mission of the school appears to place a higher value on the English-medium section of the curriculum (see Section 4.7).

- The school does not itself organise home language classes and fails to persuade parents of the need to arrange home language tuition outside school (see Section 5.5 in this chapter).
- Specialist English teaching takes place in separated-out classes using language textbooks – as opposed to in-class or small-group classes where teaching is linked to the needs of the curriculum and practised via authentic learning activities (see Section 7.4).
- English is an official language alongside others in the home country and is used interchangeably with another national language in the student's family. When students from these backgrounds enter an English-medium school it sometimes proves difficult to sustain their use of the non-English national language either inside the family or in the home community as a whole.

Text Box 5.6 Examples of home languages being under pressure from English

Two examples of a change in language usage resulting from students attending English-medium schools occurred during the focus group session carried out in the course of the research enquiry described in Appendix B. In both cases, the global prestige of English seemed to result in the children of some families either refusing to commit themselves to becoming literate in a second national language or to using it at all.

The first example concerned a mother from Malta, where English is one of two national languages. In this case, the mother recognised with sadness that her older children showed no interest in becoming literate in Maltese. They mixed exclusively with others from similar English-speaking educational backgrounds both outside and inside Malta and they needed Maltese only to speak to local tradespeople and older family members. They intended to find work outside Malta eventually and she could see that their attachment to Maltese was falling away although they still saw Malta as their home.

The second example concerns a mother from the state of Tamil Nadu in India where there is a major political movement to reinstate Tamil as the language of everyday usage. This mother expressed the pain she felt at her son's changed view of his home language after a short time in an English-medium school. She recognised that already English exerted a great fascination for her son among his peer group at home in Chennai. She expressed her feelings in this way: 'Me particularly, when I am a little excited, I try to talk to him in my own language. And my son rebukes me: Mama, I don't like the sound of it anymore.' She clearly felt great pain

(Continued)

> **Text Box 5.6** Examples of home languages being under
> pressure from English (*Continued*)
>
> on hearing her son say this, especially as one set of grandparents spoke only Tamil.
> She could see that his time in an English-medium international school had con-
> firmed him in his view of English as the language he wished to identify with.

- Students in bilingual schools whose home language is neither of the school languages may fail to achieve multilingualism or biliteracy. This is the case, for instance,
  when a German student arrives in Buenos Aires where he attends a Spanish/English
  bilingual international school. Most schools in this situation offer English language
  support, but where third language students are very few they may experience a sense
  of exclusion from the mainstream of school life both linguistically and culturally.
- Extreme dislocation and multiple moves, perhaps mid-year, may be the cause of
  students failing to reach a level in either or any of their languages that allows them
  to participate fully in school (see Chapter 2 for more on mobile families).
- Break-up in the family, or other disruptive family circumstances leading to changes
  in the languages that are used in the home.

Note: Readers interested in investigating the causes of subtractive bilingualism further might wish to consult the following texts, among others: Carder (2007), Collier and
Thomas (1997); Gallagher (2008); Hakuta *et al.* (2000).

5.3 The Benefits of Being an 'Elective' Bilingual

Students in international schools fall into the category of bilingual individuals who
may be described as 'elective bilinguals' (*Note*: not to be confused in this discussion with
'emergent'). As the term suggests, the parents of these students have chosen, or elected,
to place their children in an English-medium or bilingual school where one of the languages of instruction is English. Irrespective of whether the families involved lead a
globally mobile existence or are settled long term in a location, they tend to have similar
aspirations for their children. They view the English language as a valuable tool for their
children's future and they appreciate the usefulness to their children of gaining a globally recognised qualification at the end of their studies.

Anne-Marie de Mejía (2002) describes the family profile of elective bilinguals. She
contrasts the experience of elective bilinguals whose parents choose to send them to
English-medium schools with that of circumstantial bilinguals who are obliged to attend
majority language schools. Circumstantial bilinguals as members of minority language
communities are required to negotiate their positions in a majority language context
that may threaten to overwhelm their affiliation to their home language and culture.
Elective bilinguals approach their experience in English-medium schools with the confidence of personal entitlement and security in their linguistic and cultural identities.

Text Box 5.7 Comparing the experiences of 'elective' and 'circumstantial' bilinguals

Nine-year-old Agatha is an example of an elective bilingual. Her home is a large city in Brazil. Her mother has a Greek/Italian background and her father is from a German/Brazilian family. The family languages are Portuguese, English and Italian. Her father works for the Brazilian affiliate of a large US company; her mother works as an interpreter. When she was four, Agatha entered a school accredited as an 'experimental bilingual school' by the city education authorities. Eighty-five per cent of the students are Brazilian. The teaching is substantially in English and is based on a UK curriculum model with Brazilian references incorporated into the subject areas. Portuguese language and Brazilian studies are taught in separate classes. All the teachers speak both English and Portuguese. Students gain Brazilian qualifications (Ensino Fundamental and Ensino Médio) alongside the UK IGCSE 16+ examination. In the final two years of school, students take the IB Diploma.

Agatha's parents expect her to go to college in Brazil, with the option of later moving to an English-speaking university. Agatha has many of the advantages that are held to be typical of elective language learners; based on her family background and her schooling, she is in a strong position to achieve an additive multilingual outcome.

The obvious advantages of Agatha's situation can be compared with a child from the Somali community that has gathered in Islington, a suburb of north London that was once the author's home. Children from this community arrive in the UK as asylum seekers and refugees fleeing from civil war in Somalia. Of the adults only a few of the men can speak any English when they arrive in the UK and the mothers almost universally speak only Somali Arabic. The children are placed in the local schools, often representing quite large percentages of the total number of pupils. These children are thus exposed to a world where the language, culture, expected behaviours and ways of learning are completely unfamiliar, although they remain surrounded by fellow Somali incomers. This is a situation where so-called 'circumstantial' bilinguals, especially those who have histories of disruption and trauma of this type, are potentially at risk of experiencing a subtractive outcome.

In talking to a local primary school head teacher in the same neighbourhood, it was clear, however, that it is wrong to make blanket statements about learning outcomes. She talked of the difference that strong family support and high expectations could make and how schools could develop and grow in the ways that supported such students. The school had received funding for extensive bilingual support for the Somali pupils. Pointing out the diversity of the children playing nearby, she said: 'We are used to welcoming children from all over the world – we know how to help them to achieve.'

5.3.1 The family profile of elective bilingual students in international schools

An established feature among the families who choose an English-medium education in an international school for their children is their perception of the advantages for their children of being proficient users of English and of having access to globally recognised qualifications. A further feature which is highly significant is that most retain a continuing value for their home language and culture and take positive steps to see that their children keep in touch with their home language and home schooling system. Where parents display a positive, proactive approach to their children's overall bilingual development, as has been shown in an earlier section of this chapter, the children concerned are in an advantageous position with regard to educational outcomes. The following viewpoints and experiences are typical of the families who elect to send their children to international schools and are key elements in contributing to an additive experience.

English and the value of an English-speaking education

- The parent(s) and other family members are already accustomed to using English in one or other aspect of their lives.
- Both students and parents recognise the power and usefulness of English.
- Parents feel entitled to give their children access to the perceived advantages of an English-medium education.
- They view globally recognised qualifications as a useful tool in extending opportunity for their children.
- They may envisage the possibility of their children receiving all or part of their higher education in an English-speaking country.
- They are in a position (or their employers are willing) to pay the generally high fees required by English-medium schools.
- They view English as an additional advantageous medium of communication (rather than as a more powerful replacement for the use of the home language) – the global 'lingua franca' as one mother put it in the course of the research enquiry described in Appendix B.
- They embrace the idea that being conversant with English and being able to function effectively in English-speaking settings will give their children membership of the broader international community with all the possible advantages this may bring.

Continuing views regarding their home language, schooling system and culture

- Their general social and economic status in the home setting leads parents and students to retain a high regard for their home language and culture.
- They have a well-established and enjoyable family and social life in the home setting that takes place in the home language – children are motivated to continue to use their home language in order to remain part of these gatherings.

- Maintaining the home language and contact with their home schooling system enables parents to send their children to home universities for their first degree, leaving open the choice of an overseas English-speaking university for further study.
- They see the advantages of their children developing a high level of biliteracy in the home language in order to keep options open with regard to employment opportunities.

Text Box 5.8 Elective bilinguals in Turkey

A group of schools in Turkey answers the needs of parents who wish their children to become proficient in English and to have access to English-speaking higher education opportunities without diminishing their commitment to the Turkish nation and the Turkish language. One of the schools, the American Collegiate Institute in Izmir, makes this clear on its website (www.aci.k12.tr), where the preamble to its list of objectives reads: 'We aim to enable our students to be strong bilinguals in English and Turkish.' Later the first objective states: 'Our aim is to produce students who practise a clear commitment to the ideals of Attaturk' [the founder of the modern Turkish nation].

The students at the Izmir school and at Robert College, a renowned school in Istanbul with a somewhat similar profile and foundation (http://webportal.robcol. k12.tr), are rigorously selected at the age of 11 and spend their first year following an intensive course in the English language. On the basis of a week's visit to the Izmir school it appears that the standard of spoken and written English at the end of the year is astonishing. Subjects are taught in Turkish and English as mandated by the Turkish Ministry for Education.

Students at the Izmir school take the IB in the final year alongside some mandated national courses, while students at Robert College in Istanbul have the choice of taking US Advanced Placement tests or the Turkish National Entrance Exam (ÖSS). Of the 176 students who graduated from Robert College in 2011, 123 went to prestigious Turkish universities (scoring in the top percentiles for students in private schools), while 53 went overseas to the USA, the UK and Canada. The list of famous alumni of both schools is interesting since it indicates the extent to which students remain connected with and contribute to Turkish society. Their education has enabled them to gain access to what the English-speaking world has to offer while remaining deeply Turkish at heart.

5.4 Elective Bilinguals in International Schools and Their View of English

This section looks further at the way in which English is viewed by families who elect to send their children to English-medium international schools (or bilingual international schools where one of the languages is English). It considers the position that such families assign to English and investigates the role that they expect English to play within their overall language repertoires. It underlines the sense of entitlement that elective bilinguals and their families may increasingly feel in their use of English.

For parents who send their children to international schools, English and a familiarity with English-speaking education systems are additional tools for their children rather than overwhelming necessities which they must acquire. This view of English as an advantageous means of communication seems to sit well with two ways of describing English – one is the idea of English as a lingua franca (ELF) and the second is the concept of English as an international language (EIL). Several pointers in the research enquiries described in Appendices A and B seemed to suggest that these were the functional roles which students and parents ascribed to the ways they tended to use English.

5.4.1 English as a lingua franca (ELF)

As mentioned earlier, a Spanish mother in the focus group session associated with the research enquiry described in Appendix B herself mentioned the idea of ELF. 'People like us', she said, need to learn English. She went on to expand in this way: 'it's the *lingua franca* of international people: if you speak English you fit in immediately and your children have friends.' Her husband, she said, needed English in his work.

The same mother was very clear, however, that she intended her children to maintain and develop their links with the home language and with Spain. As she pointed out, they went on frequent visits home and expected to return there permanently at some point. The children needed to speak the family language to talk to their grandparents and to be able to enter a Spanish-speaking school again if necessary. In any case, they were constantly using Skype and Facebook to keep in touch with their cousins in Spanish. This mother viewed Spain, the Spanish language and Spanish life as something precious and to be valued. Part of her role as a Spanish mother was to ensure that her children continued that deep sense of attachment and familiarity with their national culture.

The ease with the concept of ELF may be due to its capacity to stand aside from close association with the economic and cultural aspects of American or British or Antipodean English. In the case of families whose children are elective bilinguals, the idea of English as a communication medium may give it a more neutral profile – a profile that leaves space for rich continuing development in the home language.

Text Box 5.9 What is a lingua franca?

The term 'lingua franca' was coined in the Levant when a language evolved, largely based on Italian, that was used among traders of diverse backgrounds to communicate with one another (Mansel, 2010: 14). The name itself derives from the colloquial Arabic word, Franj, which was used to describe Westerners in the coastal cities of the Eastern Mediterranean (Maalouf, 2006). Various languages had been used throughout history to enable speakers of different languages to communicate with one another and a language used in this way came to be described as a lingua franca. Latin, Arabic and French have each been used as a lingua franca at different historical periods by diplomats, merchants and travellers. Arguably, at the present time English is the language used most widely as a lingua franca (English as a lingua franca; ELF), although it is possible that other languages will replace English in that role in the future. In different places ELF reflects aspects of the local language, and may vary in grammatical form. However, its core remains recognisable to the speakers who use it and as such it is considered desirable as a pathway to global opportunities (Jenkins, 2007; Seidlhofer, 2001).

The term lingua franca when used in connection with English probably has more resonance with speakers of European languages due to its latinate origins. Within the European Union, for instance, the description of ELF is common currency. In the wider world, other terms are used to describe the use of English as a medium of global communication, one of which is English as an international language (EIL).

5.4.2 English as an international language (EIL)

In the discussion about the use of English in the research enquiries described in Appendices A and B, the word 'international' was frequently mentioned, as might be expected, from parents, teachers and students who were involved in the world of international education. For the interviewees, the status of English and the need for people like themselves to become proficient in the language and to learn how to function in international environments appeared to be unquestionable. All the respondents who filled in the small-scale survey which formed part of the research enquiry described in Appendix B, when asked to rate their reasons for choosing to send their children to an English-medium international school, rated the need to learn English as 'essential' or 'very important'. (The next most highly rated reason was that the school felt 'international'.) The overwhelming feedback on the topic throughout the two enquiries was that people who sent their children to international schools viewed English as the essential medium of global and international communication 'for people like us'.

Their view of English as 'the international language' for many families whose children attend international schools is closely associated with English-speaking education systems and countries. The same parents who said they thought of English as the international language also said they wanted their children to go to Australia, North America or the UK for some part of their higher education.

The concept of EIL clearly retains aspects of status and empowerment, even when parents say they view English purely as a communication tool. Increasingly in the rapidly developing countries of the world, the socially mobile element of the populations in these countries wishes to appropriate the perceived power of English for themselves. One teacher interviewed made this comment which perhaps expresses the way the world is moving, at least in the case of students who are elective bilinguals. He said this of the East Asian students at the school:

They will take from you what they can use and dismiss immediately that they learnt it from you. Now it's theirs. And the Chinese are like that too, to some extent. They're going to take anything they can get.

Some of the features associated with EIL

- EIL has the potential to remove English from its association with the linguistic and cultural imperialism associated with British colonial times or the 20th-century economic and cultural dominance of the USA.
  - *In certain settings, in the Middle East and East Asia, English and Western-style education is being used as a means to enhance the already powerful or developing economic status of countries in these areas. An article in a UK newspaper begins with the heading: 'Battle intensifies for $2 billion English-teaching business in China'. The same article describes the use of American, Canadian and British teachers to teach Chinese students in school and in extracurricular classes.*

    Few would argue that the Chinese people feel any lack of pride in and attachment to their own history, culture and language and yet aspiring Chinese parents feel driven to enable their children to acquire English. Clearly there is a discussion to be had here about the precise role that English is playing in this circumstance.
- EIL leaves space for the development and acceptance of World Englishes – forms that emerge locally in different areas of the world. World Englishes tend to develop local differences of grammar, vocabulary and usage. A variety of this sort may be used concurrently with more standard forms in settings such as the Indian subcontinent.
- EIL as a concept may remove the pressure for individuals and groups to aspire to so-called standard forms of American or British English.

Note: Scholars who have addressed the topic of EIL over the years include, among others: Pennycook (1991, 1998, 2007), Phan (2008), Sharifian (2009).

5.5 Promoting Mother Tongue Maintenance and Development in International Schools

In recent years, more international schools are offering in-school or after-school classes in students' mother tongues. There are a number of reasons for adopting this approach. One is the increasing numbers of emergent bilingual students in international schools, both those that serve globally mobile students and those whose student body is largely made up of local students. In these cases, the provision of in-school mother tongue classes is partly a response to demand on the part of the parent body.

A further reason is the consistent advocacy by a small number of international school educators convinced of the right of emergent bilingual students to receive in-school tuition in their mother tongue in order to ensure an additive outcome from their years of education in an English-medium school (see Carder, 2007; Gallagher, 2008). Finally, some international school organisations and programme providers, chiefly the IBO, have championed the cause of mother tongue maintenance as an integral part of a school's academic offering. The bilingual option available at IB Diploma level also contributes a real sense of purposefulness to the continuing maintenance and development of students' mother tongues.

Note: The emphasis in this section is specifically on mother tongue classes. The value of incorporating students' mother tongues into the ongoing work of the mainstream classroom as a means of promoting their learning of both the school and home languages is addressed in Section 9.2.

5.5.1 Schools' motivation in making mother tongue provision

The value of incorporating mother tongue classes in the school's programme, or at least providing venues and teachers for after-school classes, is based on an understanding of the benefits to emergent bilingual students. Schools that promote mother tongue provision spell out the advantages to their students on their websites. One school, the International School of The Hague in The Netherlands, provides the following introduction on their Mother Tongue Programme link:

> It is crucial for children to develop their own mother tongue (MT). It is the language they use to communicate with their family and friends. It facilitates a possible relocation to their home country, national school or university and it gives them access to their own culture and family background. Research shows that a strong mother tongue helps in the development of a strong second language. At the International School of The Hague we recognise the importance of children maintaining their own mother tongue and our vision is: 'Every child is empowered to develop his/her mother tongue within the curriculum'. (http://www.studiov.info/ish/primary/eal_mother_tongue)

5.5.2 Commitment to mother tongue maintenance in international schools

Embedded mother tongue classes

Increasing numbers of international schools offer time during the school day for regular mother tongue classes. As far as possible, where teachers are available, the students follow a national programme. Few schools at the present time offer classes in the languages of all the students in the school due to lack of viability of numbers and of available teachers. Thus most schools, as is the case with Utahloy International School of Guangzhou in China, tend to offer in-school classes only in the most highly represented languages. In the case of this school, those currently available at the time of writing were Chinese, Finnish, French, German, Italian, Japanese, Korean and Spanish. (www.utahloy.com/gz/mother_tongue/mt_overview.html).

One or two schools, notably the International School of London (www.islschools. org/london), commit to providing in-school mother tongue teaching in all the languages represented in the school.

Extracurricular mother tongue classes

Some schools, partly in response to small numbers of students in a language group or because of timetable restrictions, choose to schedule mother tongue classes after school. Often in these cases, the school offers accommodation and facilities to parents who organise mother tongue classes privately.

The United Nations International School of Hanoi in Vietnam, for instance, offers a high level of support for mother tongue classes by offering coordination to so-called MT community groups. These groups are responsible for finding and funding the teacher and the classes take place in school where there is time or after school. (see 'Mother tongue programme' link on the school's website at www.unishanoi.org/).

One or two national governments have a consistent approach to ensuring the maintenance of the national language in the children of expatriate families. The obvious example is The Netherlands, which has a policy of providing and funding teachers to teach Dutch nationals in major expatriate locations.

In-school or after-school provision for preparing students for local school examinations

This happens most frequently in English-medium schools with large numbers of local students, often in response to parents' wishes to keep their children in touch with their home language and local school system.

A policy of supplying information giving options in the local community for language teaching in students' mother tongues

Where schools do not provide school-sponsored mother tongue classes, perhaps due to lack of funding or availability of teachers, they have a role in explicitly informing parents of the value of mother tongue maintenance.

Such information might include the following options, according to availability in the locality:

- After-school or Saturday morning classes at a national expatriate school. (For example, Japanese schools based in major cities usually offer intensive classes which are popular with Japanese parents.)
- Classes offered by such national expatriate language and cultural centres as the Alliance Française (French) and the Goethe Institute (German).
- Privately organised individual and small-group tuition sessions.
- Correspondence and online courses such as the French government-sponsored programme, the Centre National d'Enseignement à Distance (CNED; www.cned.fr/) – not always accepted easily or gracefully by students.

5.6 Language Policies in International Schools

In line with some national schooling systems, many international schools now group together their language policies and practice under the heading of a single school language policy. In most schools these policies are used to ensure that the language rights of all the students are acknowledged, particularly the right of emergent bilingual students to receive tuition in their mother tongues. Language policies tend to be beneficial for emergent bilinguals since their directives involve teachers in acknowledging and making strategic decisions which lead to more favourable outcomes for these students (see Carder, 2007; Gallagher, 2008).

5.6.1 Who requires schools to write language policies?

The IBO (www.ibo.org) has been a prime mover in establishing the practice of writing language policies. As it sets out on its weblink entitled 'Guidelines for developing a school language policy', 'Every IB World School authorized to offer one or more of the three IB programmes is required to have a written language policy'. The document goes on to quote one of the IB's mandated programme standards (2005):

> The school has a written language policy (including provision for second-language teaching and mother-tongue language support) that meets the needs of the students and reflects the principles of the programme.

The reputable accreditation organisations also include criteria in their accreditation self-studies requiring schools to make provision for the language-learning needs of all their students. However, they tend to avoid specifying what form such provision should take and hence the provision of mother tongue classes in international schools tends to be patchy.

5.6.2 Effective approaches to writing a language policy

Quality language policies are written by groups of stakeholders, including the teachers who will implement the policy. This tends to be a more effective practice than importing another school's language policy wholesale. The process is described clearly, with emphasis on the primary area, in the chapter written by Jane Scott (2011), entitled: 'Writing and implementing a language policy in the primary section of a linguistically diverse school'. It can still be a useful strategy to look at the language policies of schools accredited by reputable organisations and also to refer to the publications issued by the IB in this area.

5.6.3 The content of language policies

As is often the case with international schools, the content and implementation of these policies can vary considerably, with each school adopting language teaching programmes that suit its student profile and academic offerings.

Language policies usually include statements relating to the following areas:

- the school's overall philosophy about language usage and teaching in the school;
- the balance between the use of languages in bilingual schools;

- the admissions policy of the school in relation to incoming students' proficiency in the school language(s);
- provision for emergent bilingual students to become fully proficient in the school's language(s) of instruction (specialist English teaching programmes);
- the level of the school's commitment to multilingualism and multiculturalism;
- the level of the school's commitment to ensuring an additive outcome for its emergent bilingual students by acknowledging and promoting the maintenance and development of students' home languages and cultures;
- how the school implements its policy of maintaining and developing students' home languages and the financial implications, if any, for families;
- the school's commitment to training all its teachers in the strategies that include emergent bilingual students in mainstream classrooms;
- parent education about the value of maintaining the development of students' home languages;
- the teaching of the host country language(s);
- foreign language teaching and practice.

Note: A list of links relating to language policies, including examples of policies posted by international schools and documents published by the IBO is included in the Resources section at the end of the chapter (see also Scott, 2011).

Key Points in This Chapter

- Bilingualism and biculturalism is a way of life for emergent bilingual students in international schools.
- International schools contain increasing numbers of emergent bilingual students. Often now they are the substantial majority.
- Teachers will find that an understanding of bilingualism will help them to be more effective in their work with emergent bilingual students.
- Bilingualism can be expressed as a continuum of language use.
- Simultaneous bilingualism occurs when an individual learns two languages at the same time (as in babyhood).
- Sequential bilingualism is said to occur when individuals learn their second language after they have acquired their first (as when an emergent bilingual student arrives at an English-medium school for the first time).
- Bilingualism brings potential benefits in cognitive development and metalinguistic awareness.
- Students who are emergent bilinguals may experience both additive or subtractive outcomes.
- Maintaining a student's home language and culture is a vital element in ensuring an additive outcome.

- Students from minority ethnic groups may experience subtractive outcomes as a result of being educated in majority language schools.
- Students in international schools come largely from a group known as 'elective bilinguals'.
- Elective bilinguals have built-in advantages which tend to contribute to more positive outcomes to their education in English-medium schools.
- English-medium schools are increasingly committed to making provision for classes in students' mother tongues.
- Schools that set out their philosophy and practice in language policies tend to offer a more effective language-learning experience to emergent bilingual students.

Resources

Websites and links
International schools used as examples in this chapter
American Collegiate Institute, Izmir, Turkey: www.aci.k12.tr.
International School of Tanganyika, Dar es Salaam, Tanzania: www.istafrica.com.
Robert College, Istanbul, Turkey: http://webportal.robcol.k12.tr.

Bilingualism
Cambridge Bilingualism Network: www.cam.ac.uk/research/news/bilingualism-is-good-for-learning.
Diaz and Klinger (1991) have made available online a very accessible overview of the interaction between bilingualism and cognitive development: www.english6.net/d/diaz-klinger-interaction-between-bilingualism-and-cognitive-e9465-pdf.pdf.

Additive and subtractive bilingualism
International Baccalaureate Organisation: 'The language is the learning' website: www.ibo.org/ibworld/jan09/languageisthelearning.cfm.

Mother tongue provision in international schools
International school of The Hague: http://www.studiov.info/ish/primary/eal_mother_tongue.
United Nations International School of Hanoi in Vietnam – see 'Mother tongue programme' link on the school's website at: www.unishanoi.org/.
Utahloy International School of Guangzhou in China: www.utahloy.com/gz/mother_tongue/mt_overview.html.

Example of a distance learning programme provided by governments for the children of expatriate nationals
Centre National d'Enseignement à Distance (CNED) – distance-learning course for French-speaking students sponsored by the French Ministry of Education: www.cned.fr/.

Language policies in international schools
Canadian Academy, Kobe, Japan: http://www.canacad.ac.jp/page.cfm?p=3276.
Guidelines for developing a school language policy, issued by the IBO: https://ibweb.idu.edu.pl/files/dokumenty/guidelines_for_developing_a_school_language_policy.pdf.
Language policy link for Atlanta International School, USA: www.aischool.org/page.cfm?p=4944.
Mashrek International School, Amman, Jordan (a bilingual Arabic/English school): www.mashrek.edu.jo.

References

Baker, C. (2011) *Foundations of Bilingual Education and Bilingualism* (5th edn). Bristol: Multilingual Matters.

Baker, C. (2014) *A Parents' and Teachers' Guide to Bilingualism* (4th edn). Bristol: Multilingual Matters.

Bialystok. E. (1991) *Language Processing in Bilingual Children*. Cambridge: Cambridge University Press.

Bourdieu, P. (1991) *Language and Symbolic Power* (trans. G. Raymond and M. Adamson). Cambridge, MA: Harvard University Press.

Carder, M. (2007) *Bilingualism in International Schools: A Model for Enriching Language Education*. Clevedon: Multilingual Matters.

Collier, V. and Thomas, W. (1997) *School Effectiveness for Language Minority Students*. NCBE Resource Collection 9. Washington, DC: NCBE George Washington University, Centre for the Study of Language Education.

Cummins, J. (2000a) *Language, Power and Pedagogy: Bilingual Children in the Crossfire*. Clevedon: Multilingual Matters.

de Mejía, A.-M. (2002) *Power, Prestige and Bilingualism: International Perspectives on Elite Bilingual Education*. Clevedon: Multilingual Matters.

Diaz, R. and Klinger, C. (1991) Towards an exploratory model of the interaction between bilingualism and cognitive development. In E. Bialystok (ed.) *Language Processing in Bilingual Children* (pp. 167–192). Cambridge: Cambridge University Press.

Gallagher, E. (2008) *Equal Rights to the Curriculum: Many Languages, One Message*. Clevedon: Multilingual Matters. An outline of the pedagogical approach set out in Eithne Gallagher's book from the perspective of multilingual students can be viewed at: http://www.youtube.com/watch?v=TFAOIPeSjU&feature-related.

Hakuta, K., Butler, Y.G. and Witt, D. (2000) How Long Does it Take English Learners to Attain Proficiency? University of California Linguistic Minority Research Institute Policy Report No. 2000-1. Santa Barbara, CA: University of California.

Jenkins, J. (2007) *English as a Lingua Franca: Attitude and Identity*. Oxford: Oxford University Press.

Kubota, R. and Lin. A. (eds) (2009) *Race, Culture, and Identities in Second Language Education: Exploring Critically Engaged Practice*. London: Routledge.

Luke, A. (2009) Race and language as capital in school: A sociological template for language-education reform. In R. Kubota and A. Lin (eds) *Race, Culture, and Identities in Second Language Education*. London: Routledge.

Maalouf, A. (2006) *The Crusades Through Arab Eyes* (trans. J. Rothschild). London: Saqi.

Mansel, P. (2010) *Levant: Splendour and Catastrophe on the Mediterranean*. London: John Murray.

Pennycook, A. (1994) *The Cultural Politics of English as an International Language*. London: Longman.

Pennycook, A. (1998) *English and the Discourses of Colonialism*. London: Routledge.

Pennycook, A. (2007) The myth of English as an international language. In S. Makoni and A. Pennycook (eds) *Disinventing and Reconstituting Languages*. Clevedon: Multilingual Matters.

Phan, L.H. (2008) *Teaching English as an International Language: Identity, Resistance and Negotiation*. Clevedon: Multilingual Matters.

Phillipson, R. (1992) *Linguistic Imperialism*. Oxford: Oxford University Press.

Scott, J. (2011) Writing and implementing a language policy in the primary section of a linguistically diverse school. In E. Murphy (ed.) *Welcoming Linguistic Diversity in Early Childhood Classrooms*. Bristol: Multilingual Matters.

Seidlhofer, B. (2001) Closing a conceptual gap: The case for a description of English as a lingua franca. *International Journal of Applied Linguistics* 11 (2), 133–158.

Sharifian, F. (ed.) (2009) *English as an International Language: Perspectives and Pedagogical Issues*. Bristol: Multilingual Matters.

6 Being Informed About Language Learning

This chapter is concerned with the process of language learning. The aim is to help teachers become knowledgeable about significant aspects of language learning so that they can offer more effective support to students and parents.

The sequence of Chapter 6 is as follows:

- Introduction: why it is useful to understand the language-learning process.
- Individual variations in language learning.
- What sort of language do students need to acquire?
- The factors that lead to success in language learning.
- How long does it take to learn a language to the required level?
- Issues relating to the language-learning process.

Text Box 6.1 Terms and ideas that appear in this chapter

Note: The following terms are part of everyday usage in international schools and are frequently used in the naming of specialist English language classes and as a shorthand means of describing students' present level of language-learning achievement. They are problematic as accurate descriptions because students rarely learn a language at an even rate across the skills (see Section 6.2). These terms are used as ballpark descriptions which enable students to be broadly categorised for school purposes. Assessment instruments that divide students into these categories by means of cut-off points related to numerical scores should be treated with caution.

Beginners, beginning students, early learners: Students are generally described as beginners when their spoken English is limited to short answers to expected questions in a social and classroom context. Beginners are not yet able to understand what they hear outside the most concrete and context-related speech. In the classroom, teachers need to provide beginners with highly differentiated learning activities and to offer scaffolds and frames to help them to accomplish learning

(Continued)

Text Box 6.1 Terms and ideas that appear in this chapter (*Continued*)

tasks. Schools that are accredited by one of the reputable organisations are expected to provide either in-class English language teaching for beginners or pull-out classes.

Intermediate students: This classification is frequently divided into lower intermediate and upper intermediate since this phase covers a wide range of potentially uneven language proficiency. Intermediate students are at the beginning of the continuum of moving from concrete, context-specific language usage to being able to function in a concept-based environment such as a classroom. As they progress, they are increasingly able to understand decontextualised speech and to answer higher level questions involving the 'hows' and 'whys' of a topic. They are able to read appropriately graded texts and to begin to construct longer pieces of writing. They continue to make errors of construction and grammar, but have the ability to make themselves understood. They will continue to need differentiated learning activities that include, for instance, shorter quantities of reading material, and many intermediate students continue to need scaffolding and modelling of learning tasks. Most international schools continue to provide specialist English language tuition in some form for intermediate students.

Advanced: Advanced students are held to have mastered the basic skills of listening, understanding, speaking, reading and writing. They can contribute in classroom conversations both in whole class and in small groups. They can read class texts and take part in whole-class writing activities. They have reached a level at which they can search out new vocabulary for themselves and, in theory, build on their existing knowledge of English to add new advanced grammatical constructions. There is some controversy about whether schools should give advanced students further specialist tuition in the school language. Some administrations feel that mainstream teachers should now be responsible for refining and expanding advanced students' skills in the classroom. Other teachers feel that students at this level can fail to reach their full potential as users of English and as successful learners in general if they are not offered further targeted skills teaching.

Proficiency: This is a term that is widely used and yet has no commonly accepted descriptors attached to it. It is also used as a label to describe English language textbooks and in the naming of examinations. It is recognised that the term 'proficiency' covers a range of competencies. It is not a fixed point on a language-learning continuum. Probably the most useful way to view the adjective 'proficient' is to see it as a way to describe successful users of a language in a specific setting. In other words, proficiency in a school setting means that students are able to participate fully in the academic programme of the school as well as playing their full part in social and extracurricular activities.

Introduction: Why Is It Useful to Understand the Language-learning Process?

Classrooms in international schools contain emergent bilingual students at all stages of proficiency in the language of instruction. Some of the newly arrived students may be complete beginners. Others, whether newly arrived or longer term, are at an intermediate stage and show a variation of proficiency level across the different language skills typical of students at that stage of learning a new language. Lastly, there are emergent bilingual students who are quite proficient in their use of English but who continue to need targeted teaching in order to achieve their potential as successful students. Side by side with the emergent bilingual population there are usually first-language users of English, with the whole class exhibiting the range of general ability and motivation which is to be found in any classroom.

Diverse classrooms in international schools: Mobility and parental anxiety

Diverse classes are to be found all over the world in locations that attract large numbers of incomers or which serve multilingual populations. Teachers in these settings become accustomed to working with students who speak many home languages and represent different cultures. International school classrooms typically display a similar range of student experience. The aspects that may be unique to international school classes are the degree of coming and going among students in schools that serve a globally mobile population and the high expectations that are typical of parents who place their children in international schools. Given that a high proportion of the students are emergent bilinguals at different levels of proficiency in the language of instruction, it makes sense for teachers to search out knowledge and understandings that will help them to face the evident challenges in their classroom.

Learning about language learning

This chapter is designed to address some key features of the language-learning process with the focus being on the practical implications for the management of a classroom. The aim is for teachers to feel better informed about the issues and thus to be able to work more effectively with both students and parents.

The first section of Chapter 6 draws attention to a basic fact about language learning, which is that students learn a language at different rates and in different ways. The difference in the ways that individuals move along the language-learning continuum has practical implications for teachers and affects every aspect of practice in the classroom.

Section 6.2 is devoted to describing the sort of language students need to acquire if they are to participate fully in the academic classroom. Later sections expand on this topic by discussing the myths surrounding the age at which students learn a language most easily, the features that positively affect language learning and the length of time that it takes students to acquire academic language skills. Finally Section 6.6 discusses some of the issues that may arise as emergent bilinguals move along the language-learning continuum.

6.1 Language Learners Are Individuals: They Learn at Different Rates and in Different Ways

Learning a new language is something that many individuals undertake. However, behind the theory of language learning that describes the process in general lies the reality that individual learners show great variety in the ways they develop in learning the new language. Language learning progresses by fits and starts and its development in many cases is patchy rather than seamless.

6.1.1 Individual students may develop language skills at uneven rates

Learning a language is often broken down into the different aspects of the way individuals use language. These are frequently described in textbooks as the four skills of language and are generally listed as listening, speaking, reading and writing. For teachers working for the first time with students learning a new language, the uneven progress in acquiring these skills that is quite typical may come as a surprise. Experienced teachers recognise that there can sometimes be an extraordinary degree of difference in levels of development at a given stage in the language-learning process. It is quite common to find students who can clearly understand quite well and yet are unwilling, or unable, to speak out in class. Other students may speak quite fluently, but show signs of a lack of understanding of what they hear. Many students find it easier to speak and read than to write effectively.

6.1.2 Individual students take different lengths of time to reach proficiency

Language learners are individuals who approach the learning of a language with a variety of different abilities, aptitudes, motivation and experiences. These personal variables result in differing outcomes among students who have experienced similar levels of specialist language teaching and mainstream classroom support. Experienced teachers are accustomed to these differences and expect to provide practical and emotional support for as long as it takes. They recognise that understanding and assessing each student's present level of proficiency across the language skills is essential since only with this understanding can they supply learning support at an appropriate level. Applying general approaches to work with emergent bilingual students in a classroom is rarely effective.

6.2 What Sort of English Do Students Need to Learn?

An understanding of the sort of English that emergent bilinguals need to learn is a key factor in ensuring positive outcomes for these students. Students who are successful learners in English-medium international schools are able to function effectively across the skills and to show a high level of cognitive development in the new language. It is not enough for students to be able to function adequately in the social sphere; to succeed in school they must acquire the academic language needed for participation in all the learning activities of the classroom. Cummins (1984) describes the range of language use by contrasting the 'evolved language skills' needed for success in the classroom with 'surface fluency'.

6.2.1 Cummins' distinction between basic interpersonal communicative skills (BICS) and cognitive/academic language proficiency (CALP)

In a number of publications (Cummins, 2000b, 2008, among others), Jim Cummins has developed a theory that characterises the sort of language that students must acquire in order to succeed in school. He begins by describing the initial language that students learn as 'basic interpersonal communicative skills' (BICS). These skills include ordinary social talk, asking, and answering 'What', 'When' and 'Who' questions and basic reading and writing tasks. BICS language is generally held to be 'context embedded'. That is, the situation in which the language activity takes place includes many supportive aspects. To quote Colin Baker (2011):

> BICS is said to occur when there are contextual supports and props for language delivery. Face-to-face, 'context-embedded' situations provide, for example, non-verbal support to secure understanding. Actions with eyes and hands, instant feedback, cues and clues support verbal language. (Baker, 2011: 170)

BICS is the sort of language used when younger students are playing outside during recess or when older students are taking part in activities on the sports field. In both these settings, students are relaxed and engaged in physical activity. Their peers quickly show them what to do and they gain instant feedback both emotionally and practically if they join in effectively.

In the classroom, students are working in the BICS mode when they participate in recognised and routine classroom activities and when they engage in activities online or on paper that are fact based, pre-structured and which involve only a limited amount of new language.

Cognitive/academic language proficiency

According to Cummins (1979), students need to develop 'evolved skills' if they are to perform successfully on the higher order learning activities involved in more advanced class work. This is true of classrooms that contain even the youngest students. He describes this type of usage as cognitive/academic language proficiency (CALP). Put simply, BICS is everyday conversational language while CALP is academic language. Experienced teachers recognise that a student with seemingly good conversational skills may not have the evolved academic language to operate successfully in the classroom.

CALP is characterised as being context reduced. That is, students are given few visual clues or prior information about a reading text or in carrying out written work. CALP includes the thinking activities that students are asked to carry out when working with texts or creating a piece of writing at this level. These include analysis, hypothesising, inferring, generalising, predicting and classifying. Activities of this sort require students to use conceptual language in contexts with few visual or near-at-hand cues. Answering the questions 'Why' and 'How' generally requires students to use higher level language.

Text Box 6.2 What BICS and CALP look like in the classroom

The following learning activities illustrate the way in which the ideas of basic competence (BICS) and cognitive academic language skills (CALP) translate into classroom tasks.

Explorers

Activities requiring basic competence (basic interpersonal communication skills; BICS)

- Who are the famous explorers? Search for explorers that set out from your home country or who visited your country. (Encourage emergent bilingual students to be wide ranging: include Arab explorers such as Ibn Battuta and the early Chinese explorers as well as explorers such as Vasco da Gama and John Cabot who set out from Europe; get the students to consult books, apps and the internet and to ask their parents.)
- Follow the travels of these explorers on a map.
- Make a poster illustrating their travels.
- Research the objects and discoveries they introduced when they returned home.
- Construct a piece of writing, make an oral presentation or create a three-dimensional object that informs the class about the explorer that interests you most.

Offer frames and outlines to support students; give them the opportunity to find drawings, photos and graphics to illustrate their reports; suggest apps and internet material as sources of information; suggest relief maps, travelogues and journals as a means of presenting the information. (Chapters 10–13 are devoted to scaffolding the learning of emergent bilingual students in the mainstream classroom.)

Activities that require higher level 'academic' language (cognitive/academic language proficiency; CALP)

Set up groups or ask students individually to investigate the following topics; ask them to present their information in a creative form by producing an oral presentation, an online interactive poster via an application such as Glogster (www.glogster.com), a PowerPoint presentation or a written document.

Why did people in history feel the need to explore?

- Consider modern day explorers – why do they feel the need to explore?
- Are there common characteristics of explorers?
- How does exploration affect the region being 'discovered'?
- Who sponsors explorers and what do they gain from such sponsorship?

6.2.2 Caveats about the BICS and CALP approach

Cummins' BICS and CALP approach resonates with teachers for several reasons. It keeps awareness of the difference between early language proficiency and more advanced evolved language skills at the front of their minds. It seems to account for the real-life needs of students in the academic programme. It gives many useful pointers to the ways that teachers can target their support of emergent bilingual students.

However, some scholars (see MacSwan & Rolstad, 2003; Wiley, 2005) feel uneasy about aspects of Cummins' theory. They argue that there is no clear-cut division between basic competence and higher level 'academic' language. Students, as was mentioned at the beginning of this section, move forwards at different rates in the different language skills. They do not display basic competence at one moment and then immediately leap to a mastery of higher level language proficiency across all aspects of their language usage. The pattern is more patchy. Scholars also query the supposition that cognitive development goes hand in hand with linguistic competence in a second language. Both of these aspects are influenced by many factors, including the level of students' home language competence and their prior experiences of education.

In the field of higher education, the language students need for success in the academic context is described as 'English for academic purposes'. In some ways this is a less problematic idea than Cummins' approach. It indicates that academic activity requires a certain sort of language without the need to introduce a cut-off point in the continuum of language learning and cognitive development.

Text Box 6.3 Trying to understand why a student is struggling in the mainstream classroom

The story of nine-year-old Arun touches upon several of the issues that are raised in this chapter. He arrived in an international school from India, having been educated up to that point in an independent English-medium school within the Indian

(Continued)

Text Box 6.3 Trying to understand why a student is struggling in the mainstream classroom *(Continued)*

system. He spoke English which he used at home side by side with Hindi. On the early entrance tests he displayed a good knowledge of grammar and vocabulary and could read out loud with ease. It was only when Arun was asked to carry out some authentic learning tasks, including a listening comprehension and some mathematics problems, that his teachers became concerned about his ability to cope within the mainstream classroom. After closer monitoring, it became clear that Arun had not yet acquired the cognitive/academic language he needed to engage in higher order activities in the classroom. He found it difficult to engage in speculative or conceptual discussion and found any sort of writing other than purely narrative very challenging. Most significantly, Arun found it difficult to carry out conceptual tasks that related to what he had read.

The teachers in his new school had no way of knowing whether the problem lay in his unfamiliarity with this type of learning or whether he had not yet developed his cognitive abilities to the necessary level. His parents and Arun himself were surprised and upset when it was suggested that he join an intermediate specialist English language teaching class. After many meetings, finally it was agreed that Arun should join the specialist class for the rest of the school year, when the situation would be reviewed.

It would be pleasant to be able to say that Arun flourished in this class and showed marked progress in his regular classroom. Unfortunately this was not really the case. Arun found it difficult to change the way he functioned in school and continued to find conceptual learning tasks of all sorts difficult. His teachers decided that his failure to thrive in the school was due to two main reasons: Arun had been used to a different mode of teaching and learning in his Indian school and he had not yet reached a high enough cognitive level in either English or Hindi. Arun continued to receive specialist support until the time came for his return to India.

6.3 What is the Best Age for Language Learning? Myth Versus Reality

6.3.1 Young children learn a language more easily!

In the world of international schools it is quite common to hear parents discussing the advantages of learning a language when very young. Often they make the comparison with their own efforts to learn a foreign language in school and mention how much they wish they had been able to start their language learning at a younger age. Sometimes these thoughts lead parents to send their children to nursery or playgroup in the local language of the community in which the school is based before entering them into an English-medium international school.

There are many points to be made about an optimum age for language learning. First, a distinction needs to be made between 'picking up a language naturally' (a phrase often used by parents) and learning a language for use in school. Most children have the ability to acquire words and phrases in another language when they hear them used during the course of play or structured physical or manual activity. This is the ideal situation for language learning. The children are relaxed and the language they hear is associated with near-at-hand, concrete examples. This is a different circumstance from the need to use verbal language to describe and explain and to learn to read and write in a new language.

Secondly, children who move in and out of languages when they are very young seldom retain more than the memory of learning the language, although it can be argued that these memories predispose them to further language learning at a later stage. In other words, it may be true that it is easy to 'pick up a language' when very young, but the chances of a child gaining and retaining a useful working knowledge of the language, unless they continue to be exposed to it, are rather low.

6.3.2 The facts about learning a language as a child

Scholars who have carried out research studies into the impact of learning a language at a young age offer the following findings (Baker, 2011, 2014; Cenoz, 2009; Singleton & Ryan, 2004).

- Children who begin to learn a language at a young age and continue to learn the language throughout their schooling tend to gain a higher level of proficiency than students who start in their teens. This is partly due to length of exposure but may also be due to factors such as motivation, good quality teaching and parental support.
- The classrooms of young children lend themselves to the initial acquisition of language. Teaching and learning activities tend to involve concrete and near-at-hand content which is good for language learning. The classes of older students tend to involve more decontextualised and conceptual material. Beginning students in these classes require specific teaching in the school language of instruction in order to make progress.
- Children who start to learn a language at a young age tend to find pronunciation easier or less challenging.

On the other hand:

- Teenagers and adults are capable of reaching equivalent levels of language proficiency to children who started to learn the language at a young age. This is providing their levels of motivation are high and they receive adequate exposure to high-quality

teaching, and they have aptitude. They may not achieve a high level of accuracy in pronunciation.
- Teenagers and adults can potentially learn a language faster than a young child as they are more cognitively advanced.

6.4 Features That Affect the Language-learning Outcomes of Emergent Bilinguals

There are a number of features that are generally held to contribute to learning a new language successfully. In the case of students in school or higher education the aim is for them to acquire the target language to a level that allows full participation in the academic programme. Researchers, scholars and experienced practitioners generally include the following items in a list of features that positively influence language-learning outcomes (see Baker, 2011; Gallagher, 2008; Krashen, 1985; and the CAL Digest (2008) 'Principles of instructed second language acquisition': web address given in the Resources section at the end of the chapter).

Adequate exposure to the target language

Adequate exposure to the target language in an English-medium classroom may seem to be a given state of affairs. However, adequate exposure refers to the nature of the language that students are exposed to as well as the length of time they experience the language in use. In order to be helpful, the exposure needs to take place in a classroom that takes account of the needs of emergent bilingual students.

Comprehensible input

Sometimes called 'caretaker speech', mainstream teachers can facilitate their emergent bilingual students' learning by using speech that is slightly ahead of their present level of competence. This has the effect of allowing them access to the meaning while encouraging the acquisition of new language. Such speech uses modified vocabulary and simpler sentence constructions. Often teachers express the same information or instruction in different ways in order to make the meaning more comprehensible (Baker, 2011) (see Text Box 6.4 for more on Stephen Krashen's input hypothesis).

Low-anxiety classrooms

Reducing students' level of anxiety is not only a kindness but is also conducive to effective language learning. Most language learners of all ages recognise that they learn better when they do not feel under pressure from unrealistic expectations and are free to make mistakes without fear of reprimand or comment. Emergent bilinguals flourish in classrooms with the sort of upbeat, friendly and positive ambience that encourages them to take risks and to feel valued members of the classroom community. This is the sort of classroom that Krashen advocates in his affective filter hypothesis (Krashen, 1981, 1985, and other publications) (see Text Box 6.5).

Text Box 6.4 Stephen Krashen's input hypothesis

Stephen Krashen (1981, 1985, among other texts) describes language that is designed to be accessible to emergent bilingual learners as 'comprehensible input'. This description is associated with his input hypothesis, one of five hypotheses related to language acquisition. In this hypothesis, Krashen suggested that individuals learn a language when they receive input that is only marginally ahead of their present linguistic competence. If the gap is too great between what they can understand and what is being said they may be overwhelmed by the number of unfamiliar language items and unable to make sense of the communication. Where the gap is small enough, their existing understanding, which Krashen called 'i', allows them to make sense of the new linguistic elements in the input. Krashen described this ideally effective input as 'i' + 1.

Krashen's hypothesis has been questioned over the years, but the idea of comprehensible input continues to retain its credence because it seems to explain what learners and teachers perceive to be the case in real life. Language learners of all ages and at all stages can cite instances when the language they hear is too far above their existing level of understanding for them to be able to make sense of it. Examples of this experience range from asking a local resident to give directions when lost in a car on a foreign holiday, to trying to make sense of a news item in the new language on television.

Text Box 6.5 Krashen's affective filter hypothesis

The term 'anxiety-free' classroom is familiar to many teachers and reflects the thinking behind Stephen Krashen's affective filter hypothesis. According to his hypothesis, certain features interfere with a student's acquisition of a new language. The features include a low level of motivation, the absence of a positive attitude to learning the language in question, the degree of anxiety felt by the student and a reduced level of self-confidence and self-esteem. Krashen describes these features as 'affective' and suggests that they serve as a negative filter or barrier to students' progress in learning a language.

According to Krashen, the presence of negative affective features reduces students' ability to engage proactively and effectively with the target language. Some of the features relate to the personality and experience of individual students; others may be brought about by the actions of others. In the case of students in a school, the teacher's approach and actions and the ambience of the classroom are potential factors in raising or lowering a student's affective filter. Where students feel ill at ease and under pressure, their affective filter is raised and it is difficult for language learning to take place in an optimum manner.

(Continued)

Text Box 6.5 Krashen's affective filter hypothesis *(Continued)*

Critics (Gregg, 1984; Lightbown & Spada, 2013, among others) of the affective filter hypothesis argue that it is impossible to establish by experiment whether such an explanation for unsuccessful language learning is valid. Most teachers who work with emergent bilingual students, however, recognise that students make better progress in acquiring a new language when they are highly motivated and confident in their language learning and when the classroom environment is encouraging and free from unrealistic expectations.

See Frankfurt International School's ESL link for more about Krashen's theories and their practical implications; web address given in the Resources section at end of this chapter.

Students' level of motivation

Several factors affect students' motivation to learn a language. Some relate to life in school, others to society at large. As a new student in a school an obvious reason for learning English is to survive in the school setting and to be able to make friends and engage in social life and extracurricular activities. Being able to make sense of what is going on in the classroom and to participate in the academic programme is an equally powerful motivational force. Lastly, in the case of many students in international schools, they and their families appreciate the opportunities that are open to them if they acquire English to a high level of proficiency (Baker, 2011).

Mainstream classrooms where teachers integrate the language and content-area learning of emergent bilingual students

Note: Chapters 10–13 are devoted to describing practice in content-based classrooms such as these.

Continuing development of the home language

The importance of maintaining and developing the home language (or mother tongue as it is referred to in international schools) has been emphasised in Chapter 5. It is an essential element in ensuring that emergent bilingual students in English-medium schools experience an additive outcome from their educational experience. Maintaining the home language is also an important element in the overall effective learning of a second language. It ensures that students' cognitive development continues alongside the learning of the new language; research shows that skills in the home language transfer effectively to the learning of a second or further language. (See Sections 5.2 and 9.2 for a fuller discussion of aspects of this topic.)

Aptitude and ability

Aptitude and ability here refer to an aspect of language learning that is used in common talk – the equivalent of saying that someone has 'a good ear for languages'. Being 'good at languages' is a phrase unlikely to be mentioned in scholarly books about second language learning, and yet most of us know individuals who are effective and rapid language learners. We also know people in apparently similar circumstances who make slower progress in learning a language. In international schools the majority of students acquire English to a level that allows them to succeed in the social and academic programmes of the school. This is partly due to their status as 'elective bilinguals' and partly due to the generally favourable conditions for language learning that they experience within their families and at school. Setting aside students who have specific learning issues, the impact of ability and aptitude can probably only be seen in the different lengths of time it takes individual students to reach a high level of proficiency.

6.5 How Long Does It Take Emergent Bilingual Students in International Schools to Acquire the Necessary Academic Language?

The length of time it takes students to learn a new language has an impact on emergent bilingual students, their parents and the school as a whole. Most emergent bilingual students entering an English-medium school as beginning or intermediate students of English are happy to leave behind dependence on specialist help. Their parents are pleased when their children are able to cope apparently unaided in the mainstream classroom and to attend foreign language classes with their peers if that has not been open to them. The school is happy to move students out of specialist classes that require extensive funding.

The measure of a student's readiness to leave a specialist English language teaching programme (not necessarily exactly the same thing as having acquired the academic language needed to participate in the mainstream programme) is often assessed in terms of what is known as 'grade-level equivalence'.

6.5.1 What does equivalence mean?

Much of the research that has been carried out on students learning English as a school language (e.g. Collier, 1989) has been carried out in national schooling systems. The focus of much of the research is to find out how long it takes students to reach 'grade-level equivalence' (as it is often termed in US publications) with their first language peers. In these studies, the students tend to come from minority ethnic groups and to fall into the category known as 'circumstantial bilinguals' (see Section 5.2). A further variable in many cases is that the students being tested have received varying amounts of specialist language teaching support which has taken different forms and lasted for differing periods of time.

There is much discussion about what this sort of equivalence entails. Does it mean that students can perform in class and on language tests to a minimum accepted standard, or is achieving an individual student's full learning potential across the curriculum the desired outcome? Administrators and teachers in international schools would argue that fulfilling a student's learning potential is the goal, without perhaps realising the length of time it takes students to reach this level.

6.5.2 How long does it take immersed students in national systems to reach the same level as their English-speaking peers?

Some findings that made a big impact on thinking in international schools some years ago were those of Collier and Thomas, written up in Collier (1989). Their large-scale research survey, based on thousands of test results from English as a second language (ESL) students in the USA indicated that it took between five and seven years, and sometimes as many as 10, to reach grade-level equivalence. The most significant variable (the factor that made the difference) appeared to be the amount of formal schooling that students had previously received in their home language (Baker, 2011). A later study by Hakuta *et al.* (2000) found that English oral proficiency takes three to five years to develop, but that academic English proficiency can take four to seven years in immersion situations.

6.5.3 How long do students in international schools take to learn academic English?

Despite the research findings indicating that emergent bilingual students need as much as seven years to reach the same level of English proficiency as their English-speaking peers, international schools work on a different assumption. The majority of students are expected to reach a level of English proficiency that enables them to work in the mainstream classroom without specialist help after an average of three years (or fewer) of in-class or withdrawal support. After that period, administrators in many schools tend to question the continuing presence of students in specialist English language programmes. They argue that it is the mainstream teacher's role to provide further opportunities for students to refine their language skills.

This expectation that students can work unaided in mainstream classrooms after only three years of specialist teaching may seem to run counter to the findings of research. Most experienced teachers in international schools, however, would recognise that many emergent bilingual students are ready to exit specialist English teaching programmes after this time, especially if they are younger. Their English at this point may not be uniformly proficient in all areas of the language required for success in the academic programme, but most are equipped to develop their language skills further in the mainstream classroom.

6.5.4 Factors that contribute to language acquisition among emergent bilinguals in international schools

Various factors contribute to this pattern of English language acquisition and to the possibility of language learning continuing in the mainstream classroom. The first is the status of most emergent bilingual students in international schools as 'elective bilinguals' (see Section 5.3 for a discussion of the advantages of being an elective bilingual). Another factor is the relatively high commitment on the part of parents who send their children to international schools to maintaining and developing the home language with all the advantages this brings to learning a further language.

An additional beneficial feature is the expertise to be found among many teachers in international schools in integrating language and content-area learning in the mainstream classroom (see Chapter 10 for a discussion of this approach). Finally, there are two further factors that tend to be true of international school classrooms which affect language-learning outcomes in general. The first is the practice of individualising learning and the second is the smaller class sizes generally to be found in international schools. Taken together, these factors mean that students' learning needs are more likely to be recognised and addressed.

6.5.5 Students and parents questioning continuing attendance in withdrawal classes

Students and their parents, as well as school administrators, may question continuing attendance in withdrawal English classes. This seldom happens when students are absolute beginners. At this stage, there is an obvious need for immediate and extensive language teaching. It is later in the language-learning process that students and parents may feel that their value is no longer obvious.

Sometimes the discussion arises because withdrawal English language classes are scheduled at the same time as the proficient English speakers attend foreign language classes. When this is the case, it is understandable that parents may feel their children are missing out on a valuable learning opportunity, especially when the foreign language carries prestige as in the case of French or Mandarin, for instance.

Students sometimes express very strongly that they wish to leave the specialist English teaching programme. Students who have been high achievers in their home school systems may feel a sense of shame and separation when they leave the classroom to attend their English language classes. Others resent it when the teacher providing in-class support separates them out for special treatment. The atmosphere and situation of the classroom and the school as a whole are the elements that make a difference to this way of thinking. Where there are large numbers of emergent bilingual students and where there is a matter-of-fact, cheerful acceptance that everybody is a language learner, generally students accept help with their English language learning quite readily.

Text Box 6.6 Listening to students

The story of Anya, an 11-year-old student from Ukraine, indicates the importance of taking into account the feelings of students when making educational decisions. Anya was a lively, articulate person who was tested on entrance to the school and placed in an upper intermediate specialist English language class. The classroom was a stimulating and encouraging environment which the other students appeared to enjoy and where they made substantial progress. Anya, however, did not settle in the class. In

(Continued)

Text Box 6.6 Listening to students (*Continued*)

fact she was sometimes disruptive and clearly felt negative about many aspects of what she was asked to do. After some weeks the specialist teacher raised the matter with her class teacher who agreed to talk to Anya about how she felt about the English class.

Anya was very clear about her reasons for disliking the class. Her best friend was in the advanced class and she thought that the things she was asked to do in the intermediate class were stupid. When it was pointed out that she was not achieving at a very high level in the intermediate class, Anya replied by saying: 'well, I don't really try because I don't like being there'. In an old-style schooling system probably Anya would have been required to remain in the class. However, in this international school after meetings with the parents and the counsellor it was decided that Anya could move to the advanced class. Before she entered the class, she was asked to sit down with all the teachers involved and they talked over with Anya how she was expected to behave in her new class. The result was a changed Anya – she was a smiling, positive presence in the class who tried her best to contribute verbally and to complete the learning tasks. At first she found them difficult but very soon she began to make rapid and sustained progress.

The lesson for teachers from this story is that the personality and motivation of the student are major features in successful language learning. Many educators would argue that a student like Anya should be shown that she cannot expect special treatment and that if she is allowed to choose which class she attends other students will expect the same. On the other hand, Anya was clearly demotivated and disinclined to work in the class that she disliked and immediately became a positive, hard-working student in the new class. Perhaps it is a good thing for the smooth running of schools that most students are less assertive and forceful than Anya.

6.6 Issues Relating to the Language-learning Process

This section is concerned with some of the aspects of learning a language which may raise questions in teachers' minds as they track the language-learning development of their emergent bilingual students. These topics are discussed from a practical point of view rather than from a theoretical standpoint. (Readers should consult Baker (2011), among other publications, for a fuller account.)

6.6.1 Pronunciation issues

When emergent bilingual students initially start to speak a language, there are likely to be letters or groups of letters that they find difficult to pronounce and which may limit the understanding of listeners. It is useful to remember that, over time, most young language learners in an immersed situation will learn to speak in a way that is familiar to those around them. Teachers need to be wary of making their students anxious or afraid to speak by constantly correcting their pronunciation. Confidence is important in speaking a language; anxiety can be undermining and make students unwilling to take risks.

However, it is part of the teacher's role to help students become more comprehensible and to be able to play their part in the social and academically related conversations of the classroom. They can help students by tactfully rephrasing any mispronounced words and phrases and they should consult a student's specialist English language teacher if there appear to be major difficulties. Sometimes speech issues can be related to hearing problems and this is an area that should be checked. However, at other times they may reflect the stereotypical (but nevertheless real) pronunciation difficulties that students from some groups have with letter sounds that do not occur in their own languages. It is a good idea to point out pronunciation issues one to one or in a smaller group; there are successful strategies and games that encourage emergent bilinguals to produce a more recognisable pronunciation.

6.6.2 Intonation issues

Language teachers tend to point out that students' command of intonation is more significant in making themselves understood than issues with pronunciation. Intonation is the sound pattern (or 'tune') of a language and contributes a good deal of meaning in both formal and informal settings. Intonation also includes emphasis and voice quality. Intonation differs between languages, and if students fail to attune themselves to the intonation of the target language it makes it more difficult for their listeners to grasp the general intent of a piece of dialogue or to fill in gaps in meaning.

A piece of advice that is sometimes given to teachers of emergent bilingual students is to speak slowly and clearly. Clarity is always a good thing but too much slowing down can have the effect of distorting the natural intonation pattern that individuals customarily use. Teachers can help their students to produce a more recognisable intonation by repeating phrases and sentences that cause difficulty and tactfully pointing out the differences in detail. One to one or in small groups, teachers can have fun with their students by using all sorts of chants and raps to help establish a more recognisable usage.

6.6.3 Plateaux of language learning

It has already been suggested that language learning does not progress at an even pace. Within this overall pattern of uneven development, there is a further recognisable phase that may occur during the language-learning process which is sometimes described as a plateau. It occurs with many but not all students.

A plateau in students' language learning may occur after a period of steady development in their skills and takes the form of a delay in progress for varying periods of time. A plateau does not seem to be linked to a sudden decrease in application on the part of the student or necessarily to be related to an external factor. For no apparent reason, students just mark time for a while.

Sometimes this period can be related to general fatigue arising from the need to make so many adjustments in the new location, something that teachers recognise in many of their emergent bilingual students. On other occasions it appears that a student needs time to consolidate after a period of rapid and positive learning. The most difficult type of learning delay for students and teachers is where students are finding the whole process of language learning very challenging. In this case, students can become disheartened and demotivated.

Understandably, this is a sapping experience for the students involved, and teachers need to be aware of their role in supporting them during this phase. Non-intrusive, one-to-one conversations about all sorts of topics are valuable – students need to feel liked and included in ways that are separate from their status as language learners. Praise and encouragement are all important. Teachers need to be ready to reassure parents that their children are not unusual and to describe the delay as a typical period of useful consolidation. During this period, students need to be offered creative and stimulating learning activities which keep their interest engaged. Technology is often a useful source for this type of activity. They should also encourage students to take part in a sporting or other extracurricular activity where they can continue their use of language in less pressurised, more near-at-hand situations.

Suspecting that underlying learning issues may be affecting students' language-learning progress

There are times when teachers will suspect that a delay in an emergent bilingual's progress may be due to underlying learning issues. In this case, an evident delay in a student's language learning is rarely the only sign that leads teachers to take this view. Usually there are other factors that supply evidence suggesting that further monitoring and assessment is needed. (This complex subject is addressed in Section 6.5.)

A silent period

A further feature that teachers may observe in early emergent bilingual students is sometimes described as a silent period. There are different reasons why students prefer to keep silent for varying periods of time rather than speak. In some cases it appears to derive from a reluctance to make mistakes in public. They would rather wait to speak out in a class discussion until they feel able to speak without fear of shaming themselves. Other students appear to make their first steps in learning a language via the written word rather than via speech. They wait until they have gained some confidence in the language via their ability to read before speaking out. Many students are happier to join in talk in the playground or on the sports field before they are prepared to make the more structured contributions that are required in class.

Whatever the reason, teachers should avoid putting overt pressure on students who prefer to remain silent by obviously asking questions at every opportunity. On the other hand, teachers need to monitor students who remain silent in order to assess their level of understanding. This can be done by watching the ways they interact with their classmates and the ways they respond to written and spoken instructions. If the silent period

Text Box 6.7 'Managing' an extended silent period

Ingrid, a six-year-old Danish student, arrived in school with her older brother and seemed to enter school quite happily. She was placed in a withdrawal beginners' class for specialist English teaching as well as being assigned in-class support for some hours a week. She seemed to settle well and quite soon acquired a small group of friends with whom she played during break time. Her class teachers and the other specialist teachers who worked with Ingrid noted her reluctance to speak but it was not until some weeks had passed without her saying a word either in the classroom or outside that they viewed the situation as something to be closely monitored. Talking to her parents, it was established that Ingrid was a fluent and indeed chatty Danish speaker. She was in general a happy and well-adjusted child who had not appeared to be unduly upset about making the move from Denmark to her new home.

After three months of silence, teachers and parents were becoming frustrated and concerned about Ingrid's total silence in school. It was clear, also, that she was putting herself under pressure in order to preserve this conscious silence. The counsellor suggested that it might be Ingrid's means of exerting control over her life – she might accept the fact of the move but she wasn't going to make things easy either for herself or for those around her by accepting the need to learn a new language. Her parents by this time were extremely anxious and the mother in particular felt guilty for what she saw as her part in placing her daughter under stress. Meanwhile Ingrid continued to speak Danish as normal and in particular loved the Danish language activity and music classes she attended outside school.

An overall strategy was agreed by all the adults who cared for Ingrid. Since she functioned in Danish at an age-appropriate level in both aural language and early literacy, it was decided not to put her through the ordeal of testing to establish the presence of hearing issues. Her level of comprehension would be systematically monitored in a variety of settings, and support would be provided to the parents and teachers via sessions with the counsellor. It was agreed that the adults around her would not single her out for special treatment by pressing her to answer questions or to contribute in class.

Ingrid kept silent for a further two months, and then one day it was reported by the teacher who was supervising playtime that she was chattering to her friends in the playground in English – not in perfect English, but in understandable and noticeably quite well pronounced phrases and single words. A further month passed before Ingrid began speaking in class and from then on she made rapid progress in all areas of English acquisition. It had been agreed that no adult would make any comment when she chose to begin speaking, and unfortunately Ingrid only stayed in the school a further year before she moved on to another foreign posting. Everybody would have welcomed the possibility, when she was old enough to be asked, of finding out the reasons Ingrid herself might give for her silence. It is still unclear why an apparently well-adjusted and linguistically competent little girl chose to take this path.

extends over a period of more than a few weeks or months, it may be necessary to check for hearing or other issues. In every case, teachers should be consulting with other professionals and talking to parents if they are concerned.

6.6.4 Register: Appropriate language for the situation

Sometimes in class and around school, teachers will notice that their emergent bilingual students are using inappropriate ways of expressing themselves in a new language with adults or other authority figures. This can take the form of informal language, an overuse of slang terms or an over-familiar tone. Usually, it is quite obvious that the student concerned does not intend any rudeness.

Being aware of the need to use appropriate language in certain social situations relates to the aspect of language learning known as register. Most people adapt their use of language to fit in with a context as a matter of course. They do this when they interact in a social or more formal setting with people who are perceived to have seniority or are deserving of respect. This adjustment may involve some of the following ways of talking and interacting:

- using courteous turns of phrase: 'What would you like?' rather than 'And how about you?';
- using more formal vocabulary rather than informal terms: 'children' in place of 'kids', for instance;
- choosing more formal ways of putting over information: 'I would like to talk to you about my working relationship with Angie' as opposed to 'Angie is driving me crazy';
- the tone of voice and overall demeanour and body language of the speaker;
- waiting for the respondent to reply.

Register is an issue for speakers of many languages when they interact with other individuals in different settings. In some cases, students may be accustomed to using different forms of the language in specific situations. In Japan, for instance, senior people are addressed using a different range of grammar and vocabulary items from those used with individuals who are the speaker's equal. In other cases, speakers make their choices from a pool of vocabulary and grammatical items as in English.

Most emergent bilingual students will understand the need for adopting appropriate language when it is made clear to them. However, some new emergent bilingual students, noticeably those from educational systems where there is a different set of expectations about the relationship between students and teachers, sometimes misread the informal and friendly communication that exists between those two groups in international schools. It is not easy for them to perceive the subtle distinctions that continue to exist between students and teachers even when they appear to be chatting in a friendly way together. It is up to classroom teachers and others to model explicitly the sort of language that is appropriate.

Key Points in This Chapter

* Understanding the language-learning process enables teachers to support their students and to communicate more effectively with parents.
* Being knowledgeable about the process enables teachers to recognise where hitches occur or when progress falters.
* Individuals learn the skills of a language at different rates (listening and speaking, reading and writing); they rarely move forward at an even pace across the skills.
* Individuals take different lengths of time to reach proficiency in a language.
* There is an important distinction between early superficial fluency and the academic language needed to perform on higher order learning tasks.
* In order to function at their full potential, emergent bilingual students need to attain CALP, as theorised by Cummins..
* Teenagers who learn a school language in positive circumstances achieve a similar level of proficiency to students who start their language learning at a very young age.
* Research on immersed second language students in US state systems suggests that students in these settings take between five and seven years to reach grade-level equivalence.
* In international schools, students customarily achieve a level of proficiency that allows them to take part in mainstream class work after three or more years.
* Being knowledgeable about the length of time it takes to learn a language enables teachers to communicate effectively with school administrations, parents and students.
* Students in international schools generally achieve recognisable pronunciation and intonation over time.
* Language learners sometimes experience periods of delay in making progress, known as plateaux.
* Beginning students sometimes keep silent for differing periods of time before they are ready to speak out.
* Students may not perceive the type of language that is appropriate in a given situation, such as when talking to teachers.

Resources

Note: A link entitled 'A Guide to Learning English' on the Frankfurt International School website (http://esl.fis.edu/) gives a useful summary for teachers wishing to know more about Krashen's theories and their practical implications. The read-only document, copyright Paul Shoebottom (1993–2013), was written prior to a visit by Stephen Krashen to the school for a two-day workshop.

Center for Applied Linguistics (CAL) (2008) Digest: 'Principles of instructed second language acquisition', available at: http://www.cal.org/resource-center/briefs-digests/digests/(offset)/75.

Technology application

Glogster: an interactive visual learning platform: this platform offers students the possibility of creating interactive posters and other graphic forms that allow them to download text, photos, audio and video clips and for their peers to post comment. See www.glogster.com.

References

Baker, C. (2011) *Foundations of Bilingual Education and Bilingualism* (5th edn). Bristol: Multilingual Matters.

Baker, C. (2014) *A Parents' and Teachers' Guide to Bilingualism* (4th edn). Bristol: Multilingual Matters.

Cenoz, J. (2009) *Multilingual Education: Basque Educational Research from an International Perspective.* Bristol: Multilingual Matters.

Collier, V.P. (1989) How long? A synthesis of research on academic achievement in a second language. *TESOL Quarterly* 23 (3), 509–531.

Cummins, J. (1979) Cognitive/academic language proficiency, linguistic interdependence, the optimum age question. *Working Papers on Bilingualism* 19, 121–129.

Cummins, J. (1984) *Bilingualism and Special Education Issues in Assessment and Pedagogy.* Clevedon: Multilingual Matters.

Cummins, J. (2000b) Putting language proficiency in its place: Responding to critiques of the conversational/academic language distinction. In J. Cenoz and U. Jessner (eds) *English in Europe: The Acquisition of a Third Language.* Clevedon: Multilingual Matters.

Cummins, J. (2008) BICS and CALP: Empirical and theoretical status of the distinction. In B. Street and N.H. Hornberger (eds) *Encyclopedia of Language and Education. Vol. 2: Literacy* (2nd edn). New York: Springer.

Gallagher, E. (2008) *Equal Rights to the Curriculum: Many Languages, One Message.* Clevedon: Multilingual Matters.

Gregg, K.R. (1984) Krashen's monitor and Occam's razor. *Applied Linguistics* 5, 79–100.

Hakuta, J., Butler, Y.G. and Witt, D. (2000) How long does it take English learners to reach proficiency? University of California Linguistic Minority Research Institute Policy Report 1. UC LMRI.

Krashen, S.D. (1981) *Second Language Acquisition and Second Language Learning.* Oxford: Pergamon.

Krashen, S.D. (1985) *The Input Hypothesis: Issues and Implications.* Oxford: Pergamon.

Lightbown, P. and Spada, N. (2013) *How Languages are Learned* (4th edn). Oxford: Oxford University Press.

MacSwan, J. and Rolstad, K. (2003) Linguistic diversity, schooling and social class: Rethinking our conception of language proficiency in language minority education. In C.B. Paulston and G.R. Tucker (eds) *Sociolinguistics: The Essential Readings.* Oxford: Blackwell.

Singleton, D. and Ryan, L. (2004) *Language Acquisition: The Age Factor* (2nd edn). Clevedon: Multilingual Matters.

Wiley, T.G. (2005) *Literacy and Language Diversity in the United States* (2nd edn). McHenry, IL: Center for Applied Linguistics and Delts Systems.

Part 4

Day-to-Day Life in Mainstream Classrooms Containing Emergent Bilingual Students

Part 4 is concerned with day-to-day life in classrooms that contain emergent bilingual students. It focuses on resources that are available to enhance the learning of these students, including the types of English language specialist teaching programmes that tend to be available in international schools. It sets out the need for teachers to explain the learning culture of the school to students and parents and it suggests practical strategies that enable emergent bilingual students to access the language of the classroom.

7 Using School-wide Approaches and Resources to Promote the Learning of Emergent Bilingual Students

The aim of Chapter 7 is to introduce the different areas of school provision and practice that contribute to the learning and sense of wellbeing of emergent bilingual students. The areas considered in the chapter include the uses of assessment for work with emergent bilingual students and how resources such as technology and the library/media centre serve to enhance the learning of this group of students. It also spells out the types of in-school provision that are available to support the English language learning of emergent bilingual students and addresses such issues as the appropriate ways to assess whether students should be included in such programmes and when they should leave them. Finally, the chapter offers some thoughts on how to recognise and assess emergent bilingual students who appear to be struggling in class.

The sequence of Chapter 7 is as follows:

- Introduction: school provision and practice that contribute to the learning of emergent bilinguals.
- Effective assessment of emergent bilingual students' learning.
- The value and uses of technology.
- Effective use of the library/media centre.
- The role of specific English language teaching specialists.
- Learning disabilities in emergent bilingual students.

Introduction

This chapter groups together the elements and aspects of an international school that teachers can draw on to promote the learning of emergent bilingual students in their classrooms. Most teachers will be accustomed to incorporating these elements into their day-to-day teaching. The focus in this chapter is on their special uses with emergent bilingual students.

Section 7.1 sets out the assessment approaches that are generally to be found in international schools and addresses the uses of effective assessment in work with emergent bilingual students. This is followed by sections on the potential benefits of embedded technology and the possibilities offered by well-equipped libraries/media centres.

Later sections are concerned with two areas that are of vital importance to the well-being of emergent bilingual students. Section 7.4 discusses the nature of specialist English language teaching programmes in international schools. It looks at the different ways that such teaching is delivered and it goes on to explore the topics of placing students in these programmes and of managing their exit from specialist teaching. The focus of the last section is on emergent bilingual students who are struggling with learning the school language and with learning in general. It suggests some ways of diagnosing what is going on with such students and offers some thoughts on the issues that surround testing and communicating with parents.

7.1 Assessing Emergent Bilingual Students in International Schools

A real knowledge and understanding of the individual learning profiles of emergent bilinguals is at the heart of effective work with these students. When teachers understand not only where students fit on the learning continuum in general, but also the pattern of their English language development in particular, they are in a position to offer the sort of targeted learning support that achieves real success. Other aspects of a student's learner profile are also critical in offering effective support. These aspects include the student's level of independence as a learner, her or his willingness to take risks in their language learning, and the degree to which they are able to build on what they know in order to make sense of new language items they encounter.

7.1.1 Assessment in international schools

Assessment in international schools, as in national schooling systems, is designed to give two sorts of information. One sort is to evaluate students' mastery of what they have been taught in the classroom. This is termed summative assessment and generally takes the form of tasks and tests that can be measured or scored. Often summative assessment activities take place at critical times during a student's life in school such as at the end of the academic year or at the end of some years of study. Summative assessment may be generated in-school by teachers or be administered by an external body where the results may be used as a basis for university or college entrance.

The second type of assessment aims to assess a student's progress along a learning continuum. The purpose of formative assessment of this type is for teachers to be able to use the knowledge gained from the process to inform future instruction. An effective piece of formative assessment tracks student learning and makes it clear where a student needs further targeted input from the teacher in order to move forward.

Both these forms of assessment are to be found in international schools, but usually with variations that reflect the school's historical links and initiatives on the part of individual administrators and teachers. In general most schools follow the basic assessment approaches that are linked to their curricula and programmes of study. Often, however, schools use other assessment tools, drawn from a range of sources, alongside those embedded in the curriculum offered at the school.

Assessment approaches found in international schools

- Summative assessment, used to establish a student's knowledge, skills and understandings around a topic at one moment in time, may involve tests and examinations. International schools offering enquiry-based or discovery learning approaches may use other means to assess overall student achievement. These include posters, oral and written and online presentations, video clips and the use of apps and web-based material.
- Normative assessment of individual student's work is used to inform future teacher instruction. Normative approaches to assessment include the use of checklists which give descriptions of the learning targets that it is hoped students will master in a given area. Teachers track students' progress against these learning targets and use the information supplied by qualitative and quantitative measures to focus their instruction more effectively on the areas where students need further help.
- Many international schools use checklists to assess students' progress along a learning continuum in a content-area subject. The State of Western Australia's 'First Steps' literacy programme, used in a number of international schools, provides criteria to assess student progress in literacy learning at each grade level (www.det. wa.edu.au/stepsresources).
- Within some programmes, notably the Primary Years Programme (PYP) and Middle Years Programme (MYP) of the International Baccalaureate Organisation (IBO), teachers draw up sets of criteria against which they assess a final learning task. In some cases students and teachers may collaborate in drawing up their own sets of criteria which are used throughout a learning activity to guide the final version (see www.ibo.org/pyp/assessed/index.cfm; www.ibo.org/myp/assessment).
- Students are encouraged to reflect on and assess their own learning. Student-led parent conferences are customary in many international schools, at which students exhibit their learning to parents using exemplary pieces as evidence.
- Many schools (often with students involved in making the choices) collect exemplary pieces of student work in binders or in online portfolios to keep as permanent records. These collections of work are useful to send on to the next school in the case of a globally mobile student. (Portfolios are a requirement for IB PYP schools.)
- Some schools use standardised tests derived from a provincial, state or national schooling system in one of the English-speaking countries as a means of assessing

the progress of students being educated in an international school against national norms. (Many stakeholders in the school community welcome these tests as a way of proving that students' education is 'keeping up' with those at home – problematic in the case of emergent bilingual students who originate from none of the countries on which these tests are normed.)
- Other schools prefer to use one of the sets of standardised assessment tests designed for use with international students. The International Schools' Assessment (ISA) created by the Australian Council of Educational Resources (ACER; www.acer.edu.au/isa) is an example of this type of assessment approach. ACER works closely with the IBO to measure IB students' outcomes against those of other international students.

7.1.2 Assessing emergent bilingual students appropriately

The issues that surround the assessment of emergent bilingual students largely relate to summative assessment where these students may be tested and graded using models that were designed for a different population of English-speaking students. In most schools, bilingual students are assessed as if they were monolinguals in the language being tested. It is rare for a students' competence in both their languages to be assessed as a whole.

Both school-based and externally assessed tests and examinations are problematic in several ways when they are used to evaluate the learning of emergent bilingual students. It is unfair, unproductive and potentially distressing to developing learners to ask them take tests that are designed for proficient users of the school language. Schools need to have a policy in place about the testing of emergent learners of the school language and about the need to explain this policy to both parents and students.

The same is true for the ways in which schools use letter and numerical grades on school reports that go home to parents. Many schools make the distinction between grades for effort and those for achievement or use different ways of signalling emergent bilinguals' progress in the first months and even years. The aspect to underline is that grading for emergent bilinguals should be used as a means of conveying useful and positive information rather than serving to undermine students' self-confidence and motivation.

Note: The subject of assessment is addressed elsewhere in this Handbook. Section 8.2.1(h) deals with the cultural implications of unfamiliar forms of assessment and Section 11.2 suggests ways of planning the assessment of a new unit of study.

7.2 Technology Provision in International Schools

The potential value and use of technology is similar for all schooling systems. However, many international schools exist separately from other school systems and in isolated locations, so that the ability to access the wider world is of special value. In the case of emergent bilinguals of all ages, the possibilities offered by the range of technological devices and applications have the power to enhance their learning in many ways.

7.2.1 The 'digital divide'

The so-called 'digital divide', which relates to differences in the level of student ownership of, and access to, fixed and mobile technological devices operates also to some extent in the world of international education. Where schools have fast, continuous broadband access and adequate financial resources, international schools tend to be at the forefront of technological innovation and provision. In the bigger international schools it is now common for students to have access to one-to-one mobile devices such as laptops and tablets. A school in Qatar, for instance, has invested so largely in the hardware and software of one company that the organisation concerned has supplied an accompanying technician to troubleshoot in the school.

Families whose children attend international schools tend to be motivated and financially able to equip their children with the latest technology. As a result, students in many international schools are fortunate in having high-quality access to all the benefits that technology can offer. However, the diversity of educational backgrounds among students new to the school and the transience of students and teachers are factors that need to be taken into account when setting up training programmes in the use of the latest technology.

7.2.2 International schools at different levels of technology provision

Other international schools may be limited by the nature of the internet access available and by financial considerations. In many regions, internet access is limited by the number of hours that a country or province has access to a server, or by an intermittent power supply. Not so long ago, for instance, international schools in Botswana in southern Africa were dependent for their internet provision on the few hours available to their area on a server in Johannesburg in South Africa.

Internet access is increasing rapidly, but teachers cannot always assume that they will be able to incorporate technology into their teaching. This does to some extent deprive teachers and students of the use of a valuable tool for teaching and learning. As experienced educators recognise, however, the quality of a classroom depends on the nature of the interaction between teacher and students. It still remains possible to create stimulating, inclusive and engaging classrooms without the use of technology.

7.2.3 e-Safety

International schools are wise to have a 'digital citizenship policy' in place. Policies of this sort set out the school's expectations about e-safety in school. Most generally set limits on access and usage, and most lay down specific rules about the use of social media because of the possibility of bullying. Teachers need to ensure that all students observe the school's policy and that emergent bilinguals are able to understand the language in which it is framed. Where such a policy does not exist, teachers should take it upon themselves to see that technology is used appropriately in their classrooms.

7.2.4 Issues relating to the embedded use of technology in schools

Schools need to make clear to students and parents their views on how information derived from apps and websites should be used. Unfortunately, it is rather easy for students to be tempted into copying sentences and whole paragraphs from these sources and presenting them as their own work. Sometimes, it is true, new students are not aware of the concept of plagiarism and may believe that they are carrying out a legitimate activity. In general, it is better from the first for the school to set out its policy with regard to the use of internet material and to point out that copying of this type reduces the quality of student learning in the long run.

It is understandable that fatigued emergent bilingual students may wish to make use of internet material in this way. Teachers need to make it clear that they would prefer shorter pieces of writing that are clearly created by the students themselves rather than any amount of (obviously) downloaded material.

7.2.5 Provision of technology

The provision in international schools includes all or some of the following technological devices and applications:

- The provision of separate labs with numbers of computers and linked screens (although these have disappeared in some schools where the emphasis is now placed on embedded technology in the classroom).
- The purchase by the school, or by individual parents for their children, of laptop computers which students carry with them from class to class.
- School-provided or personally purchased mobile devices (tablets). In many schools, all the tablets in a school are sourced from one major supplier as in the case of iPads. In other schools, students are free to bring in their own devices which run on a variety of operating systems; this is often referred to as a 'bring your own device' (BYOD) policy.
- Access to a school-selected range of apps and programs accessible on a range of technological devices.
- SmartBoards/interactive whiteboards or smart TVs, often linked to teachers' and students' computers or mobile devices.
- Smartphones (many schools are grappling with the use of smartphones in school because of the opportunities for bullying or for inappropriate access to unmonitored material that they may make possible).
- Library/media centres that contain wifi capability and numbers of computers.
- Restricted intranet links on school websites which typically include parent and student portals. Many schools run their communications with parents and students via a virtual learning environment (VLE) which allows the school and teachers to post interactive material.

7.2.6 Technology and emergent bilinguals

Technology offers rich possibilities for enhancing the teaching and learning of emergent bilingual students both in the content areas and in learning the school language(s). Technology opens up the classroom and enables students to extend their learning in many ways.

The overall uses of technology in the teaching and learning of emergent bilinguals

- Technology brings the outside world into the classroom. It has the potential to bring international-mindedness into every school by offering links and apps that widen the frame of reference that teachers and students can draw on.
- Technology enables students to draw on the internet to research references to the language, culture, history and geography of their home country and region.
- Technology offers immediate access to home language sites via alternative keyboards, e.g. Arabic, Chinese.
- Technology allows students to use their home languages to understand new content-area learning.
- Technology allows students to search out information on a new topic prior to or after its introduction in class.
- Technology empowers by allowing emergent bilingual students to investigate new topics and content at their own pace. It has the capacity to make content more accessible by presenting subject matter in bite-sized chunks with graphic and audio components.
- Technology fosters independent learning in emergent bilinguals who may sometimes feel disempowered in the classroom. It offers the capacity for students to manage their own learning.
- Technology enables students to exercise choice and to work in areas of interest to them.
- Technology facilitates the authentic and relaxed use of the school language while students are grouped around the computer. Students reluctant to speak out in class will contribute while focused on accomplishing a group task.
- Technology provides non-judgmental feedback. It is neutral – it does not 'put down' emergent bilingual students.
- Technology offers activities, exercises and games that include immediate feedback and instant assessment of the student's performance. In response to the feedback, students are motivated to redo the activity and improve their score.
- Technology provides ready-made frames, graphic organisers, flow charts, timelines and interactive displays that can be used to provide instructional scaffolding. (See Chapters 10–13 for more on scaffolding student learning.)
- Technology provides a user-friendly means for students to create presentations and to display their learning.
- Technology motivates students who find pencil-and-paper tasks challenging.
- Technology offers possibilities for collaborative learning.
- Technology builds friendships among technology enthusiasts.

Text Box 7.1 Two examples of the use and value of technology

In the classrooms of international schools in the early morning before school starts it is common to see small groups of students gathered around computers. The groups typically contain students at different levels of English proficiency including early beginners. The students appear entirely engaged and usually there is excited talk about what is on the screen, often a mathematics or literacy game. Even where groups are made up entirely of students who share a single common language, as in the case of three Korean boys seen in an international school in Switzerland, it becomes obvious that they are using their home language to negotiate the use of English on screen. This is a simple example of the way that technology allows students to practise the school language in a relaxed, unselfconscious manner.

A second example involves the use of a SmartBoard (interactive whiteboard) linked via the teacher's computer to the students' tablets. The school where this use of technology was observed was situated in Vienna, Austria, where there is a museum that contains a number of paintings by the Flemish artist Pieter Breugel the Elder. A group of emergent bilingual students was due to visit the museum as part of their Cultural Studies course, and the EAL teacher had put up on the SmartBoard a large-scale version of Breugel's painting, 'Children's Games', which is to be found in the museum. Her first aim was to introduce the vocabulary needed to discuss art and artists so that students would be well prepared for the visit. A second aim was to offer them an authentic context in which to practise the continuous present tense (they are playing hopscotch, he is juggling, she is skipping, etc.) and later the simple past tense (we went out to play, she did a hundred skips, I fell over, etc.).

She had started by taking the students along to the art room where she had arranged for the art teacher to demonstrate all the things that artists need to make their work. This discussion covered elements such as the use of easels, types of brushes, names of colours, types of paint, and so on. Later, with the students grouped in front of the SmartBoard, she and the students pointed out the different games that the children were playing in the painting. The students then participated in uploading a descriptive sentence using the continuous present tense next to the image on the screen. Finally, after their visit, the students were invited to download the image of the painting on to their tablets and were asked to write an account of the festival day using the simple past tense as if they were one of the children in the painting.

These two examples would be recognised by many teachers as quite run-of-the-mill uses of technology. For teachers working with emergent bilinguals they are an indication of the power and potential for engaging these students in authentic activities involving the use of the school language.

Note: This section deals with the overall aspects of technology provision in school. Detailed practical uses are suggested in later chapters.

7.3 The Library/Media Centre

I thought, wow, this is a big school. I liked the playground and I liked the way we could play football at recess. But what I really like is the library. I can go there and sit in a big chair and just read or I can look at a computer. And I know I can always ask Mrs Ferguson to help me. (Daniel, aged 9, from Poland; taken from a student account collected during the research enquiry described in Appendix A)

Libraries, or Media Centres as they are often called today, offer welcoming spaces where emergent bilingual students can access information in many forms, including books and other hard-copy print media as well as via electronic means. Many such spaces in international schools draw on technology in all its aspects, from its use in checking out books to offering access to the internet in the form of desktop or laptop computers. Many offer wifi capacity which allows students to work in the library on their own computers, tablets and smartphones.

Text Box 7.2 Libraries in international schools

Libraries in international schools offer a valuable resource to parents as well as children and most schools welcome parents into libraries to help their children select books and to participate in special activities and events. In many schools parents act as long-term volunteers and become vital and valued members of the library team. As Jeffrey Brewster, an experienced international school librarian has written:

Many families may come from a culture without a school library or from a culture that has an approach to education which is clearly 'please leave your child at the school door and we will do the rest'. These families need to have us reach out to them. . . . We must make the initial approach. It is essential that the library staff see students as members of families that can benefit from involvement with library programs and services. Careful consideration of library lending policies and opening hours is required. Do the policies and procedures support families?' (Brewster, 2011: 163)

For further illuminating discussion of ways that the library can be used to enhance and augment the learning of young emergent bilingual students, Jeffrey Brewster's chapter entitled, 'The role of the library in supporting young language learners and their families' appears in Murphy (2011).

In most international schools nowadays, it is common to find selections of non-fiction and fiction books in the home languages of emergent bilingual students. This type of provision is generally linked to an overall school language policy that spells out the school's commitment to promoting and maintaining students' home languages.

7.3.1 Librarians linked to learning in mainstream classrooms

In most schools, librarians and media specialists are linked in to the ongoing learning of the classroom and it is usual for classes to be allotted a scheduled time for visiting the library both to withdraw media and to learn investigative and research skills. Librarians are frequently included in meetings held to plan new IB Units of Inquiry or class topics, and teachers welcome their help in sourcing and selecting resources to share with students.

Many librarians in international schools seek to widen the choice of databases as well as reading material for students by including non-fiction and fiction texts in the home languages of students at the school. The parents of emergent bilinguals are a valuable resource in this area – they can be asked to search out bilingual texts, dictionaries, guidebooks and biographies on their visits home. These offer an additional source of readily available information for emergent bilinguals to stand alongside technological media in their own languages.

7.3.2 Reading for enjoyment and entertainment

Modern school libraries offer emergent bilingual students the opportunity to gain enjoyment and entertainment from reading in a variety of media. Most libraries in international schools are friendly, stimulating and inclusive environments, frequently including armchairs and reading corners. Many schools use the library for exhibitions of artwork and for displaying cultural artefacts. They are lively places where students are invited to participate actively and to engage with the environment.

For younger emergent bilingual students the provision of a variety of colourful, well-illustrated books in a range of formats supplies a non-stressful means of engaging in reading in the new language. One of the most enjoyable times in the school week for many students, particularly the very young, is their library visit at which teachers or librarians introduce new books or read stories aloud. Most school libraries recruit assistants and volunteer parents to engage with younger students and to help them choose age-appropriate reading material at an accessible reading level.

7.3.3 The librarian as mentor and guide

Older emergent bilingual students frequently find the librarian to be an encouraging presence in their life in the school. Librarians are in a position to give targeted help to individual students and can act as mentors and guides in academic matters. It is very helpful if emergent bilingual students feel they can go to the librarian to ask for aid in finding print material or in investigating a topic.

Text Box 7.3 'Welcome to the library! We are here to help you'

This is the notice on the banner above the door in a library in an international school in Indonesia. Like many libraries in international schools, it is a well-resourced welcoming space where a prime aim of the librarians is to offer targeted practical help to students in carrying out classroom learning tasks. The following list was displayed on the wall above the line of computers.

Preparing research for your enquiry:

(1) Decide exactly what you want to find out.
(2) Think about where to find the information.
(3) Locate the information. Choose what you need.
(4) Extract the information from your sources:
    (a) a museum visit
    (b) posters
    (c) CDs/DVDs
    (d) radio
    (e) TV
    (f) books
    (g) websites
    (h) apps
    (i) encyclopaedia
    (j) interviewing a person
(5) Put the information together from the different sources.
(6) Present the information.
(7) Reflect on what you have done. Evaluate the finished piece of work. Did you ask the right question? Did you search in the most effective resources? Have you added your own take on the topic? Have you lifted passages wholesale? Have you presented it in an effective and meaningful way?

The research process: question – plan – gather – consider and process information – evaluate – present – reflect

7.4 Specialist English-teaching Provision for Emergent Bilingual Students

7.4.1 The school's responsibility in offering an effective English language teaching programme to emergent bilingual students

Schools that are accredited by the major agencies and schools that adopt programmes of study from bodies such as the IBO are required to offer effective teaching to emergent bilingual students in the school's language or languages of instruction. These bodies do not lay down the form of this provision but most set out criteria for what these programmes should aim to accomplish.

7.4.2 Names that are given to specialist English language teaching programmes

Specialist English language teaching for emergent bilingual students in international schools goes under a number of names. The range of names reflects the ways that programmes directed at emergent bilingual students have historically been described in English-speaking schooling systems across the world. There is a constant search in internationals schools for a term to describe specialist English language classes that is empowering and respectful of emergent bilingual students. Some of the terms used at present to describe these programmes include English as a second language (ESL), English as an additional language (EAL), English language learners (ELLs) and English language support.

7.4.3 The development of specialist English language teaching programmes in international schools

Over the years, the view of what comprises an effective English language teaching programme for emergent bilinguals in international schools has been altered and refined. To some extent the changes reflect the policy and practice found in national schooling systems. However, there are acknowledged differences in the profile and experiences of many students in international schools which have led to divergences from the thinking in national systems about the nature of effective English language support.

English language teaching programmes tend to evolve in response to the traditions of the school and its location, to the latest thinking, and to changes in the make-up of the student body in a school. Often the provision in an individual school reflects the advocacy and practical input of an individual or small group of specialist English teachers. In an increasing number of schools the philosophy behind the provision for the language learning of emergent bilingual students in the school is set out in a Language Policy (see Section 5.6).

7.4.4 Linking specialist English provision with a mother tongue teaching programme

In an increasing number of international schools, the school's contribution to developing students' mother tongues is described in paper or online documents alongside the provision for specialist English language teaching, often under an overall heading such as 'ESL and mother tongue programme'. This approach is designed to ensure that emergent bilinguals enjoy the type of school experience that leads to an additive outcome (see Section 5.2).

This link is a positive step forward in provision for emergent bilingual students since it emphasises the potential value of a holistic approach to the education of bilingual students. Viewing the continuing development of both languages in an emergent bilingual student's repertoire as interlinked and mutually beneficial underpins pedagogic initiatives in the mainstream classroom such as the 'interlingual' and 'translanguaging' approaches. (See Section 9.2 for a discussion of the use of students' mother tongues in mainstream classrooms.)

7.4.5 Variety of provision and scheduling

The provision and scheduling arrangements for the teaching of English to emergent bilingual students in an international school vary from school to school. The programmes tend to differ in the breadth of provision as well as in the detail.

Most specialist English language teaching and support programmes have one thing in common: they tend to be logistically complex. It is common for teachers to have to consult numerous schedules and programme documents in order to understand the detail. The complexity arises because specialist English language and mother tongue provision (where an in-school programme exists) typically involve cross-class scheduling with classes at multiple levels. Newly arrived teachers in a school may need to consult year-level colleagues and specialist English language teachers in order to understand how the programme offerings affect the day-to-day running of an individual class.

7.4.6 English language teaching programmes in international schools

English language teaching programmes in international schools take two forms: these are withdrawal programmes (or pull-out programmes) and in-class support. Until recently there was a considerable ongoing debate about the merits of each approach. Nowadays in many schools it is common to find both types of specialist English language support for emergent bilingual students existing side by side. It is still possible to find schools that restrict their programme to a withdrawal model, but the general trend is towards a flexible model where specialist support staff work more closely with mainstream classroom teachers.

Withdrawal (or pull-out) programmes

In a withdrawal programme, emergent bilingual students are withdrawn from the mainstream classroom for English language tuition individually or in small groups. These classes are designed initially to 'kick start' students' learning of English and to offer them collective support during their early days and months in an English-medium environment. Later time in the programmes is designed to extend students' overall grasp of the language and support their learning in the mainstream classroom. Students are usually placed in groups that reflect their level of proficiency. In order to make such classes feasible they are generally formed of students from all the classes at a year level or even across two year levels. Typically the classes are called names such as 'beginner', 'intermediate' and 'advanced'. Beginning students are frequently offered longer periods of so-called 'intensive' teaching.

Effective withdrawal or pull-out programmes take the following forms:

- Introducing vocabulary and grammatical structures:
  - *The teaching of vocabulary and grammatical structures should reflect the real-life needs of students. This includes the language needed to take part in enquiry-based programmes and other forms of classroom learning. There is a place for English language textbooks and other published materials but the ultimate aim of an effective English language teaching and learning programme is to equip students to engage in authentic social and academic activities.*
- Offering small-group support and encouragement in a space where the needs of emergent bilinguals are the focus of activity:
  - *One of the potential advantages of a pull-out programme is that emergent bilinguals can gain confidence and positive feedback in a small group. In the mainstream classroom early learners of English may feel themselves constantly at a disadvantage. In the small-group situation, teachers can deliver language at a level that is comprehensible to students and provide them with targeted learning activities that offer a manageable degree of challenge.*
- Ensuring that emergent bilingual students acquire the cognitive/academic language skills necessary for full participation in mainstream classroom learning (see Section 6.2 for a discussion of what is meant by cognitive/academic English):
  - *Supporters of withdrawal classes suggest that students benefit from receiving small-group tuition in higher level listening, speaking, reading and writing activities. They argue that such an approach makes it less likely that students will stop short of acquiring the advanced language skills they need for success in the academic programme. Other language specialists suggest that emergent bilingual students acquire these skills more effectively in authentic learning situations in the classroom. Here, they argue, students have the advantage of working alongside proficient English speakers who model the language used when engaged in higher level tasks. Collaboration and liaison between classroom and specialist teachers is the answer to providing an effective programme whichever approach is in place.*

Text Box 7.4 Learning to solve mathematics problems in English

A small group of newly arrived eight-year-old beginner EAL students were withdrawn each day during the time when proficient English speakers went to German classes. They had recently started working on language-based mathematics problems in the mainstream classroom. Two of them had clearly been used to word-based mathematics problems in their previous schools but were struggling with the language. The other three students came from schooling systems where the approach to mathematics had been largely arithmetical. These students had not only to contend with the unfamiliar language but also with the concept of language-based mathematics. The EAL class met four times a week, with one of the classes being on a Friday afternoon.

It was in the Friday class, when the energy level of the students tended to be at a low level, that the EAL teacher brought out a some synthetic modelling clay in different colours and asked the students to make models of all sorts of food items, including what they ate at home. They were asked to concentrate on foods that could be divided up. The activity appealed to the students and there was a lot of laughter and talk surrounding the modelling. Ryoko made intricate pieces of sushi, while Kristof produced a large piece of salami which he carefully sliced. Stina produced eight cinnamon buns and the two other students made a large pizza and a basket of apples. With the time left over, a number of birthday cakes with candles were constructed. The aim, ultimately, was for the students to write simple mathematics problems on topics such as the cost of each portion of food and methods of dividing the portions fairly between family members. Incidentally, the activity involved students in using new language such as 'kneading', 'squashing', 'slicing', 'rolling', and so on.

The following Monday, the students were asked to sit in two groups and write their mathematics problems. They were given several examples such as: 'I have 12 slices of salami – what is the fairest way to divide these up in a family of four people?' 'I have 5 euros and the apples cost €1.50 each. How many can I buy?' Several of the students mastered this process very rapidly and began to make more salami slices and more apples so that they could write harder problems. The Swedish student wrote several where the answer was not a whole number. All the students soon broke away from the model problems and began creating problems that involved new mathematical concepts.

During the next class, each group asked the other group to solve the problems they had written. Each team was required to illustrate their answer by using the food items themselves to describe the solution. On some occasions the teacher asked the students to offer an alternative answer. In a fourth class, real-life problems from their mathematics textbook were discussed, with students being encouraged to use graphs and drawings to explain their methods and describe their learning. The whole series of classes had been productive of a great deal of authentic language while providing support for real-life learning in the mathematics classroom.

In-class support

The second form of English language tuition is often described as 'in-class support'. This type of support is delivered in several ways. One, often seen in national systems, involves teaching assistants who speak the student's home language. They sit with students to act as interpreters and mediators by explaining what the teacher is saying and to help them as they work through the learning activities of the classroom. A second type of in-class support involves specialist English language teachers in collaboration with the class teacher. This approach includes co-teaching, where the classroom teacher and the specialist teacher plan the management of a new content topic together with the aim of including the whole class in ongoing learning. The contributions of the specialist teacher may include the creation of differentiated materials, researching useful frames and scaffolds on the web or via apps and individual help for early learners of English.

Effective in-class support includes the following activities:

- Overall encouragement and emotional support for new or struggling emergent bilingual students:
  – *Some students welcome the presence of a supportive adult of whom they can ask questions and from whom they can gain moral support – other students are empowered by viewing themselves as independent learners and dislike being singled out for special treatment in a classroom.*
- Engaging with students during each phase of a unit of work in the content areas:
  – *This approach involves introducing and reinforcing the learning of the vocabulary and language structures required for participation in the new unit of work.*
- Supplying individually targeted differentiated learning activities related to ongoing content-area instruction:
  – *This contribution may include the provision of informational texts at different reading levels and the supply of differentiated levels of support via scaffolds and frames for writing activities.*
- Offering targeted support in teaching literacy skills to emergent bilinguals:
  – *In order to be effective in this role, specialist English teachers should be included in in-service training given to mainstream teachers in the areas of literacy teaching and learning. It is vital that they employ an identical methodology in the teaching of reading and writing to that of the mainstream teacher.*
- Supplying language support to students engaged in word-based problem-solving activities in the mathematics classroom:
  – *Word-based problems in mathematics are an established area where emergent bilingual students may experience high levels of frustration. This is especially true if the student has been used to achieving at a high level in the subject. In-class support that introduces students to the language that is commonly used in mathematics problems tends to increase students' sense of wellbeing and independence. (See Section 13.2 for further discussion of this issue.)*
- Using the possibilities of embedded technology to supply visual and graphic support for learning in the content areas:
  – *This can involve the use of apps designed with specific content areas in mind, or the use of generic material.*
- Encouraging emergent bilingual students to search widely for material and references that relate to their prior experience and home culture, history and geographic locations:
  – *This can be carried out via textual and technological means at school and at home. It can also include interviews and discussion with far-flung family members and friends via Skype or email in the home language.*
- Pointing out ways in which emergent bilingual students can use their home languages to enhance and reinforce their learning in the content areas:
  – *Sometimes students retain informational texts in their home languages from their previous school. At other times parents may be willing to source materials on their visits home during*

the holiday periods when warned in advance of upcoming themes and topics. Emergent bilinguals gain greatly from reading about a subject in their home language prior to learning about the topic in English in the classroom.
- *Note: This is a different approach from the doubtful procedure of using a dictionary to translate classroom content word by word.*

7.4.7 Debate about the merits of in-class support and pull-out classes

For a period in international schools, there was fierce debate about the comparative benefits and disadvantages of the two forms of specialist English language teaching. Advocates of the in-class approach maintained that removing emergent bilinguals from the mainstream classroom singled them out as deficient in some way. They pointed out that withdrawing emergent bilingual students removed them from the language-rich environment of the mainstream classroom. It was a far more effective and inclusive policy for the specialist teacher to collaborate with the classroom teacher in making classroom content accessible. By working with their proficient English-speaking peers, emergent bilingual students were given opportunities to acquire the language necessary to complete authentic tasks.

Supporters of the withdrawal model emphasised the positive, nurturing aspect of the small-group situation. It was felt that the classroom teacher could not alone provide emergent bilingual students with the specific language teaching that was essential if they were to flourish within the school. Carefully targeted teaching in small groups would be more likely to ensure that students made rapid progress in their language learning.

Note: See the September 2012 edition of the *Teachitworld Teacher Training Bulletin*, available at http://www.teachitelt.com/custom_content/newsletters/twn_sept12_long_1.html, to read a fuller discussion of the pros and cons of the different types of English language specialist teaching.

7.4.8 Programmes and practice in international schools

In many international schools the debate has been resolved by offering both forms of specialist teaching. Starting with very young students, much of the support takes place within the classroom. With the younger age group it is felt to be more appropriate for students to stay with their peers and to receive immediate targeted support relating to the ongoing activities and happenings of the class.

Moving up the school, withdrawal tuition is introduced most often for beginning students and intermediate students. In many schools in-class support continues until the end of the elementary (or primary) years, based on collaboration between the class teacher and the specialist teacher. This approach ensures that emergent bilingual students are offered further language teaching that links to what is going on in the classroom.

A link on the website of the Bavarian International School sets out an exemplary specialist English language teaching programme in an available-to-read handbook entitled *The English as an Additional Language Programme Handbook* (www.bis-school.com/page.cfm?p=365).

The necessity for scheduled planning time for classroom and specialist teachers

Opportunities for teachers to liaise and to plan together are essential elements in providing an effective English language teaching programme for emergent bilingual students. The classroom teacher and the English specialist are in a position to offer a more effective learning experience to emergent bilingual students if they liaise closely in monitoring their progress. This is clearly the case where specialist English teachers are providing in-class support. However, it is also vital if the content of withdrawal programmes is to reflect the work of the mainstream classroom.

7.4.9 Initial placement in a specialist English-teaching programme and exiting criteria

Parents who apply to an international school are generally asked to fill in an admission form giving details about the prior educational history of their children together with relevant details about the family as a whole. The required information includes the children's history of language use and may indicate their status as emergent bilinguals. The decision to place new students in a specialist English language programme is usually based on evidence gathered by specialist English teachers with input from the class teacher.

Effective ways of assessing a student's use of English are designed ultimately to measure their competence on authentic learning tasks. Simple tests of vocabulary or grammatical exercises may give an indication of what the student has learnt in a previous school or from private tuition, but they do not give sufficient guidance as to how a student will perform in the classroom. The tests should be administered consistently and cover a range of language activities.

Effective placement tests include the following assessment approaches:

* Consideration of any records or learning portfolios from previous schools.
* Interview with the student, primarily to assess a child's apparent confidence and independence as a learner:
    - *It used to be common practice to use the interview as a guide to a student's performance in class. Now there is a realisation that competence in face-to-face informal English is not a reliable indicator of a student's ability to participate in the classroom to the required cognitive/academic level. (See Section 6.2 for a discussion of what is meant by cognitive-academic English.)*
* Tests of students' performance on authentic classroom tasks:
    - *These might include language-based mathematics problems, activities that require students to give evidence of reading comprehension and tasks that require students to utilise a range of writing skills.*
* Testing on published tests designed to measure emergent bilinguals' ability to use the cognitive-academic English they need to achieve in a mainstream classroom:
    - *There are a number of reputable batteries of assessment tests designed for use with multicultural and multilingual students and to test students' cognitive/academic abilities in*

English. These are appropriate for use in the context of an international school. The names of the providers are listed in the Resources section at the end of this chapter.

- Input from the classroom teacher concerning a new student's apparent learning profile and ability to contribute in class. Where students' level of English allows them to participate, information from beginning-of-the-year mainstream classroom tests in literacy and mathematics is useful.

Criteria for exiting the specialist English language teaching programme

In order to assess the appropriate time for students to leave the programme, specialist English teachers generally apply a range of criteria to measure students' competence in English. The tests take different forms in different schools. They may include published English language tests, assessment of student performance on reading and writing tasks and evidence from the classroom and other teachers. Often the stated aim of testing is to measure a student's ability to perform at 'year-level' competence, in other words to be able to participate without support in the mainstream classroom. For this reason, it is essential for the assessment regime to include tests of students' competence on authentic pieces of work.

Some schools still continue the practice of using numerically scored tests to establish a student's readiness to leave the specialist English language support programme. When students reach a certain score they are considered ready to leave the programme. For school administrators, students and parents this has the advantage of limiting the discussion about an appropriate time for exiting the programme. However, such tests fail to measure a student's capacity to function on authentic learning tasks and many schools have abandoned this approach.

The following measures are used to assess students' readiness to exit a specialist English language programme:

- Evidence from the listening, speaking, reading and writing criteria that are used in the mainstream classroom to track all students' learning at a year level (including the Australian 'First Steps' literacy programme mentioned in Section 7.1).
- In the case of younger students, evidence from the reading assessments used in the mainstream literacy programme to measure students' progress in reading. (An example of this type of assessment is the approach known as 'Running Records' (www.learnnc.org/lp/editions/readassess/977). This system, originally devised by the New Zealand educator, Marie Clay, is designed to track the strategies that young students bring into use when decoding and making sense of their reading. Marie Clay's renowned Reading Recovery programme delivers effective short-term intervention to struggling readers. (See Section 12.1 for more on the topic of young students' literacy learning.)
- Retesting on published tests such as those used to assess students for placement in an English language programme.
- Input from the class teacher about the student's profile as a learner in the mainstream classroom.

7.4.10 The classroom teacher as sole English language specialist

Small schools, newly established schools or schools in isolated locations may not be in a position to offer a comprehensive programme of English teaching. Teachers who are employed as classroom teachers in schools of this type may find that they are responsible to a large extent for the English language learning of their emergent bilingual students. This can be a challenging situation, although many emergent bilinguals offer stories of very productive years spent in the company of an inspiring teacher.

7.4.11 Looking for help on the internet

Where teachers have access to the internet, there are now many organisations and individuals offering practical language teaching strategies together with discussions of the issues that may arise. Some of the most useful websites are grouped together in the Resources section at the end of this chapter.

7.5 Understanding and Addressing the Causes of Slow Progress in Emergent Bilingual Students

The challenge of trying to understand the causes of a delay or a longer period of slow progress in an emergent bilingual student is one of the most often cited reasons for concern mentioned by teachers. The difficulty lies in trying to distinguish between the profile of a student as a language learner and the potential presence of specific learning disabilities. Baker (2014: 96) makes it clear that the student's move into a second or further language is rarely in itself the cause of the delay, although it is accepted that constant changes of school and language may increase the impact of any underlying learning disability.

Teachers who suspect underlying learning disabilities may notice the following patterns in a student's way of working and behaving:

- Even when students are learning to write in a new script and spelling system where difficulty in forming the letters of the Roman letters accurately and spelling mistakes can be expected to occur, experienced teachers may notice features in the way that students approach the physical act of writing and of setting out script on a page that give cause for concern. Significant spelling difficulties can become evident from the early days, although teachers should not rush to conclusions.
- Students give evidence of finding it difficult to engage in classroom activities whether spoken or written, and may appear restless and unfocused (although the possibility of the student being unfamiliar with expected learning behaviours should be taken into account).
- Disparity between a student's evident intelligence and achievement. Even when students are beginning learners of English, teachers may become aware of significant differences between a student's verbal contributions and her or his capacity to make progress in reading or writing.

7.5.1 Possible sources of further information about a student's learning profile

- Teachers should check any information provided by the previous school as a matter of course. They should give more credence to evidence based on recognised tests or other assessments that were carried out in the student's home language.
- Teachers should talk to parents, although they should treat the subject of a potential learning disability with great sensitivity. In some national education systems and national cultures, learning disabilities are not acknowledged and may be considered a source of shame.
- Consulting with colleagues about the way that the student acts and reacts in different situations in school is a useful approach. Are there situations such as on the sports field where the student appears confident and in control? Are there consistent areas where the student evidently shows unease or even distress?
- Consider whether it is feasible to contact the previous school if this was not done at the time of admission.

7.5.2 Possible causes for apparent learning disabilities

In globally mobile emergent bilingual students there are number of causes for apparent learning issues that may be the result of a life of extreme mobility and constant change. These factors are compounded by any change in the make-up of the family and shifts in languages.

- Students who have experienced multiple moves and different schooling systems, sometimes entering a school mid-year, may fail to develop a solid basis in either (or any) of their languages. They may have been moved or have experienced a profound change at home that has resulted in inconsistent exposure to a settled number of languages. The lack of a firm basis in either of a bilingual's languages places them at a disadvantage when they are expected to learn in an existing language or in a new language. (See Section 5.2 and Baker, 2014: 95.)
- Teachers should bear in mind the possibility that a student's failure to make progress may derive from an extreme cultural mismatch in learning expectations and classroom behaviour. Some students are uncomfortable with the idea of taking independent steps in their learning, always preferring to wait for the teacher to lead them through the next phase. Other students come from schooling systems where students are not expected to contribute their own thoughts and where achievement is measured by their ability to repeat what they have heard from the teacher. In these cases, it is useful once more to observe students in different situations to find out what is going on. Many students, for instance, are transformed when working with others around a computer. It is a sign for concern, however, if a student appears to be continually alone and to make little contact with peers speaking the same language.
- Students who appear to have extreme difficulty in replicating the sounds of English on a consistent basis should be checked for hearing issues. Similarly, sight testing

should be suggested if teachers suspect that vision problems may be a cause of a student's failure to progress.

7.5.3 School referral policies and communication with parents

Accredited international schools are expected to have referral policies and procedures in place for the times when a student shows consistent signs of struggling. Most experienced teachers recognise the challenges of assessing the factors behind an emergent bilingual student's failure to thrive. The referral process usually involves some or all of the following elements:

* perusal of baseline and assessment data;
* the student's profile as a learner based on the observations of all the teachers concerned;
* monitoring and observation by learning disabilities professionals or the school psychologist;
* meetings between the senior staff and teachers concerned.

Parents are a key element in the process of establishing the nature of a potential learning disability or emotional issue but, as mentioned above, conversation with parents should be handled with great sensitivity.

When all the initial stages of the referral process have been achieved, often the school recommends testing with the parents' permission. Not all schools are themselves equipped to administer recognised tests; in some cases professionals in the expatriate or local community provide the appropriate level of expertise.

7.5.4 Issues over testing

There are some well-established concerns about the administration of tests for learning disabilities on populations for whom the tests were not originally designed. Tests in English-medium schools are generally drawn from English-speaking countries with content and scoring modes that match the expectations of teaching and learning in those settings. For the findings of these tests to have validity, certain challenges have to be recognised and addressed:

* Some of the tests contain in-built issues relating to the use of language and cultural symbols. Quite elementary aspects of these tests such as the range of animals used in a recognition test for young children raise questions about the validity of the findings. In other cases, students being tested may be expected to make guesses or to imagine certain outcomes from sets of pictures. Guessing and speculating are not customary activities in many schooling systems and tests of this type may fail to provide useful information for students from these backgrounds.
* A further concern relating to testing is that of using the language that the student is struggling to learn as the vehicle for taking the test. Ideally, the tests should be

administered in the student's strongest language with the tester able to speak the same language. At the very least, the test-giver should be a friendly non-threatening presence who explains the language used on the test so that the student is not penalised from the start. In some locations with large expatriate populations it is possible to find qualified personnel who are able to administer tests in the student's home language – an approach which is clearly the preferred option.

Possible outcomes

Experienced learning disabilities teachers frequently recommend that schools should not wait until a firm diagnosis is established before offering small-group and individual learning support to students with suspected learning disabilities. Waiting for such a diagnosis tends to allow the student to lose confidence and motivation and to fall further behind.

Most professionals recommend rapid targeted intervention in the areas that appear to be the source of a learning delay. An intervention may take the form of extra support in a small writing or reading group and/or sessions with a speech and language therapist or school counsellor. In many cases, the intervention takes the form of in-class support for the student concerned, with the collaboration of the class teacher and English language teaching specialist.

Note: The following publications offer further information relating to this complex subject: Baker (2014), Bekhechi (2011) and Hamayan *et al.* (2013).

Key Points in This Chapter

Assessment

- Most international schools draw on the assessment approaches embedded in the programmes and curricula they offer.
- Many schools use further assessment tools which derive from English-speaking countries.
- Schools need to develop policies and practices that are appropriate for use in assessing the learning of emergent bilingual students as they develop their mastery of the school language.

Technology and the library/media centre

- Many international schools are in a position to provide extensive resources to support the learning of students.
- Technology empowers emergent bilingual students by enabling them to manage their own learning.
- Technology offers multiple opportunities to expand students' perspectives by bringing the world into the classroom.
- Technology offers a ready means for students to access information in their home languages.

- Many international schools have well-equipped libraries or media centres containing an array of printed texts and electronic media.
- Librarians are integrated into class learning and support emergent bilingual students in carrying out investigative projects.

Specialist English language teaching programmes

- International schools accredited by the major organisations supply comprehensive programmes of specialist English language teaching.
- Many international schools offer specialist English language classes in the form of in-class support and withdrawal classes.
- The aim of both types of support is to enable emergent bilingual students to participate in mainstream classroom learning activity.
- Adequate liaison and planning time between classroom and specialist teachers is an essential element in an effective programme.
- Placement in these programmes and readiness to exit should be assessed against a wide range of language tasks and activities and ultimately on a student's performance in authentic classroom learning tasks.

Understanding the reasons behind slow progress

- The challenge of understanding the reasons behind a learning delay in the case of an emergent bilingual student is in distinguishing whether the issue is related to language learning or an underlying learning disability.
- Multiple moves resulting in changing language exposure and experience of different schooling systems can result in an emergent bilingual student failing to acquire a firm basis in either or any language.
- Lack of a developed primary language can be the cause of delayed progress in an English-medium classroom.
- Tests designed for use with English speakers should be regarded with caution when used with emergent bilingual students having difficulty in learning that language.

Resources

Assessment in international schools: Links to organisations and providers

IBO assessment websites: www.ibo.org/pyp/assessed/index.cfm and www.ibo.org/myp/assessment.

International Schools' Assessment, created by the Australian Council for Educational Research: www.acer.edu.au/tests/isa.

Running Records assessment approach: www.learnnc.org/lp/editions/readassess/977.

Stanford Achievement Test Series (10th edn), published by Pearson in the US: http://www.pearsonassessments.com/learningassessments/products/100000415/stanford-achievement-test-series-tenth-edition.html.

State of Western Australia First Steps literacy programme criteria: www.det.wa.edu.au/stepsresources/.

Woodcock-Munoz Language Survey Revised – Normative Update (2011) (WMLS-R), published by Nelson in the UK: www.assess.nelson.com/test-ind/wmls-r.html.

Organisations offering online practical advice for mainstream teachers who have sole responsibility for the language learning of emergent bilingual students in their classes

Organisations and associations devoted to the improvement of English language teaching to emergent bilinguals:

- UK-based National Association for Language Development in the Curriculum (NALDIC): www.naldic.org.uk.
- US-based TESOL International Association: www.tesol.org.

Major publishers of English language teaching textbooks and software. These sites include hints, suggestions and whole lesson plans relating to the inclusion of bilingual students in mainstream classrooms. Among them are:
- Pearson Global Schools' site, entitled 'English Language Learning': www.pearsonglobalschools.com.

Bodies that administer education in the local authorities, states and provinces of Australia, Canada, New Zealand, the UK and the USA which offer useful strategic and practical advice as well as example lesson plans. Use Google to find the education links on the sites of these bodies.

Help in print

A printed text written by a former teacher in an international school offers a useful guide to the components of a specialist English language teaching programme. Caroline Scott's book, *Teaching Children as an Additional Language: A Programme for 7–11 Year Olds* (2009) also provides assessment checklists and criteria, as well as attractive resources to photocopy. Teachers who find themselves the sole source of English language teaching in a classroom containing emergent bilingual students will find this book to be a valuable addition to their store of materials.

An example of a current English language teaching programme

See the link on the Bavarian International School website, giving a read-only version of the school's 'English as an Additional Language Programme Handbook': www.bis-school.com/page.cfm?p=365.

The pros and cons of in-class and withdrawal specialist English language teaching

Teachitworld Teacher Training Bulletin (September 2012 edn). Check out this website (http://www.teachitelt.com/custom_content/newsletters/twn_sept12_long_1.html) to find a fuller discussion of the pros and cons of the different types of English language specialist teaching.

References

Baker, C. (2014) *A Parents' and Teachers' Guide to Bilingualism* (4th edn). Bristol: Multilingual Matters.

Bekhechi, F. (2011) Meeting the needs of young second-language learners who struggle. In E. Murphy (ed.) *Welcoming Linguistic Diversity in Early Childhood Classrooms*. Bristol: Multilingual Matters.

Brewster, J. (2011) The role of the library in supporting young language learners and their families. In E. Murphy (ed.) *Welcoming Linguistic Diversity in Early Childhood Classrooms*. Bristol: Multilingual Matters.

Hamayan, E., Marler, B., Sanchez-Lopez, C. and Damico, J. (2013) *Special Education Considerations for English Language Learners: Delivering a Continuum of Services* (2nd edn). Philadelphia, PA: Caslon.

Scott, C. (2009) *Teaching Children as an Additional Language: A Programme for 7–11 Year Olds*. London: Routledge.

8 Explaining the Learning Culture of the School to Students and Parents

Chapter 8 sets out the aspects of daily life in the classroom and in the school as a whole that may cause questioning and unease in students and parents accustomed to different educational norms. Explaining the school culture and the rationale behind the school's policies and practices is an essential part of the teacher's role in an international school.

The sequence of Chapter 8 is as follows:

- Introduction: why teachers need to explain the school culture to students and parents.
- Entering the new school: placing the student in an appropriate class and the school's communication with parents.
- Aspects of classroom and school life that may need explaining to parents and students.
- Parent expectations and concerns about language learning.

Introduction: Why Teachers Need to Explain the School Culture to Students and Parents

Parents who place their children in an international school for the first time may be struck by differences in many aspects of school life that cause them to ask questions and perhaps give them a sense of unease. Families in this situation tend to arrive with expectations about teaching and learning that derive from their previous experiences and which reflect the norms current in other settings. Where this is the case, it is a major part of a teacher's role to explain the rationale behind the school's policies and practices and to demonstrate their effectiveness in a classroom containing a diverse population of students, many of whom have experienced multiple moves.

The school as an expression of culture

Issues of culture and intercultural learning are the factors that underlie the practical content of this chapter. International schools are places where cultural adjustment is a daily fact of life. New families are faced with the need to adjust not only to a new location but also to their first experience of international schooling. International schools are not all the same, however. Experienced movers recognise that each international school tends to evolve a unique school culture reflecting its history, location and the sources from which it takes its ethos and practice. (This topic is discussed in Section 3.5.) As a result of these multiple influences, each international school has a unique flavour, even if all international schools also have much in common. The individual characteristics of each school require further adjustment from all new members of the school community.

Explaining the way the school functions to new parents and students is a means of ensuring that families understand how to gain the most from the school experience and how to lessen the stress involved in adapting to the new environment.

The content of this chapter

The first section of this chapter addresses two areas that relate to the early experiences of students and families in a new school. The first is the challenge of deciding the correct class placement for a student who moves to an international school from another schooling system. The second area describes the impact on new parents of becoming accustomed to a level of communication and expected involvement in their child's life at school that may be unfamiliar.

Section 8.2 introduces a selection of classroom practices that sometimes cause misunderstanding and unease in families who are new to the school. Practical suggestions for communicating with parents about these topics of potential concern are included. Finally, in Section 8.3, some of the issues that parents raise about their children's experience of learning the school language are introduced and commented upon.

8.1 Two Aspects of International Education That May Be New to Parents

Two features that immediately strike many parents new to international schools as different are class placement policies for new students and the degree of communication that they receive from the school from the moment of registering their children. Both these aspects are school wide rather than classroom based, although they inevitably involve class teachers.

8.1.1 Class placement policy in the new school

The class and even the year level in which their children are placed on arrival at the new school can, unfortunately, be an immediate source of concern to new parents.

It is rare for the opening of a new school year to pass without a debate over which class one or more students should be placed in. Generally, a senior member of the administration is the person who communicates with parents about this area, but teachers can be caught up in the consequences if parents remain unhappy about the school's decision. The reason why placement is a potential source for misunderstanding and disagreement is because the structure of school systems across the world varies in many ways.

Policy of placing student with peers in the same age group

The general policy in most international schools accredited by reputable organisations is to place students with children of a similar age, regardless of their prior school experiences, level of English language proficiency and level of maturation. The general view on the part of schools is that students rarely function successfully in the social or academic areas of school life if they are separated from their own age groups. They argue that small class sizes and teachers experienced in working with diverse, mobile populations allow the school to cater for students' individual needs when they are placed with their age-group peers. This policy is sometimes difficult to sustain in the face of the significant differences in prior educational experience that occur among mobile populations of new students. The reality is that any given year group/class in an international school may have students representing an 18-month age span.

Text Box 8.1 The age at which children start school varies around the world

A further element that leads to parental anxiety about class placement in the new school arises from the differences in the ages that students start school across the world.

In the British system, and other national systems that tend to reflect it such as those in India and Pakistan, children are placed in school at the age of five (occasionally even at four). Parents from these systems may be concerned when their children enter an international school which broadly speaking starts formal education at the age of six. They argue that their children are further along the continuum of learning than the rest of the children in the class, and point out that their children will be disadvantaged when they return to their home system.

Other parents from national systems such as those in Scandinavia, where children do not enter school until six and do not start formal learning until the age of seven, are concerned for different reasons. They are used to children starting school in the mornings only, or in some other flexible arrangement. They argue that their children will be placed under unacceptable pressure by being required to engage in formal learning too early.

Administrators and teachers in international schools are accustomed to discussing these areas of concern with parents. They point out that personnel in international schools are used to working with newly arrived students from all education systems. They explain that classroom strategies such as differentiation are available so that students work at their own level. They give evidence, if they are wise, that students from all educational backgrounds in the school are achieving similar levels of outcome by the ages of nine or 10. Nevertheless, parents who are concerned with this issue rarely reduce their level of anxiety until they see their children happily settled and making progress.

Differences in the cut-off dates at a year level

Most international schools, being independent foundations, make their own decisions about the cut-off dates for the age of children at a year level (the age group for which each class caters). In some schools these dates reflect customary American or British practice. In other schools the decision on cut-off dates reflects the schooling system in the surrounding community. In any case, parents who are about to enter their children in an international school may find that the cut-off dates in the new school are different from the school that their children previously attended. This is an area that concerns parents greatly because they feel their children will either miss out on part of the school year or, alternatively, be compelled to repeat what they have already learnt.

Sometimes the confusion lies in the way that classes at a year level are named. Parents may not recognise the American grade-level system of naming, for instance, or can have no way of knowing what level of teaching and learning goes on in classes named simply Year 1, Year 2, and so on.

Differences in timing of school years which lead to placement issues

A further cause for potential placement issues occurs when families cross hemispheres in making a new move. In areas such as Europe and North America which lie in the northern hemisphere, the school year runs from autumn through to early summer. In the national schooling systems of South America, southern Africa or Australia, on the other hand, the school year runs from the end of January until the beginning of December. Thus children from the northern hemisphere moving to the southern hemisphere find that they arrive during the middle of the school year and vice versa.

There are further differences around the world. The Japanese school year starts in April and ends in March. In South Korea, the school year starts in mid-March and ends in mid-February. Intense discussion about appropriate classes for new students in these circumstances is understandable and common.

Implications for teachers

These concerns, where they occur, can be a source of stress for new teachers who are hoping to begin their relationship with new parents on a positive basis. In many cases, the answer is to explain to parents that international schools at the start of the school are accustomed to carry out informal (and sometimes formal) tests in order to understand where individual students are placed on the learning continuum. This is invariably the case with mathematics, where future learning depends on a solid basis of prior knowledge. Gradually building up a picture of a student's learning profile and breadth of schooling is the only way that makes sense in classes of this sort. In the case of emergent bilingual students, the issue of their English language development is a further element that requires careful assessment and placement, if necessary, in a specialist English language teaching programme.

The essential communication that teachers need to make to parents is that their children are carefully monitored and that the approach in the classroom is to take students forward in their learning from their existing level of knowledge and understanding.

Text Box 8.2 Teachers need to be culture learners too: Naming students correctly

Teachers in international schools need to be sensitive to cultural differences in their dealings with students and parents. An area where this is the case is the correct naming of students and parents. New teachers may be working for the first time with students whose naming systems are unfamiliar to them and which differ from the conventions they are used to. They may be faced on the first day when parents bring their children into school with an embarrassing situation: which of the names written down on the class list should the teacher use with a student; how should the parents be addressed?

Chinese, Japanese and Korean names, for instance, are customarily written in these languages with the family name first and the given name second. In the case of Ban Ki-moon, the present Secretary-General of the United Nations who comes from Korea, for instance, Ban is the family name and Ki-moon is the given name. On the other hand, many international families from these backgrounds present their children's names in ways that reflect Western usage when they are out of their home country. Calling children by their correct names is a vital part of making them feel at home in the new school. Teachers should not shrink from asking parents exactly how they and their children wish to be addressed.

Some naming systems make distinctions related to gender – those of Russia and Iceland are obvious examples here – and other systems reflect genealogical and cultural considerations. Teachers should ask experienced colleagues for advice in this area. Several websites offer information and advice; they are included in the Resources section at the end of this chapter.

8.1.2 Written communication with parents

High-quality communication with parents is a core aim in many international schools in line with their mission of including parents in the life and learning of the whole school community. Depending on the availability of internet connections, many schools have opted to send out their communications via a parent portal on the school's website. Other schools retain a paper-based method of communication, often sending letters home on a specific day in a plastic pouch to ensure that they reach home safely.

In English-medium schools the language of communication tends to be English, although some schools employ volunteer parents to translate or convey key messages in other languages. In bilingual schools, or schools where the student population contains many students of one language group, the communications are usually also delivered in those languages.

Increasingly, classroom teachers are expected to communicate regularly with parents online about weekly or even daily life in the classroom. In some schools it is now common practice for homework to be posted on the class link and for the regular newsletter relating to class activity to be sent out via the parent portal. Other uses for the internet include posting blogs and photographs to describe residential school trips and sporting fixtures.

Occasionally parents describe a feeling of being overwhelmed by this level of communication from the school. Such parents tend to come from schooling systems where such a high level of communication about every aspect of their child's life is unusual. One Russian parent described how she felt in this way: 'We are not used to knowing about every second of our child's day. I don't think it's necessary. We just need a written report at the end of each term.' However, most parents come to welcome the regular contact with the school as a whole and their child's teacher in particular. In today's world of immediate communication it seems unlikely that the flow will diminish in the future, given the possibilities presented by parent portals on school websites and other technological pathways.

8.2 Explaining Day-to-Day Practice in International School Classrooms

Some of the aspects of life in an international school that lead to parental concern relate to day-to-day practice in the classroom. The classroom culture in international schools has evolved in response to the diverse needs of a globally mobile student body. The programmes and curricula offered in most schools are similarly tailored to provide an educational experience that meshes with the lives of this group of students and which equips them for further education and eventual employment. The resultant classroom practice can seem very different from the way things are done in national schooling systems. It is understandable that new parents should have many queries about practice in their children's classrooms.

8.2.1 The balancing act for teachers working with diverse students

Teachers are engaged in a balancing act when they explain the workings of the classroom to parents and students in an English-medium international school. It is vital that students feel at ease in the culture of the school so that they feel included and can learn effectively. However, this ease should not come at the expense of students being required to set aside the distinctive elements that derive from their own cultural and linguistic backgrounds. Experienced teachers recognise that it is possible to embrace diversity in a meaningful manner while at the same time making clear the ground rules and overall approaches that underpin classroom life in the school.

The following areas are frequently the cause of queries from students and parents:

(a)   the generally informal atmosphere in the classroom;
(b)   the way the classroom is set out;
(c)   differences in learning behaviours;
(d)   differences in the age that formal literacy teaching begins;
(e)   teaching 'different' mathematics;
(f)   discipline (or the apparent lack of it);
(g)   homework policy;
(h)   assessment;
(i)   grouping and seating arrangements.

Explanations and suggestions relating to these areas are set out below, headed by typical comments or queries that teachers regularly hear from parents. A recommended overall strategy for teachers is to avoid being defensive if parents occasionally sound critical. The reason for their unease is that the school's policies and practice are unfamiliar. The most effective approach for teachers is to explain why the school has adopted these practices and to give evidence of why they are effective with the sorts of students who attend the school.

(a) The generally informal atmosphere in the classroom
Parent comments and queries:

> Piotr has found it far easier to settle in the class than we expected – he knows he can ask the teacher whenever he doesn't know what to do.

> The thing that made Sa'ad feel so welcome was the way Mrs Cunningham asked him to be her special helper.

> We like the teachers being so friendly here, but we are used to the students having to show more respect. The teacher is always right for us.

To students and parents accustomed to school systems where there is a less easy and friendly relationship with teachers, the informality and frequent interaction that they see in international school classrooms between teacher and student and between student and student may be confusing. In the early days in an international school, it is clear that sometimes new students misunderstand the general friendliness of teachers, which leads them to be over-familiar and to use very informal language. Some parents question whether classrooms of this sort can deliver a rigorous curriculum. Teachers need to explain that this approach helps globally mobile students to settle and is a means of students becoming collaborative learners, ready to share in critical thinking and problem solving.

(b) The way the classroom is set out
Parent comments and queries:

> We feel that Keiji is being disturbed by the other children at the table. He is used to having quiet in class so that he can get on with his work.

Families used to classrooms that contain rows of desks facing the teacher may find it difficult to interpret the type of classroom where students sit in groups around tables. Teachers need to emphasise the value of this arrangement, which allows for different groupings of students and enables shared learning to take place. Parents are likely to be convinced only when they see the quality of their child's spoken and written assignments.

(c) Differences in learning behaviours
Parent comments and queries:

> I am sorry you are not pleased with Young-Kyun's behaviour. In Korean schools they were punished if they talked in class. Here he does not understand how he should behave.

> I know Felicien is being a nuisance in your class. The thing is, at his French school, he had to sit still all day and wait to be told what to do. He's finding it difficult to get used to being more independent and being allowed to move around.

Students used to 'traditional' classrooms are likely to need help in learning the behaviours that are usual in the classrooms of international schools. Some students mistake the buzz of focused talk for general chatter and find it difficult to join in constructively. If they have been used only to working independently, they may find it difficult to work collaboratively as may be required in an enquiry-based or investigative programme. Placing emergent bilinguals in carefully selected groups and monitoring the interaction is one way of instructing students in the desired form of behaviour for students used to a teacher-directed classroom.

(d) Age at which formal literacy teaching starts
Parent comments and queries:

> We're surprised that Arun does not bring a reading book home yet. In India he was already reading well.

> I feel childhood is a time for playing and learning about the world, not being forced to sit down at a desk all day. Ingrid is not used to it.

In ways that are similar to concerns about the appropriate time to begin formal school-ing, parents have expectations about when young children should learn to read and write. Some parents, such as those whose systems historically derive from the British system, are used to school systems that start children's literacy teaching and learning at the age of five; others, such as those in Scandinavia, are used to formal literacy learning starting at the age of seven.

Because of the differences between schooling systems, it is common to find newly arrived children at different stages of pre-literacy and literacy development in early childhood classrooms. Fortunately, classes in international schools are usually small enough to allow teachers to take children forward from the point they have reached in their literacy studies. Nevertheless, many parents remain anxious about this subject. Parents from areas such as the Indian subcontinent may feel that the school is not suf-ficiently demanding, and parents from systems that leave formal literacy teaching until later are constantly on the lookout for signs of stress in their children.

Text Box 8.3 Questions about emergent bilinguals and literacy learning

A topic that the parents of very young children sometimes raise is the order in which their children should learn to read and write in their two languages. There is no clear-cut answer to this question and teachers may not be privy to all the cir-cumstances that might guide the decision. In bilingual schools young children learn to read and write in both languages at the same time. Where young children are being educated in an English-medium school there is a tendency to suggest that teaching in their home language should focus primarily on oral acquisition while they move through the early stages of learning to read and write. That is, they should learn to read and write in English before moving on to literacy learning in the new language. However, the circumstances in individual families may make that an unrealistic proposition – and maybe an unwise one.

Japanese parents, for instance, are usually anxious that their children should keep in contact with the literacy curriculum customary in Japanese schools from the time they start formal education in any language. The reasoning behind this thinking has to do with the structure of literacy teaching and learning in Japanese schools. Japanese children are expected to acquire a specified range of kanji at each year level as they move through the school. For families who expect their children to return to the Japanese system or who are committed to their children maintain-ing and developing their proficiency in Japanese, there is a need for children to keep in step with every stage of the Japanese system.

Some experienced teachers argue that a student's likely stability or mobility are key issues. Where students are expected to continue their education in English in a series of international schools, it might seem to make more sense for children to concentrate solely on learning to read and write in English. Where students are settled in a stable two-language environment, or the parents expect their children to return to their home schooling system, it is more apparent that should continue to pursue their literacy lessons in both languages side by side.

The situation is different with new students who are older and who have a firm literacy basis in their home language. In this instance, the research clearly establishes the value of students maintaining their home language literacy studies, since the skills of reading and writing in the home language transfer readily to literacy learning in a second. Where this is the case, students have a head start in learning to read and write in English. The chapter called 'Reading and writing questions' in Baker (2014) is devoted to this complex topic.

(e) Teaching of mathematics

Parent comments and queries:

> *Aygul is having a very difficult time with math. She did all this math before in her Turkish school, but she can't do the problems because she doesn't understand the English.*

> *We're worried about the maths taught in school. It's not the same as in India. Naija won't be able to get into a good school at home if she hasn't done the right maths.*

Several areas surrounding the teaching of mathematics in international schools may give cause for concern among students and parents who are used to different approaches.

Students from schooling systems with high levels of mathematics teaching and learning

Students from some education systems, including those of China, Japan, Singapore and South Korea among others, may feel that the mathematics teaching in an international school lags behind the level that they have already mastered. Evidence indicates that this is likely to be the case: students from these settings are used to a more highly paced and challenging mathematics programme (the OECD 2012 PISA test scores confirm this view; see www.oecd.org/pisa/). At the same time, emergent bilingual students from these backgrounds may lack the language skills to engage in problem solving and are likely to experience frustration and a sense of failure at being unable to participate fully in this type of activity.

In school, specialist English teachers and classroom teachers need to teach and model the vocabulary and structures required for the learning of mathematics (see Section 13.2 for a practical discussion of this issue). Out of school, parents sometimes address the issue by placing their children in specialist mathematics classes (such as the Japanese system of Kumon: http://en.wikipedia.org/wiki/Kumon). Parents' worries about the standard of their children's mathematics lead to a high take-up of the Saturday morning classes offered by most Korean and Japanese expatriate schools.

'The wrong type of mathematics'

Students and parents from some backgrounds, including the Indian subcontinent, may find that the type of mathematics taught in an international school does not match that in their home systems. These are systems that tend to place more weight on an arithmetic approach to the learning of mathematics than on a problem-solving peda-gogy. Parents become anxious that their children will not be able to succeed in the highly competitive Indian examination system if they are unaccustomed to working in the ways that are expected. (There is huge competition for entry into prestigious schools in the Indian subcontinent. Students who are not practised in carrying out arithmetical calculations at speed may find themselves at a disadvantage.)

The anxiety persists about the style of mathematics taught in international schools even where families acknowledge that the problem-solving approach equips students eventually to take globally recognised examinations. The worry is for parents who expect to return to the Indian system when their children are 10 or 11 years old and must compete to get into secondary schools. This concern is understandable and well-founded. In the case of families returning to the Indian system, international schools sometimes recommend that parents arrange the appropriate style of tuition so that their children will not be at a disadvantage when they return home.

(f) Discipline (or the apparent lack of it)
Parent comments and queries:

> *There's a boy in Sari's class who is very noisy and disturbing. Why don't you do something about it?*

> *I don't understand why there aren't more real school rules. How do the children know how to behave?*

Both students and parents may find the approach to discipline in international schools difficult to understand. Instead of specific rules and a formal system of punishment, there is usually a list of expected behaviours which may have been generated in consulta-tion with students. Where behaviour does not meet expectations, students tend to be taken aside, invited to consider the effect of their behaviour and encouraged to behave differently in the future. There may be formal sanctions but these also tend to be based on discussion which may ultimately include the Head and parents.

The aim is to change student behaviour rather than to punish poor conduct. This approach can seem ineffective and weak to students and parents accustomed to a differ-ent disciplinary style that may include corporal punishment in a few but decreasing areas of the world. To help new students understand the ways in which they are expected to behave, teachers need to spell out clearly the conduct that is expected in school and to be consistent when students show signs of not understanding what is expected.

(g) Homework policy
Parent comments and queries:

> *In Finland, we don't think young children should have to do homework. They've been shut up in school all day and need to play and relax when they get home.*

I don't feel you are giving Chunmei enough homework. He gets it finished in 40 minutes and I don't think that is enough for a boy of his age.

I dread it when Fedir comes home with a project to do. I think, who is attending this school, him or me?

The homework policy in an international school may differ from what students and parents are used to. Parents from some systems may feel there is too little homework; parents from systems where children begin formal schooling at a later date may dislike the idea of homework altogether. Many parents are unaccustomed to the idea that parental help and involvement is acceptable in many instances (especially in the case of new emergent bilingual students).

The essential element in a discussion about homework is an established school homework policy which is available for parents to read online or in paper form. In general, teachers need both to explain the school's homework policy and to spell out the expectations about homework clearly and in writing. In the case of emergent bilingual students, teachers need to ensure that there is an open line of communication with parents. Where this is the case, teachers may hear that homework is becoming burdensome and counter-productive for students whose English is not yet well developed.

(h) Assessment

Parent comments and queries:

I don't understand why you don't mark every mistake in Leila's writing. How can she learn if you don't let her know when she's wrong.

I think the idea of criteria is modern, but they should be tested as well. [This concern refers to the methods of assessment used in the IB programmes, where students are assessed against a range of criteria. These criteria describe the looked-for outcomes that a piece of work should display. See Sections 4.3 and 4.4.]

At first, I thought how strange to have the children talking at the parent conference. I thought it was a way of not letting us know what was going on, perhaps. But when I heard Mashiko talking in English about her own progress and showing us her best work, I felt proud and when I got home I skyped my sister in Nagoya and told her about it.

The topic of assessment is also the subject of Section 7.1.

The approach to assessment that is common in international schools may be unfamiliar to parents and students who are accustomed to different forms of assessment, such as marking and grading. Many national schooling systems around the world adopt an approach to assessment that depends on tests and examinations for their measurement of a student's attainment. Marking or grading a piece of work in these systems may be carried out in red pen. It tends to involve picking out the wrong answers and giving work as a whole a numerical or letter grade. In many systems, failure to reach the required grades at the end of the year results in the student having to repeat the year.

The pattern of assessment in international schools takes a more varied form with a greater emphasis on tracking a student's learning and in using information gained from assessment to guide future instruction. Many international schools, noticeably those who offer the IB programmes, assess student work against sets of criteria to and allow a greater degree of flexibility in the ways in which students display their learning. (See Sections 4.3 and 4.4 for more on assessment in the IB programmes.)

The concerns of parents who are unfamiliar with the assessment approaches found in most international schools are generally only lessened when they are given consistent and solid evidence of their child's progress. Many parents continue to prefer a numerical grade as evidence of their child's achievement. However, most parents are impressed and won over by a carefully presented account, with evidence from completed work, of the ways their children have moved forward in their learning.

(i) Grouping and seating arrangements
Parent comments and queries:

> I am not happy that Yafit is sitting next to another Israeli girl. She will never learn English if she speaks Hebrew all day.

> It's very important to Ignacio that he sits next to Felipe. He is very sensitive boy and he needs to be near his friend.

Parents sometimes become anxious about seating and grouping arrangements in class, with different parents expressing diametrically opposed concerns. Some parents, whether new or more established in the school community, state very strongly that they would prefer that their children did not sit next to a student who speaks the same language. They see the use of the home language as diminishing their child's chances of learning English quickly and fear that the school day will be spent chatting. Other parents want their children to be supported by the presence of a speaker of the same language in the early months. These parents feel strongly that their child will suffer less stress and settle more quickly if they have the comfort of being able to communicate easily.

Teachers faced with these requests should mention that students in international school classrooms tend not to stay in one place during the whole school day – they move around while carrying out various learning tasks and are placed in different groups for different activities. Students tend to be grouped around tables in the elementary school or to change classrooms for each subject in the middle school and this limits the time that students spend in contact with a single student. It is a balancing act for teachers to make the appropriate decision in this area, as are many aspects of working with families from diverse cultural backgrounds and educational experiences. Experienced teachers often choose to seat students as their parents request and to make changes where appropriate when the child has gained confidence.

8.3 Parent Expectations About Language Learning

Parents whose children are new to an international school arrive with a range of experiences of language learning and varying levels of English proficiency. One or both of the parents may be proficient users of English because of their prior social or employment experiences. Other parents will have taken English as a foreign language in school, but have had little reason to develop their proficiency further; others have had no prior access to English. Their own experiences affect parents' expectations about how their children will learn the school language or languages and teachers should be ready to explain the school's approach to language learning and to give evidence of its effectiveness.

The following are some areas of language learning that teachers may need to address with parents. The issues that are included are those that involve parents directly or which parents themselves tend to raise.

8.3.1 Use of English at home

Some parents who themselves speak English sometimes ask the teacher whether they should speak English at home with their child rather than use their customary language. The generally accepted answer is that parents should continue using the language of the home when talking to their child. This approach is in line with the overall aim of achieving an additive outcome for the student, where the process of learning a new language does not diminish development in the home language. (See Section 5.2 for a discussion of this topic.)

Teachers should check the family situation, however, before handing out blanket advice in this area (see Sears, 2011b). In families whose children attend international schools the parents are sometimes of different nationalities and may use English in the home as the common language. In other cases, English may be used in the home since it comprises one of the national languages in the family's country of origin, as is true of much of the Indian subcontinent, Africa, Malaysia and Singapore. In this case it seems presumptuous of the teacher to express views about the language the parents should use at home with their children. Where English is used in the home it is still worth emphasising the value to the child of continuing to use and develop the other family languages. Proficiency in a number of languages including those that are used in the home country is an advantage to students – their loss represents a missed opportunity.

8.3.2 In-class use of students' home languages

Increasingly in English-medium international schools, teachers are incorporating the use of students' home languages to enhance and support teaching and learning in the mainstream classroom. This may take the form of encouraging emergent bilingual students to carry out online research in their home or primary language, or suggesting that students who speak the same language use that language to negotiate a richer meaning in English.

Parents sometimes express reservations about the use of the home language in an English-medium classroom. They feel that their children's English will improve more quickly if they use only English and occasionally they feel it necessary to point out that the learning of English was a key reason in sending their child to an international school.

Teachers should be ready to give reasons for the ways in which introducing home languages into the classroom has the potential to enhance students' learning [see Section 9.2 for a discussion of this topic]. However, it is important to avoid appearing condescending in offering advice of this sort. Parents frequently have more experience as language learners than do teachers. Teachers should make sure to enter into a two-way discussion about areas of this sort and listen carefully to parents' points of view.

8.3.3 Parents' and students' expectations about language-learning methodology

Many parents are impressed by the rate at which their children learn English in an international school and embrace the means that are used to achieve this outcome. They understand the value of a student taking part in whole-class activity in order to experience authentic language in use, and they appreciate the contribution made by specific English language teaching. A number of parents express concern, however, when their children fail to bring home vocabulary lists and grammatical exercises on a regular basis. Such parents often ask the class teacher (as well as the designated English language teacher) why their children do not bring home English language course books every night and may suggest that the school is not taking language learning seriously.

Teachers should be ready to articulate to parents the value of learning authentic English for immediate practical purposes rather than learning separated-out vocabulary and grammar. They should be prepared to offer evidence of the success achieved by emergent bilingual students in learning English in the school and describe the strategies that have led to these achievements, some of which may not be obvious to parents.

There remains a time and place for using well-constructed publishers' course books and online language-learning programmes for emergent bilingual students learning English. This comes with the proviso that the vocabulary and language is presented and eventually practised in authentic ways. Many students, particularly at the end of the school day, welcome time spent carrying out work which requires them to be less adventurous in their thinking and which allows them to build on what they already know. This applies particularly to students who have arrived in an international school from a more traditional school system.

Most of the major publishers of English language teaching (ELT) media offer an array of attractive and well-structured language- learning activities both in text and CD form as well as online. The names of several publishers are included in the Resources section at the end of this chapter.

Key Points in This Chapter

- Students and parents new to international schools arrive with expectations about teaching and learning that derive from their previous experiences of schooling.
- They may feel anxious and ill at ease with some of the standard pedagogic practices in international schools.
- Explaining the rationale behind the policies and practices in international schools is a key aspect of teachers' work with emergent bilingual students and their parents.
- Students need to understand how things work in the new school in order to succeed.
- The overall aim is to retain and build on the richness and diversity in an international school classroom, not to erase all traces of difference.
- Parents new to international schools may be surprised by the level of communication that is customary between the school and parents.
- Placing newly arrived students in an appropriate class can be a complex process and is sometimes a cause for concern with parents.
- Parents have expectations surrounding the learning of a new language which derive from their personal experiences.
- Parents have other concerns including the question of whether young students should learn to read and write in both their languages at the same time.
- Teachers should be ready to explain the language-learning methodology used in the school and to discuss language-learning issues.

Resources

Websites giving information about the way names are made up in different cultures
www.progenealogists.com/namingpattern.htm.
http://www.lacrosseconsortium.org/uploads/content_files/Good_Practice_Guideline_Names.pdf.

International education comparison scores
OECD Programme for International Student Assessment (PISA): www.oecd.org/pisa/.

Outside school tutorial classes
Kumon system classes originating in Japan: http://en.wikipedia.org/wiki/Kumon.

Links to publishers' English language teaching pages
The ELT link on the website of Oxford University Press provides an example of the range of resources available for teachers: http://elt.oup.com/catalogue.
See also Scholastic Inc: www.scholastic.com.

Online English language teaching materials

Language-learning apps and online packages also offer useful materials for use with emergent bilingual students with The Rosetta Stone (www.rosettastone.com) being one of the most well-known and widely used.

References

Baker, C. (2014) *A Parents' and Teachers' Guide to Bilingualism* (4th edn). Bristol: Multilingual Matters.

Sears, C. (2011b) Listening to parents: Acknowledging the range of linguistic and cultural experience in an early childhood classroom. In E. Murphy (ed.) *Welcoming Linguistic Diversity in Early Childhood Classrooms*. Bristol: Multilingual Matters.

9 Enabling Emergent Bilingual Students to Access the Language of the Classroom

Chapter 9 is devoted to strategies that give emergent bilingual students access to the language of the classroom. They include classroom practices that support language learning in general as well as actions on the part of the teacher designed to make individual items of communication more comprehensible.

The sequence of Chapter 9 is as follows:

- Introduction: creating a language-learning classroom.
- Factors in an effective language-learning experience.
- The role of students' mother tongues in an English-medium classroom.
- Strategies that make spoken and written communication comprehensible to emergent bilingual students.
- The language-learning value of PE, art, music, drama and extracurricular offerings.

Introduction: Creating a Classroom That Promotes Language Learning

Classrooms in most international schools contain students at differing levels of English language competence, from absolute beginners to increasing levels of proficiency. It is the teacher's responsibility to create a classroom environment that allows emergent bilinguals to access all the aspects of classroom and school life as far as possible.

Newly arrived students present the greatest challenge, whether they are beginning users of English and new to the world of international education, or more seasoned members of the international school community. In any case, teachers have an immediate need to communicate in a number of areas including:

- the day-to-day workings of school life: what time they have to be in school for registration, how they access the timetable/schedule for the day, where they go for classes, what they need to take with them, etc.;

- the basic logistics of life in school: where they can find the restrooms/toilets, the arrangements for meals, the pattern of school breaks and playtimes, where they meet the buses for their ride home, etc.;
- what they need to bring to school each day: stationery items, mobile technological devices where used (and charging instructions), PE kit, musical instruments, etc.;
- how they access information about homework assignments, future school events, class trips, drama and music rehearsals, etc. (many schools now manage communication in these areas by means of a virtual learning environment (VLE) or school website link, whereas other schools supplement their online communication with paper documentation, or via hard copy alone);
- how they can participate in class and school-related social events or school-sponsored activities such as the School Council or the school newspaper/magazine;
- how they find out when the try-outs (auditions or trials) for dramatic productions and school sports teams are scheduled (new emergent bilingual students often mention later that they missed out on trials for a team sport because they were not informed of the dates);
- access to content-area learning activities (the focus of Chapters 10–13 in this Handbook).

Many of the areas mentioned above are central to participation in school life. Very often, to be effective, communication needs to include parents as well as students. The overall aim is to prevent emergent bilingual students from feeling ill prepared or left out of the mainstream life of the school.

The content of this chapter

The first section of this chapter contains suggestions for creating classrooms that offer optimum conditions for students to learn the school language. The suggestions include the set-up of the classroom itself, the role of routines in creating an effective language-learning environment, approaches that reduce a student's level of anxiety and the value of acknowledging and reacting to emergent bilinguals' patterns of fatigue.

The focus in Section 9.2 is on the value of incorporating students' mother tongues (home or primary languages) into the ongoing teaching and learning in an English-medium classroom. This approach is increasingly being seen as making a valuable contribution to ensuring an additive outcome for emergent bilinguals. Section 9.3 contains a list of practical suggestions that make oral and written input more comprehensible to emergent bilingual students. The final section sets out the language-learning value of subjects such as PE, art, music and drama, along with that of extracurricular clubs and sporting activities.

9.1 Creating a Classroom That Promotes Language Learning

The way the classroom is set up can contribute to language learning, especially for newly arrived students. The key element is consistency: this applies to the placement of classroom supplies, the availability of reading material or audio equipment, the use of computers and the way that essential information is given or displayed.

9.1.1 Introducing students to the layout of the classroom and the use of classroom equipment

Teachers need to walk the students around the classroom, showing by example the ways in which the resources of the classroom are used, employing the same phrases and vocabulary as can be seen on the labels. Some of the new students in the class will come from school systems where independent use of classroom resources is not customary and where few technological resources are available. Classroom 'buddies' and teaching assistants are key contributors in this area, as are classroom peers, whether fellow-speakers of their language or from other language backgrounds. When students help one another, they offer both practical support and social contact.

- In the case of very young students, learning centres and play areas should be attractive, organised spaces that offer structured as well as free play opportunities.
- Elementary (primary) school students need to know where to keep their personal items and school texts, and where to find stationery and art supplies.
- All students need to be introduced to the class reference library and to be given directions about the use of the texts included in it. They need to be shown by example when it is appropriate for them to carry out independent research in this way.
- Audio and video equipment needs to be demonstrated and students need to be informed in advance and at the time when they are allowed to use it.
- All students need to understand the rules attached to computer use, including those that are connected to e-safety.
- Where a VLE is a part of school life, teachers should show by example the way that it functions and what it is used for.
- Where mobile devices are available, students should be instructed (and shown by example) how they are used in class.

9.1.2 Consistent routines: Consistent use of language

Emergent bilingual students benefit from a classroom where consistent routines are followed. This approach is valuable for all ages of students, although the routines themselves may differ. Following consistent routines is an approach that offers a degree of certainty about what is expected from students and reduces their anxiety level.

Consistent routines also offer emergent bilingual students an effective language-learning framework when the same phrases and vocabulary are used to describe regular happenings in the school day. Following this practice is in line with the acknowledged language-learning strategy of linking language with real-life activity and concrete circumstances. As the school year proceeds and students' confidence in their use of English increases, teachers can introduce different ways of expressing the same information. This serves as an effective means of widening students' knowledge of grammatical structure, phraseology and vocabulary without increasing uncertainty and anxiety.

Sometimes teachers of classes that contain students at different levels of English feel doubtful about employing strategies that may appear childish or simplistic to the proficient users of English in the class. Following consistent routines and using consistent language is a simple but effective strategy that is appropriate for use with all students. In classrooms, this approach may take the following forms with different age groups of students:

- With younger students, from the first day, teachers should follow consistent routines:
  - *Routines are supportive for young students around such events as the beginning of the school day. Young children feel more secure when they know that they are welcome and understand what is expected of them. Routines at this time of the day include being greeted consistently by the teacher and greeting other students, changing shoes, storing lunchboxes, hanging up school bags, and so on. Following routines in this manner is standard practice, in any case, with very young children. These simple activities are an opportunity for the introduction and practice of real-life language when it is used consistently.*
- In the case of elementary (primary) school students, classroom routines include activities that the students carry out independently:
  - *Activities of this type include students placing their clothing and personal items in a locker, on a peg or in a desk, having the right books to hand for a content-area class and knowing where specialist classrooms are to be found. Directing the class as they carry out these activities is an opportunity for the consistent use of language and thus for supported language learning.*
- In the case of both young and older students, English language learners benefit from a systematic approach in the content areas:
  - *One of the respondents in the research enquiry described in Appendix A mentioned that he found mathematics 'relaxing' because he always knew what was going to happen. The teacher would start with a discussion of the homework assignment on the SmartBoard, then give the class 10 minutes of 'mental math', as she called it, which the students enjoyed. Then new concepts were introduced, always with models and clear explanations, after which the teacher would write up on the board the page numbers in the textbook where students would find further examples and practice exercises. (In every class, she wrote these numbers in the same place on the board.)*

    She always, the student participant recounted, told the class that she was ready to answer questions about anything that had happened in class or about homework.

This type of structure, which is typically found in many classrooms, provides a firm foundation for language learning when consistent phraseology is used at each stage of the learning process.

9.1.3 Creating an anxiety-free classroom: Enabling students to take risks in their language learning

Being an early learner of English in an English-medium classroom carries inbuilt causes for anxiety and frustration, so the ambience of the classroom is a vital element in enabling students to feel comfortable and to reduce the overall pressure. This type of classroom can be created by avoiding actions that may make students feel insecure and by adopting strategies that boost their confidence and raise their self-esteem. (The topic of anxiety as a potential barrier to learning is discussed fully in Section 6.4.)

The following strategies are helpful in contributing to an anxiety-free classroom:

- avoiding correcting mistakes in spoken English in an overt manner;
- not pressurising students to contribute orally during an evident silent period (see Section 6.6 for an explanation of this term);
- ensuring that other students are courteous and respectful to new language learners;
- giving special explanations to emergent bilingual students on a one-to-one basis rather than during whole-class sessions;
- offering verbal cues and helpful phrases to emergent bilingual students before expecting them to answer questions out loud;
- varying the grouping of emergent bilingual students so that they are not always grouped with generally less able students;
- teachers limiting their use of idiom; idiom can be enriching and enjoyable for students who have a high level of proficiency in English but, for students who are less advanced, idiom introduces a non-comprehensible element to a piece of speech which excludes early learners of the language;
- teachers limiting humour which depends on a play on words or quick repartee; this is not to say that classrooms cannot be friendly and humorous places; it is vital, though, that early learners of English are able to join in the ongoing discourse of the classroom;
- allowing emergent bilingual students to help each other out in their home languages when that is possible and appropriate; using their home languages in an English-medium classroom reminds emergent bilinguals (and other students) of their competence and effectiveness in those languages, and it also underlines to first-language English speakers that becoming a bilingual is a challenging task which is worthy of respect;
- creating a classroom where trial and error and taking risks are applauded and treated as part of the normal mode of working;
- teachers being language learners themselves and talking about the process to students, including how challenging it can be;

- consistently employing strategies that enable emergent bilingual students to participate creditably in content-area learning (the topic of Chapters 10–13 in this
Handbook).

9.1.4 Virtual learning environments

Some schools use VLEs, or other web-based platforms, to manage the interaction
between teachers, students, parents and other members of the school community.
Access is gained by means of passwords which are made available to all appropriate
stakeholders. A VLE (sometimes known as a virtual learning platform or learning management system) supplies a set of interactive online services that provide individual
members of the school community with information, tools and resources. VLEs designed
for use in schools typically present user-friendly screens with click-on icons giving access
to interactive sites. These sites reflect such areas as administration, parents, individual
classes and content-area subjects within the school and the school community as a
whole. Most schools also have a system for setting up restricted-access student accounts.

Uses for students

Students click on the appropriate icon to find their homework assignments or to read
upcoming test content. The online capability enables teachers to expand the learning
potential of the task by suggesting learning strategies, listing printed and online
resources and setting out the assessment criteria that will be used to evaluate the work.
In some schools, VLEs allow students to upload their homework and gain access to an
immediate evaluation or correction. This approach is particularly appropriate for mathematics assignments. Some schools encourage students to make use of the application
that lists their marks/grades and test scores so that they can see the pattern of their
learning trajectory.

Further uses of VLEs

Other uses for VLEs are to post school policies and announcements for interested
members of the school community to read, and to supply platforms for communication
media such as school newsletters and limited-access blogs and chatrooms.

9.1.5 Virtual learning environments and emergent bilingual students

VLEs have the potential to enhance the language learning of emergent bilingual
students. The benefits include:

- Posting school schedules (timetables), including upcoming changes, notices about
sports teams, fixtures and travel arrangements, planned school closures, etc.
  - *The advantage for emergent bilingual students is that the information is grouped together
    on a single site and they are able to read, absorb and check the meaning of the notices in
    their own time and space. This approach also gives students time to check the content with
    their parents in their home languages. Posting important logistical information empowers
    emergent bilingual students so that they feel in control of their environment.*

- Allowing students time to read and re-read content that they may have heard only in speech or seen written on a whiteboard. This content may include classroom material, announcements, instructions, homework assignments, etc.
  - *Emergent bilingual students take longer to process and absorb spoken and written information, and are likely to need more time to note down the key points. Giving them time to read and consider the content gives them access to the same knowledge and understandings as proficient users of English who may have been quicker to pick up on vital areas of information.*
- Enabling students to upload their homework, in order to gain immediate evaluation and to receive supportive feedback from the teacher, can sustain their motivation to grapple with the challenges of language learning.
- Posting upcoming topics of study on a VLE for students and parents to read allows emergent bilingual students to carry out prior research either in their own language or in English.

9.1.6 Recognising fatigue patterns: Planning the day

Newly arrived emergent bilingual students who are early learners of English tend to suffer from fatigue as a result of being immersed in the new language. The reasons may differ from learner to learner. Some experience a sense of isolation if there is no-one present with whom they can speak their own language. Other students suffer from a sense of frustration and even humiliation because they cannot participate in the class at the level that they were previously able to attain. Many students become exhausted from trying to make sense of what they hear and from trying to find out what they are expected to do at any given point in the school day.

This fatigue tends to take on a recognisable pattern, with energy levels dipping at the end of the week and towards the end of teaching blocks. Experienced teachers in international schools accept the need to manage classroom activity so that new work is not presented in the latter part of the afternoon or the week immediately before a holiday.

The following strategies offer ways of providing a supportive learning environment during times when the concentration and energy levels of emergent bilingual students are running low.

- In the classrooms of young students, the afternoon is a time to consolidate the learning of the earlier part of the day with pleasurable activities.
  - *Sometimes quite simple manual tasks are enjoyable for fatigued young children, while still containing a useful learning component. Asking two young children from different language backgrounds to rearrange classroom supplies on shelves, or to tidy up learning or play areas, can be conducive to relaxed conversation involving colours, shapes, artefacts and objects, prepositions and verbs.*
- For students of elementary (primary) school age, where the teacher may be in a position to plan the day as a whole, the afternoon is often a good time for consolidatory

activity or for class content that is less challenging than the morning sessions of literacy and mathematics.

– *This is a time when tiring emergent bilingual students can be asked to work independently on enjoyable online material related to a class topic or to repeat an earlier activity in a new form. Best of all, perhaps, is for fatigued students to join with classmates in carrying out a communal task. Students continue to be engaged in language learning, but are not put under pressure to initiate new language themselves.*

• Older students who are beginning or intermediate English language students rarely have the luxury of a schedule or timetable where less challenging classes take place in the mornings. They may be faced with double science periods last thing in the afternoon, or may be asked to take a test at that time.

– *Where teachers have the option, this is a time when emergent bilingual students benefit most from collaborative activity with their peers. In the science classroom this can take the form of conducting experiments or creating a joint presentation online or in graphic form. In other subjects, when early users of English are wilting, it may be more conducive to learning to involve them in independent research on the computer where they can learn at their own pace rather than asking them to contribute to class discussions or to learn new material.*

9.2 The Role of Students' Home Languages in an English-medium Classroom

Emergent bilingual students benefit in many ways when they are able to draw upon their home languages within the classroom to deepen their understanding of content-area material they are studying in English. The process also contributes to an overall additive outcome by supporting and enhancing development in their home languages. A further effect of incorporating emergent bilinguals' home languages into the ongoing life of the class is to validate their identities as bilingual and bicultural individuals.

9.2.1 Moving between languages: Translanguaging

One approach to the teaching of emergent bilingual students is known as 'translanguaging'. Within this approach, students are encouraged to use their home languages as an integral part of the learning process, in contrast to classrooms where only the use of the school language is encouraged. As García (2009) states, outside the classroom:

> bilinguals translanguage to include and facilitate communication with others, but also to construct deeper understandings and make sense of their bilingual worlds. (García, 2009: 45)

In other words, left to themselves, bilinguals draw on both their languages when communicating with others and in making sense of what they experience.

According to Baker (2011):

Translanguaging is the process of making meaning, shaping experiences, under-standings and knowledge through the use of two languages. Both languages are used in an integrated and coherent way to organise and mediate mental processes in learning. (Baker, 2011: 288)

Text Box 9.1 More about translanguaging

Translanguaging as an approach to learning is based on a view of bilingualism which is different from 'diglossia'. Diglossia is a way of viewing a bilingual's languages as having boundaries, with each language having separate functions. This is the view that has underpinned the separation of languages in most bilingual schools and which has tended to result in students being taught in parallel language streams. The same thinking lies behind the practice in most English-medium schools of discouraging the use of students' home languages in mainstream classrooms. Practitioners in classrooms where translanguaging is a consistent pedagogic approach view their students' bilingualism as a rich resource for learning. They plan a systematic use of the two languages in the classroom.

Translanguaging is different from either 'code-switching' or 'translation'. Code-switching is the term used to describe moving between languages in sentences and short pieces of speech to get across an immediate meaning or to fill in gaps in knowledge of one of the languages. Translation involves the process of changing speech or text word by word into another language perhaps with the aid of a dictionary.

The process of translanguaging, according to Williams (2002), involves various cognitive skills. It entails using one language to reinforce the other in order to increase understanding and in order to augment the pupil's ability in both languages' (Williams, 2002: 40).

In classrooms where translanguaging is an integral part of the pedagogic approach, the following activities may be found:

Example 1: For a collaborative task in the content area:
(i) students discuss/reflect/negotiate content in the home language and share the results of their discussion with the rest of the class in English;
(ii) students brainstorm in the home language and write in English.

Example 2: For writing in different genres – letter writing:
(i) students use both English and the home language to write in the genre: they write letters, postcards or emails according to the language of the recipient;
(ii) students write in their home languages but negotiate editing/revising in English.

See the manual published online by the City University of New York, entitled *Translanguaging: A CUNY-NYSIEB Guide for Educators* (www.nysieb.ws.gc.cuny.edu/).

In classrooms where the use of the home language is excluded or overlooked, bilinguals are potentially denied a powerful tool for gaining access to the meaning of what they hear and read and of developing deeper understandings.

9.2.2 Translanguaging in bilingual international schools

The interest and relevance of this approach will be clear to teachers who are familiar with bilingual international schools or with English-medium international schools where most of the students in a class come from the local community and speak a single language. However, where teachers wish to introduce the translanguaging approach into a classroom that has been previously taught solely in one language, they will need to ensure that the senior management team in the school and the students' parents are comfortable with the practice. The tradition of separating a student's two languages is so deeply engrained that a great deal of discussion and practical evidence may be needed before teachers are able to introduce the embedded use of a further language.

A further aspect that needs consideration is the impact of extensive translanguaging on emergent bilingual students whose home language is neither of the languages in a bilingual school. The same concern holds good for the small numbers of students in English-medium classrooms where most of the students speak the local language. In both cases there is the obvious possibility of exclusion if teaching is carried out in two languages, neither of which is spoken by newly arrived students.

9.2.3 Translanguaging in international schools that serve a globally mobile population

In English-medium international schools that serve a globally mobile population of students, where classrooms can contain speakers of up to 20 different languages with a wide range of English language proficiency, there are similar questions to be raised about the viability of the translanguaging approach. How can teachers who may speak few of these languages monitor a classroom where students' home languages are in constant use alongside English?

The advocates of translanguaging themselves point out some of the potential issues that relate to its use in multilingual classrooms. Williams, one of the original creators of the term, himself states that translanguaging is effective in classes of stable bilingual students working in the same two languages. He also suggests that the approach is less effective with students who do not have a well-established basis in both languages (Williams, 2002). Both these elements tend to be missing in a typical international school classroom containing high numbers of emergent bilingual students, so translanguaging would need to be introduced with great care.

Nevertheless, translanguaging as an approach offers teachers of emergent bilingual students further ideas about viable ways of using the home languages of students to enhance their overall learning in an English-medium classroom. It underpins the value to students of continual development in both their languages, it helps teachers to view students' bilingualism in a more holistic light, and it provides a range of empowering strategies that can be adapted to give students more effective access to content-area learning. Strategies of this sort are included where applicable throughout this Handbook.

Note: For readers interested in finding out more about the possibilities of translanguaging, references to the following texts are set out in the Resources section at the end of the chapter: Baker (2011), García (2009), Lewis *et al.* (2012) and Williams (2002).

9.2.4 The interlingual classroom

A further contribution to the discussion about the value of incorporating students' home languages into the mainstream classroom is the concept of the 'interlingual' classroom. The chief advocate of this approach is Eithne Gallagher (2008), an experienced international school educator. For her, 'inter' stands for 'international-mindedness' and she argues that schools can only be seen to embrace international-mindedness if the languages and cultures of emergent bilingual students are a foundational part of their learning during the school day. Gallagher also emphasises the value of what she calls 'language awareness' as a means of raising the profile of all the language learning that is an integral feature of international school classrooms.

The value of incorporating students' mother tongues in day-to-day classroom teaching and learning is evident on a number of levels:

- When emergent bilingual students are encouraged to incorporate their mother tongues meaningfully into ongoing classroom activity, they retain a sense of value for their home languages and cultures.
  - *There is a tendency in an English-medium environment for students from other linguistic and cultural backgrounds to place less value on their own heritage (see Section 5.2). This is due to the potentially overwhelming status of English as a global language. Elective bilinguals in international schools may not experience this process in an extreme form, but many students learn to, or find it easier to 'smooth over' the obvious points of difference in their linguistic and cultural profiles while they are in school. One of the virtues of a 'language aware' classroom is that emergent bilingual students feel able to celebrate their status as bilingual learners.*
- Students' mother tongues can be used with good effect 'to clarify and support instruction' in an English-medium classroom (to quote a phrase taken from the *EAL Programme Handbook* on the Bavarian International school's EAL link (www.bis-school.com).

  There are several strategies involving the use of students' mother tongues that serve to underpin and reinforce their learning. These include:
  - *Ensuring that prior learning in students' home languages is brought into use when introducing a new topic or skill (e.g. science content, mathematics problems).*

- *Encouraging students to search in texts or online in their home language for outlines and information relating to a new topic. This can be a useful homework assignment. Knowledge of the general facts and overall concepts relating to a topic is an effective support for their later learning in English.*
- *Informing parents of emerging bilingual students in advance of the topics and themes that will be studied in class. In this way, parents can source appropriate materials in the home language to back up students' learning at home.*
- *Encouraging students to use their home language to search for references and examples that derive from their own history, geographical location and cultural landscape.*
- *Encouraging students to include real-life input by interviewing their family and friends overseas in their home language by means of Skype, etc.*

- When the mother tongue is placed at the centre of a student's learning, it highlights the value to emergent bilinguals of maintaining and developing their home languages.
  - *Emergent bilingual students need to be motivated to engage with studies in their home language on top of a full programme of studies in English. An assumption that their home languages and cultures are a valued and included element in their daily schooling serves to emphasise the value of maintaining these languages.*
- Teachers are key players in creating an internationally minded classroom. They exemplify this quality when they incorporate references to students' home languages and cultures into the daily work of the classroom.

Text Box 9.2 Empowering emergent bilingual students via use of the mother tongue

Every year, 11- and 12-year-old students from an international school in northern Europe make a four- or five-day field trip to the city of Florence in Italy. One year the group of around 120 students included Carlo, who had been at the school for just over 10 months and who himself came from the city. As an Italian speaker, from the first day of the preparation period, Carlo became deeply involved in the project. His teacher called upon him frequently to explain aspects of Italian culture and he was a valued facilitator during the 10-minute lessons in the Italian language that were held at the end of each day. A key element of preparation for the trip was an individual investigation by each student into an aspect of the Renaissance in Florence and its rôle in the history of art, politics, architecture, and so on. It was the custom for students to present their research in the form of an oral report standing in a location in Florence applicable to their topic.

Carlo had prepared a presentation on the topic of Machiavelli and his political text, *The Prince*. He chose to speak in front of a restaurant overlooking the Palazzo Vecchio, the seat of power of the Florentine Signoria. Wearing the strip of Fiorentina, the local soccer club (which he wore for the whole trip), Carlo launched forth on his presentation. He had prepared carefully, probably with the help of his parents, and had much to say. To start with he spoke entirely in English. Gradually he realised that an audience of local Florentines and tourists were gathering and that the people in the restaurant were listening. Quick to realise the possibilities for better communication, Carlo moved into bilingual mode and gave his presentation in both Italian and English, accompanied by copious hand gestures. At the end, as might be imagined, there was applause and shouts of 'bravo'. For the rest of the trip, it was difficult to keep Carlo's feet on the ground. It is a story that has entered the legends surrounding the yearly Florence trip.

On a more practical note, Carlo came to the fore on the trip in another rôle – as the translator and negotiator in instances where the teachers, whose combined Italian was limited, could not get their meaning across. On return to school Carlo remained a figure in the class who was perceived as advantaged by his command over two languages and cultures. The precise elements of Carlo's experience would be difficult to replicate, but the story gives an indication of the empowering effect of presenting the languages and cultures of emergent bilingual students in a celebratory and advantageous manner.

9.3 Strategies That Make Input Comprehensible to Emergent Bilinguals

As in most schools, teachers in international school classrooms deliver essential information via talk and writing. If emergent bilingual students are to participate fully in the life of the classroom, they must be able to access the meaning of what is being communicated. If they cannot comprehend much of what they hear and are expected to derive from reading, they are potentially excluded from all-school activities as well as the ongoing teaching and learning of the classroom.

9.3.1 Making input comprehensible

Note: Section 6.4 provides an account of Krashen's comprehensible input theory.

In schools that contain numbers of emergent bilingual students, it is a major part of the role of teachers to employ strategies that help to make their speech, or what they give students to read, more comprehensible. Strategies for increasing the ability of emergent bilinguals to understand what they hear and read include the following:

Talking and listening

• Make announcements and give information clearly:
  – *Teachers should announce by body language or other means that they are about to say something of importance. They should address the class in an audible voice and articulate words fully. Emergent bilingual students may not pick up on meaning if information is given as an aside or with the teacher's back to the class while writing on a whiteboard.*

- Maintain natural intonation:
  - *It is important that the major patterns of intonation are maintained in a piece of speech, although it is useful to pause in appropriate places. Emergent bilingual students need longer to process the language they hear.*
- Use body language and gestures to get meaning across.
- Use fewer idioms:
  - *As mentioned earlier in the chapter, a high use of idiom is potentially excluding and confusing.*
- Use here-and-now stimuli to introduce the topic of an announcement or an instruction:
  - *Introduce an important piece of information by setting it in a recognisable context. This can include showing a physical object or referring to something that is already familiar, as in: 'We need to talk about next week's trip to the art museum' alongside an appropriate image on a SmartBoard or an app link or brochure.*
- Rephrase using common words:
  - *When it is clear that some students may not have understood, rephrase a piece of speech in common words (although a visual prop will often be more effective). Write the original text on the class VLE link where appropriate.*
- Explain new words (or acronyms or slang not known to emergent bilingual students) using known words:
  - *Emergent bilingual students will benefit from definitions of new vocabulary that include words and concepts that they already understand. Learners' dictionaries in print and app form are useful aids for emergent bilinguals to check the meanings of words.*
- Encourage correct usage by rephrasing:
  - *When students struggle for words or make consistent errors, repeat a student's contribution in the correct form (in a tactful manner).*
- Check for understanding:
  - *Ask the whole class, and later ask individual students if they have questions about what they have just heard or read.*
- Rephrase what other students have asked or answered so that emergent bilinguals can understand.
- Allow students to explain to peers in their own language what they have heard or read:
  - *Emergent bilingual students gain a sense of support and camaraderie when they can share their understandings in their own language with peers. Teachers need to monitor this approach carefully, however. Students who are sole speakers of a language in a classroom may feel excluded if they do not have similar access.*

Writing and reading

- Write in a clean space:
  - *It is helpful to emergent bilingual students if teachers write on whiteboards and SmartBoards in a systematic and orderly manner. Where boards are covered haphazardly with script, it is more difficult for students to pick out essential information.*

- Give students time to copy:
  - *Learners of a language, especially if they are new to the use of Roman script, need more time to take down information in written form.*
- Use the same places consistently to write or post up written information:
  - *It is helpful to emergent bilingual students if teachers consistently post information relating to schedules, upcoming school events, school closures, etc. in the same places. This is true of classroom notice boards and online school sites.*
- Write answers and feedback on student work rather than using speech (or post them online on the student's link).
  - *Students may only partially understand what is said to them about their work. They will retain more from being able to see correct answers and read feedback. They can talk through the comments with their parents in their home languages.*

Time and timing
- Allow sufficient response time, sometimes called 'wait' time:
  - *Emergent bilingual students take longer to process language and to produce a response than proficient users of a language. This is true of class discussions and one-to-one sessions, and is also the case when students are expected to respond immediately to something written on a board. Teachers need to build in 'wait time' so that students do not feel under pressure to respond immediately. (Experienced teachers recognise that it is not only emergent bilingual students who will benefit from this approach.)*
- Create a classroom where students are prepared to wait quietly for their peers to process input and to construct an answer:
  - *Requiring proficient English speakers to wait quietly for their emergent bilingual peers to formulate an answer is a standard expectation in international school classrooms. Teachers can 'win' students over to an acceptance of the need to wait quietly by talking about the classroom being a community of language learners.*
- Put in place turn-taking rules so that all students get a chance to contribute in class discussions:
  - *Laying down rules for 'turn-taking' is a standard strategy in the classrooms of young students. In international school classrooms for all age groups there is a similar need to encourage all students to make a contribution in whole-class discussions. Strategies such as passing round a 'speaker's baton' or allowing individual students only one or two chances to contribute can be effective.*
- Give adequate notice of homework assignments, tests, the need to read extended reading passages, etc.:
  - *It is beneficial to emergent bilingual students if they are given as much notice as possible before a piece of work needs to be handed in, or to prepare for a test. It is helpful if this notice is given in writing either in print or online. Adequate notice enables students to consult with parents or the teacher in order to be well prepared.*
- Avoid making vital announcements just as the bell rings to mark the end of a class:
  - *Time is always short in classrooms and often teachers find themselves rushing to explain a homework assignment or the content of a test before the bell rings. This circumstance places*

emergent bilingual students under great pressure. They may be unsure of what is required of them and anxious to get to the next class.

Note: The link entitled 'A Guide to Learning English' on the website of the Frankfurt International School (http://esl.fis.edu/teachers/support/sum.htm) offers helpful information and advice for mainstream teachers in international schools. Of particular interest is the linked page, 'Feedback from ESL students' (http://esl.fis.edu/teachers/index-m.htm), where students set out the feedback that they would like to give to their mainstream teachers about their classroom experiences.

See also texts that cover the topic of making class communications comprehensible to emergent bilingual students (Carillo Syrja, 2011; Schiffer-Danoff, 2008).

9.4 The Value of PE, Music, Art, Drama and Extracurricular Offerings

Most emergent bilingual students look forward to their PE, music, art and drama classes (and IT classes where they exist separately). The practical content of these classes enables emergent bilinguals to participate on a more equal basis with their peers who are proficient users of English. Extracurricular clubs and activities have similar advantages and provide opportunities for relaxed sessions where language learning takes place alongside enjoyable participation in a chosen area of interest. Some of the advantages of participatory classes and activities of this type include:

- The nature of these classes and activities supplies the optimum setting for language learning:
  - *Teachers in classes of this type generally present new material in a concrete form. They illustrate the new item of content in a practical manner and offer models of what they want students to achieve. In most classes and clubs teachers give a practical illustration of how to achieve the desired outcome. This is an ideal way for students to be introduced to new vocabulary and structures. Such classes also provide effective opportunities to practise new language in an authentic setting. The focus on content rather than language tends to lead to a type of communication which is freer from anxiety.*
- Exhibiting a talent or being a good team player leads to positive social positioning for emergent bilingual students:
  - *Classes and activities that do not primarily rely on spoken and written language for effective participation are often the settings for changing the view of individual emergent bilinguals in a class or across the school. This is true even of schools that generally have an effective strategic approach to inclusion. Where emergent bilinguals are seen to contribute, their enthusiasm and skills lead to social inclusion and to the making of new friends. Part of a teacher's role in drawing emergent bilinguals into the mainstream of class life is to search out areas where they can display individual interests and talents.*

Such activities give students opportunities to contribute material that derives from their own cultural backgrounds. They also provide arenas where it is natural and appropriate for students to use their home languages with peers from similar backgrounds in order to engage more fully with the activity.

Text Box 9.3 Sport as a positive experience for emergent bilingual students

In an interview (transcribed as part of the research enquiry set out in Appendix A), a Japanese mother described how sport had been helpful to her daughter in building her self-confidence and in enabling her to move outside her perceived identity position as a limited speaker of English.

Researcher:	Does your daughter do any sport?
Mrs Takahashi:	Yes, she belongs to the volleyball team. She enjoys it very much.
Researcher:	Now, is that all nationalities?
Mrs Takahashi:	Almost 80% American. Yes, only two Japanese. And in the sports she can feel well accepted by others.
Researcher:	What other things would you say about volleyball?
Mrs Takahashi:	She enjoyed the activity of the volleyball and the people there were very helpful and she could give back – she could do something for the team.
Researcher:	So she could contribute. Is she quite a good player?
Mrs Takahashi:	I hope so. She feels self-confident.
Researcher:	Parents have said this to me so many times.

Key Points in This Chapter

- Effective classrooms allow emergent bilingual students to access all aspects of class and school life.
- Effective teachers of diverse classes consistently employ overall strategies that provide optimum conditions for students' language learning.
- Increasingly, students' home languages are viewed as a rich resource in the mainstream classroom.
- They can be used to good effect to clarify and support classroom instruction.
- Approaches such as translanguaging offer bilingual students the opportunities to draw on both their languages to enhance their learning and to gain deeper understandings.
- Teachers need to employ strategies to make input in speech and writing comprehensible to emergent bilingual students.

- They need to practise the consistent approaches that allow emergent bilingual students to make better sense of what they hear.
- They need to understand the consistent strategies that enable students to gain effective input from written material.
- Participative subjects such as PE, art, music and drama and extracurricular activities offer effective and enjoyable settings for language learning. The focus on content in these subjects creates an environment where the need to communicate involves less stress or potential for anxiety.

Resources

International school websites that offer useful information and advice on the topics in this chapter

The *EAL Programme Handbook* on the Bavarian International school's EAL link: www.bis-school.com. 'A guide to learning English' link on the International School of Frankfurt website: www.fis.edu/.

Translanguaging

Manual published online by the City University of New York, entitled *Translanguaging: A CUNY-NYSIEB Guide for Educators*: www.nysieb.ws.gc.cuny.edu/.

References

Baker, C. (2011) *Foundations of Bilingual Education and Bilingualism* (5th edn). Bristol: Multilingual Matters.

Carrillo Syrja, R. (2011) *How to Reach and Teach English Language Learners: Practical Strategies to Ensure Success*. San Francisco, CA: Wiley–Jossey-Bass.

Gallagher, E. (2008) *Equal Rights to the Curriculum: Many Languages, One Message*. Bristol: Multilingual Matters. An outline of the pedagogical approach set out in Eithne Gallagher's book from the perspective of multilingual students can viewed at: http://www.youtube.com/watch?v=-tFA0lPeSjU.

García, O. (2009) *Bilingual Education in the 21st Century: A Global Perspective*. Oxford: Blackwell.

Lewis, G., Jones, B. and Baker, C. (2012) Translanguaging: Developing its conceptualisation and contextualisation. *Educational Research and Evaluation: An International Journal of Theory and Practice* 18 (7), 655–670.

Schiffer-Danoff, V. (2008) *Reach & Teach English Language Learners: Levels, Strategies and Pixie Ideas*. Danbury, CT: Scholastic Inc. See www.creativeeducator.tech4learning.com for an extensive summary of the key points in the book

Williams, C. (2002) *Ennill iaith: Astudiaeth o sefyllfa drochi yn 11–16 oed* [*A Language Gained: A Study of Language Immersion at 11–16 Years of Age*]. Bangor: School of Education. See http://www.bangor.ac.uk/addysg/publications/Ennill_Iaith.pdf.

Part 5

Working With Emergent Bilingual Students in the Mainstream Academic Programme

The focus of Part 5 is on working with emergent bilingual students in the content areas of the curriculum. The concept that underpins the chapters is that classroom teachers are responsible for emergent bilinguals' language learning as well as for delivering the mainstream curriculum. Acknowledging that programmes and curricula in international schools take different forms, the suggestions in all four chapters are designed to be applicable in as many contexts as possible.

Writing About Embedded Digital Technology

Many international schools are at the forefront of the use of technology in schools. This is a field that moves forwards at an astonishing pace with new programs and mobile applications (apps) being constantly introduced. Bearing in mind the speed of change, the decision has been made to refer largely to the generic technological applications available to teachers. Where named sites and apps are mentioned, it is on the understanding that they have been introduced to provide examples. There is no intention to suggest that individual apps and programs are the sole means of providing useful input into a given area. This is an important point, since on the ground, schools generally limit the numbers of applications available to students to a carefully chosen selection. The overall aim is to suggest where technology provision can enhance the work of teachers with emergent bilingual students.

10 Key Strategies for Use With Emergent Bilingual Students in the Content Areas of the Curriculum

Chapter 10 provides the theoretical background for the pedagogic approaches that underpin the practical suggestions set out in Chapters 11, 12 and 13 of this Handbook. The chapter is based on the premise that teachers are responsible for the English language learning of the emergent bilingual students of their classrooms as well as for delivering the mainstream curriculum. Integrating content and language learning is an effective means of promoting a positive outcome for emergent bilingual students in mainstream classrooms. Professional development opportunities for teachers who work in integrated classrooms are also included.

The sequence of Chapter 10 is as follows:

- Introduction: 'Every teacher in an international school is a language teacher'.
- What is integrated content and language learning?
- Scaffolding the learning of emergent bilingual students.
- The use of differentiated instruction in classes that contain emergent bilingual students.
- Training opportunities for teachers in international schools in the integrated content and language-learning approach.

Introduction: Every Teacher in an International School is a Language Teacher

The statement 'every teacher is a language teacher' is current in international schools. It is used as a means to remind teachers in classrooms containing high numbers of emergent bilingual students of their role as language teachers as well as deliverers of the mainstream curriculum.

Note: The latest Accreditation Instrument issued jointly by the Council for International Schools (www.cois.org) and the New England Association of Schools and Colleges (www.neasc.org) includes the following statement under its standards designed to assess the quality of teaching practice in a school:

> Teaching methods [should] provide appropriately for students for whom English (or other languages of instruction) is the not the first language.

Increasing numbers of emergent bilingual students in international schools

In most international schools, especially those that cater for a mobile community, the numbers of emergent bilingual students have increased over the years. One international school in northern Europe is typical of this pattern. In the mid-1980s, only around 25% of the students in the school spoke languages other than English. By 2010, the figure was nearly 70%. This change is replicated in international schools across the world. In English-medium schools or bilingual schools that cater for local populations, the percentage of students who speak languages other than English can be as high as 95%.

With these numbers of emergent bilingual students in international schools, it is no longer feasible to view them as a minority group – they are now the mainstream. As a result of the change in student profiles, two strategic approaches have been incorporated into the policies and practice found in many international schools: that of in-class support from specialist English teachers for emergent bilingual students and the integration of language learning with content-area learning. Chapters 10–13 are concerned with the latter approach.

Integrating language and content instruction

The first section of this chapter introduces the concept of integrating the teaching of content and language. It sets out the range of theoretical and practical approaches that combine language and content instruction in the mainstream classroom.

Section 10.2 introduces the practice of instructional scaffolding as a means to integrate content and language learning. It sets out the features that are typical of effective instructional scaffolding. In Section 10.3 the use of differentiated instruction in classrooms containing emergent bilingual students is discussed and, finally, in Section 10.4 some of the professional development opportunities for teachers working in international school classrooms are explained.

Text Box 10.1 Morning mantra

There is no need for teachers to feel overwhelmed by the demands of implementing an integrated language and content learning approach to working with emergent bilingual students. Teachers entirely new to the approach are advised at first to offer a small number of carefully targeted strategic modifications until they build up confidence and experience. Whatever stage teachers have reached in their understanding and practice in these methods there remain some basic precepts for diverse classrooms that have the ability to affect positively the experience of emergent bilingual students. The most important of these is to provide an encouraging, consistent and upbeat environment. The following 'morning mantra' was well received and triggered much discussion at a number of conferences and workshops:

- Get to know your students.
- Understand the pattern of your students' English language development.
- Learn the language of the host country – become a language learner yourself.
- Build upon your students' prior learning.
- Supply models to show students what they should aim for.
- Enable your students to succeed by scaffolding their learning.
- Provide supports to lead them through a task.
- Provide technology to enhance learning and incorporate diversity into content areas.
- Have high expectations of your emergent bilingual students.
- Celebrate your students' achievements.
- Have fun in the classroom.

10.1 Approaches to Integrating Language and Content Instruction

Integrative approaches to content and language teaching have different names and have developed in different ways. They share the following goals:

- to give emergent bilingual students access to content-area knowledge and understandings delivered in the school's language of instruction;
- to promote the development of proficiency in the school language of instruction (in international schools, often English).

On the ground, the two aspects are interlinked and mutually beneficial. Focusing on content-area learning offers students chances to construct meaning from authentic language used in real-life contexts, and to practise it. Acquiring the authentic spoken and written language needed to participate in the mainstream curriculum results in students being able to engage fully in content-area learning.

Teachers in classrooms that offer an integrated approach to content and language learning take an active strategic view of the needs of emergent bilingual students. The strategies set out later in this chapter and in the following three chapters are designed to help teachers create this sort of classroom.

Integrated content and language instruction

The following definition broadly covers the teaching approaches that integrate content and language instruction:

> Through integrated content and language instruction, second language learners develop the ability to generate thoughtful spoken and written discourse about concepts in the content area and proficiency in understanding and producing the types of texts specific to that area. Students also develop the ability to carry out other content-related tasks, such as lab experiments, creative mathematics calculations, and historical enquiry. They solve problems, evaluate solutions, and collaborate effectively with one another in these activities through the use of appropriate academic language. (Sherris, A. (2008) *Integrated Content and Language Instruction.* CAL Digest. Washington, DC: Center for Applied Linguistics: www.cal.org)

The author of the CAL Digest (2008) later admits that the challenge of designing and delivering lessons that make content comprehensible and that facilitate language acquisition is 'of no small order'. However, he goes on to emphasise the positive impact that this approach has on students learning in a second language.

Varieties of integrated language and content-area instruction

Several forms of integrated language and content instruction have evolved over the years in response to different language-learning needs. The different forms are referred to by different names and newly arrived teachers may come across these programmes described in the following ways: content-based instruction (CBI), content and language integrated learning (CLIL), sheltered instruction (SI) and language across the curriculum (LAC).

Table 10.1 sets out briefly the main features of the different forms of integrated language and content-area instruction to be found in international schools. New teachers may find it helpful to understand the sort of classroom practice that is being referred to when they hear these terms.

Integrated language and content instruction in international schools

Content-based instruction (CBI) is an overall term used to describe integrated content and language instruction in a variety of contexts. These contexts include ESL-immersion, bilingual education and foreign language education.

Originally linked to the development of immersion bilingual education in Canada, CBI is used in the USA, among other locations, to improve outcomes in second language learners. This is a sector of the population in the US which, according to Thomas and Collier (2002), who have spent years in researching outcomes in American schools, has been underserved by the educational system. CBI is the form of integrated language and

Table 10.1 Features of the forms of integrated language and content-area instruction found in international schools

Form of integrated language and content instruction	Main features	Wider contexts where it is to be found	Its use in international schools	Comments
Content-Based Instruction (CBI) (See the Resources section at the end of this chapter for more weblinks)	The target language is viewed as a vehicle for content-area learning rather than an immediate object of study in itself. Gives students access to content-area learning.	Used in Canada and the US (among other locations) to improve outcomes for second language learners.	CBI under different names is the form of integrated content and language area learning that ideally underlies the practice to be found in international schools	International schools rarely refer to CBI by name, although many schools would accept the responsibility of mainstream teachers to teach language as well as content. The training courses most frequently taken up by international school teachers tend to be based on CBI.
Content and Language Integrated Learning (CLIL) (See the Resources section at the end of this chapter for more weblinks)	Students learn a target language (often a foreign language) by using it as the vehicle of communication in a content area such as social studies or science.	Generally to be found as an approach in schools in Europe, partly due to sponsorship and promotion by the EU.	CLIL in international schools tends to be used to enhance the learning of a foreign language via a content subject such as history.	In national systems in Europe, students from majority language backgrounds tend to be exposed to the CLIL approach as a means of learning a prestigious foreign language. Their status as majority language speakers in their own countries may account for the success of CLIL as shown by research.

(Continued)

Table 10.1 (Continued)

Form of integrated language and content instruction	Main features	Wider contexts where it is to be found	Its use in international schools	Comments
Sheltered Instruction (SI) (See the Resources section at the end of this chapter for more weblinks)	Used to give early learners of English access to content-area learning in subjects such as social studies and science. Teachers in SI classrooms supply a high degree of scaffolding to promote student participation and understanding. Usually provided for older students, such classes tend to be taught by subject area teachers with an interest (or training) in language learning.	Adopted in the US to promote the content-area learning of second language students with the aim of raising the overall achievement level of this group. US educational publishers offer textbook series that support sheltered classrooms.	Used in international schools generally at the upper levels to ensure that emergent bilingual students continue to develop their content-area learning while they are learning English.	Sheltered classrooms in international schools tend to be viewed as an interim support strategy. The aim is to move students on to mainstream learning as soon as possible. This is to counter the view that sheltered classrooms in national systems limit the access of second language learners to higher level mainstream learning.
Language Across the Curriculum (LAC) (See the Resources section at the end of this chapter for more weblinks)	A schooling system that adopts an LAC approach accepts the need to teach the language required to function in the content areas of the curriculum.	A broad LAC approach has led to the inclusion in several schooling systems, noticeably the UK and Hong Kong, of language-learning targets alongside content targets in the subject area such as social studies, science and mathematics.	In some British-based international schools, LAC is the approach that underpins the learning of language alongside content-area learning in the mainstream classroom.	The focus on language in the LAC approach does not necessarily include the scaffolding of content-area learning.

content instruction that best describes the approach that teachers in international schools use with diverse classes.

In international schools, the implementation of integrated language and content instruction varies from school to school and often from classroom to classroom in the same school. In international schools where there has been a commitment to train teachers by means of one of the major training programmes (mentioned in Section 10.4 below), it is possible to find widespread use of the approaches that are typical of CBI. (These approaches are the focus of Chapters 11, 12 and 13 in this Handbook.) However, in schools where that commitment has not been made, the use of integrated approaches is patchy and left largely up to individual teachers. In this case, many teachers take it upon themselves to read texts and online material and to attend conference presentations when they have the chance, in order to equip themselves to work effectively with emergent bilingual students. Sometimes it is members of specialist English language teaching departments who instigate professional development courses within their schools.

The website of the Center for Advanced Research and Language Acquisition (CARLA) gives a useful background to the development and rationale for CBI on a link entitled 'Content-based second language instruction: What is it?', available at: www.carla.umn.edu/cobaltt/cbi.html.

10.2 Scaffolding the Learning of Emergent Bilingual Students in Supportive Classrooms

Instructional scaffolding is a practical means of implementing content-based language learning. It provides emergent bilingual students with a framework of pedagogic and linguistic support which allows them access curriculum content.

> ### Text Box 10.2 A brief guide to the development of scaffolding theory and practice
>
> The term 'scaffolding' was first used by Wood *et al.* (1976) to describe the way in which parents use informal instructional formats when talking to their young children. By employing scaffolding, parents extend their children's use of language and widen their understanding of the world.
>
> Bruner, a cognitive psychologist, observed that when parents engage with their children they instinctively use language that provides a broadly comprehensible framework onto which they graft a limited amount of new material. When parents do this, their children are helped to grasp the meaning of new content by building on familiar forms of expression. A further element commonly present when parents and young children converse is the physical presence of the thing being discussed.

(Continued)

Text Box 10.2 A brief guide to the development of scaffolding theory and practice (*Continued*)

In Ninio and Bruner (1978) the idea of scaffolding was extended via an investigation into the ways that parents read stories aloud to children.

The use of scaffolding as a general learning approach parallels the work of Lev Vygotsky (1987 [1934, 1960]) and his concept of proximal development. Within this conceptual framework, a zone of proximal development lies between what learners can do unaided and what they can do with the help of an adult and, by extension, some sort of pedagogical support. Vygotsky's view was that children can be taught effectively by implementing scaffolding practices, thereby bridging the gap (i.e. the zone of proximal development) and enabling children to take on a higher level of new learning than they could do unaided.

In practice, the effectiveness of scaffolds depend on students building on what they already know in order to make sense of and take on board new knowledge. The scaffold acts as a bridge between prior knowledge and new material. Several studies written up in Bransford *et al.* (2000) indicate that students who are left to cope unaided with little personal support from the adults around them, or with few guided learning experiences, fail to develop linguistically or academically to an optimum level. These findings are in line with the research of Thomas and Collier (2002) into the experience of students in unsupported immersion classrooms.

10.2.1 The view of instructional scaffolding that underpins this Handbook

The version of instructional scaffolding to be found in this Handbook takes the widest possible view of what it comprises. Within this view, scaffolding is taken to include not only pedagogic approaches but also teacher actions that promote supportive classroom environments as a whole. The following list of features that contribute to effective scaffolding reflects this inclusive viewpoint.

10.2.2 Features of effective instructional scaffolding

Supportive classrooms for emergent bilingual students are spaces where:

- teachers have high expectations for emergent bilingual students;
- emergent bilingual students are given authentic and engaging learning tasks;
- students are encouraged to take risks and the classroom is a place that is accepting of mistakes;
- teachers guide students in acquiring the learning behaviours needed for success in the school programme;

- teachers introduce students to the practice of shared and collaborative learning in whole-class situations and small groups;
- students are provided with models of the work they are expected to produce;
- students' home languages and personal experience are incorporated into ongoing classroom activity and homework.

Teachers engage in consistent and effective planning that:

- acknowledges the needs of emergent bilingual students;
- ensures their participation in classroom activity based on an understanding of their level of English language development;
- sets out clear targets for content-area learning;
- includes explicit teaching of the language needed to participate in content-area learning;
- ensures cognitively challenging tasks that require learners to engage with cognitive academic language;
- builds in instructional groupings that provide models of authentic language in use and opportunities to practise it;
- involves collaboration between professionals working in the classroom, including teaching assistants and specialist English language teaching colleagues.

Teachers build on what emergent bilinguals know by:

- activating and incorporating students' prior knowledge and experiences into classroom learning;
- viewing emergent bilingual students' home cultures, histories, geographies and national viewpoints as valuable resources for classroom activity.

Teachers use ongoing assessment to:

- monitor and evaluate each student's progress;
- inform future instructional decisions;
- provide an appropriate level of instructional scaffolding so that students can participate in classroom learning.

Teachers provide:

- templates, frames, guides and verbal supports that enable emergent bilingual students to engage with authentic language and content-area learning (detailed suggestions and examples of the use of such scaffolds in the content areas are given in Chapters 11, 12 and 13);
- opportunities for students to draw upon the resources of technology to enhance their learning.

Instructional scaffolding is an approach that is equally valid for use in the range of programmes and curricula to be found in international schools. This includes the enquiry-based and trans-disciplinary approaches of the Primary Years Programme and Middle Years Programme of the International Baccalaureate Organisation (IBO) and others, and the teacher-directed approaches that often derive from the national curricula of English-speaking countries.

Note: See the Resources section at the end of this chapter for publications that offer further information about scaffolding.

10.3 Differentiated Instruction

Many teachers who arrive new in international schools will be familiar with the concept and practice of differentiated instruction. Differentiation provides an effective framework for classrooms that include diverse students including emergent bilingual students, students with special educational needs and students who are recognised as being gifted.

Instructional scaffolding is a form of differentiation designed primarily to support emergent bilingual students. As an approach it fits perfectly in a classroom where other forms of differentiation are practised.

10.3.1 Brief description of differentiation

Differentiation is modified instruction that helps students with diverse learning needs to master the same academic content. Effective differentiation, like effective instructional scaffolding, is dependent on an awareness of each student's current level of understanding and achievement and their individual learning needs. With this knowledge, teachers are able to provide appropriately differentiated learning tasks and activities.

10.3.2 Effective differentiated classrooms offer the following

- *Differentiated instruction based on existing evidence of students' learning:*
    When teachers have evidence of a student's present level of knowledge, skills and understanding in a given area they are able to plan instruction that provides learning activities at an appropriate level, rather than following 'a one size fits all' approach. Evidence for constructing a student's learner profile includes:
    - classroom performance assessed against criteria and tracked on checklists;
    - literacy and numeracy assessments;
    - content-area assignments and projects;
    - level of independence as a learner;
    - level of English proficiency across the skills;
    - students' view of their own learning.
    Note: See Section 7.1 for a fuller account of assessment approaches in international schools

- *Teaching and learning approaches that reflect differences in students' learning styles:*
    Differences in students' learning styles may be individual or arise out of previous experiences. Howard Gardner (1983) has suggested reasons for differences in the ways in which individuals learn with his theory of multiple intelligences. According to Gardner, there are different sorts of intelligence that individuals may bring to bear on the way they learn. An individual student may exhibit the use of one or several intelligences in approaching a learning task. These are known as a student's preferred intelligences and may include (according to Gardner) verbal-linguistic intelligence, logical-mathematical intelligence, spatial intelligence and intrapersonal intelligence, among others. In the classroom, this theory backs up the practical experiences of teachers who recognise that different students learn better via different sorts of teacher input.
    More generally, emergent bilingual students may exhibit different customary learning modes as a result of prior educational experiences in different schooling systems. Experienced teachers recognise that new emergent bilingual students may be accustomed to learning in ways that are different from those in most international schools. (See Chapter 8 for a discussion of the learning culture of international schools and its impact on new students.)
    Presenting material via multiple pathways and offering differentiated learning activities is an effective means of tapping into individual learner profiles and preferred learning styles.
- *Choices in learning activities that tap into students' interests:*
    When students' own experiences and interests are activated by the ability to make choices, this tends to motivate them to learn more effectively.

10.3.3 Practical examples of differentiation

Reading groups

It is current practice in many schools to group students by ability for reading. Students are provided with texts at different levels which offer the appropriate level of challenge. The texts may also be differentiated by such factors as level of illustration or related audio and video material. Examples of interactive texts at varying levels can be found online and are motivating to many students. Teachers or assistants interact with students to provide different levels of guidance in the skills of reading.

Grouping for mathematics

Grouping for mathematics is currently widely used. The most usual form of grouping is by ability, although sometimes students are grouped across ability levels when carrying out hands-on mathematics projects. Where the groups are divided by ability, each group may work on materials that offer different levels of challenge. Another variable factor is the degree of teacher intervention and support.

Different levels of oral input, print and online media, and video and audio clips may be used to introduce new content-area material

Different ways of accessing new material offer students a range of ways of interacting with content by tapping into different learning styles, personal interests and levels of English.

Variation in degree of learner independence offered to students

Teachers choose the level of intervention and type of support they offer to students. Able students may thrive on being left to get on with a task by themselves. Other students will react positively to support in the form of encouragement or practical suggestions. Small groups of students may be offered mini-lessons on areas of new learning according to need.

Offering differentiated ways of students displaying their knowledge

Students are given choice in the ways they can demonstrate their mastery of content. The choices may include posters, cartoons, PowerPoint presentations, annotated storyboards, newsletters, or dramatising a scene from a play to demonstrate understanding of character, narrative and concept.

Differentiated assessment methods

In a differentiated classroom, the aim is to select tools and strategies that allow students to show what they know. Being flexible in assessing student learning is particularly applicable to working with emergent bilingual students whose English may not be sufficiently developed to be able to express what they know. Options include:

- students writing about what they know in their home languages and using the text to explain their knowledge and understanding in English;
- students keeping learning logs and journals;
- students being given more time to carry out a whole-class assessment activity;
- students writing what they know about a topic in their own words rather than writing in response to questions;
- students displaying their learning via bullet points, online flowcharts, sketches, diagrams, structured paragraphs with lead questions provided by the teacher, or via teacher-created cloze tests with significant words omitted;
- students working with peers to offer an account of what they have learnt together.

See Section 7.1 for a fuller account of assessment as a whole.

Embedded technology used to differentiate levels of support, learning tasks and means of displaying learning

Technology is a powerful tool for differentiating student experiences during all the phases of content-area learning. It can be used to provide different levels of content material for individual research and enquiry, it can be used to source frames and graphic organisers with different levels of support and it can supply a range of means for students to display their learning either individually or in partnership with their peers.

10.3.4 Issues surrounding differentiation

Some aspects of differentiation, such as grouping students by ability for reading and mathematics, are so widely used in classrooms that it is easy to continue the practice without questioning some of the issues that potentially surround their use. The same is true of approaches that offer students differentiated learning tasks and alternate means of displaying their learning.

In the case of emergent bilingual students, there are a number of questions that teachers should often ask themselves:

- What are the grounds for placing individual students in ability-based reading and mathematics groups? Has the decision been made on the grounds of their understanding of content or on the level of their English language competence?
- If an appropriate level of instructional scaffolding were supplied, would emergent bilingual students remain in the same groups?
- Is there a system in place to ensure that emergent bilingual students who are competent mathematics students are encouraged to use their prior knowledge to support their learning of mathematics in English?
- What is the mechanism for ensuring that emergent bilingual students move into new groups as soon as is appropriate?
- When grouping for collaborative enquiry or carrying out a group project, what are the criteria for the formation of the groups? Where are emergent bilingual students placed? Do they get a chance to join an able group of students?
- When taking part in collaborative work, what do emergent bilingual students tend to be asked to contribute? Do they appear to be doing a great deal of map making, drawing or cutting out?
- Is embedded technology used to the best advantage in offering an appropriate degree of challenge to emergent bilingual students? Are the games and activities provided on computers and tablets always meaningful and relevant to student learning?
- Do teachers draw upon emergent bilingual students' competence in their home languages to provide alternate means of gathering information or working at a cognitively challenging level?
- Do teachers ask students to write about what they know in their home language as a means of assessing their understanding of concepts? Their English may be sufficiently developed to write about their knowledge of facts but not to explain concepts. With the help of adult or fellow speaker of the same language with a greater level of English proficiency, they may be able to express their meaning in English based on their prior work in their home language.

Note: This is an opportunity for a CAS student who speaks the same language to contribute. 'Community, Action, Service' (CAS) is a compulsory component of the IB Diploma programme. Some students choose to fulfil their CAS component by volunteering in the classrooms of younger students.

10.3.5 Emergent bilinguals in differentiated classrooms

The overall message when running a differentiated classroom is to keep in mind that emergent bilinguals may be effective learners in their own languages and school systems. It is vital that emergent bilingual students are not placed in groups based solely on their level of English at a given time. It is the teacher's responsibility to offer modifications in the form of scaffolding and differentiation that allow students to continue learning at an appropriate cognitive academic level.

Note: Weblinks that offer practical guidance about differentiation are included in the Resources section below.

10.4 Professional Development Opportunities for Teachers in International Schools

Unlike most schools in national systems, teachers in international schools do not automatically experience an ongoing programme of professional development. Most international schools are independent organisations and are responsible for setting up their own training programmes according to the school's perceived needs. The possibilities for professional development therefore tend to vary from school to school, although generally schools do accept the need to offer training opportunities to their teachers.

10.4.1 Potential professional development opportunities

Programme coordinators

As mentioned in Section 4.4, the programme or subject coordinators that most schools put in place are immediate sources of professional training and advice for newly arrived teachers. This group includes the IB coordinators that are mandated for each of its programmes as well as the curriculum and examination coordinators that exist in most schools. It is the job of these individuals to coordinate their areas of responsibility and to act as professional mentors for new teachers.

Conferences and workshops offered by regional international school associations

The conferences and workshops offered by regional international school associations provide another source of training for teachers. These conferences are either general in nature or focused on a specific subject area. The European Council of International Schools (ECIS) ESL and Mother Tongue conference held every three years is an example of a conference where language teachers and mainstream teachers from all over the world can meet for in-depth discussion of these areas and to hear about the latest research and practice. Because of the international outreach of the international school organisations, very often they have access to some of the key names in a field, and this is true in the area of second language acquisition. Most of the names mentioned in this

Handbook, for instance, have contributed to general or specialist conferences, often offering full-day workshops in the days before the conference begins which explore a topic more fully.

Conferences and workshops offered by the IBO

The IBO offers a range of conferences and workshops, usually region by region or at its various headquarters, designed to provide training to teachers engaged in its programmes. The training offered at these meetings is targeted at different groups of educational professionals, ranging from programme coordinators through to new teachers who are unfamiliar with the pedagogic approaches that are embedded in the programmes.

Universities offering programmes in international education

A further possibility for gaining focused professional development in the area of second language acquisition is to sign up for an appropriate Master's degree or PhD course at one of the universities offering programmes in international education. Some examples of university-based courses are included in the Resources section at the end of this chapter. Such universities design their courses around the working life of teachers. Thus, most of the available courses consist of summer schools held during the long summer break together with a series of assignments to be completed during the school year. To complete an extended course of this type takes a great deal of commitment and motivation on the part of a working teacher. However, educators who have completed these courses speak of the confidence and professional enrichment they have gained from the course itself and from personal and online contact with colleagues who share the same interests.

The ECIS International Teacher Certificate (ITC)

The ITC (www.internationalteachercertificate.com) is a further option for teachers in international schools. The ITC was initiated and is administered by ECIS and assessed by Cambridge International Examinations. It may sound European focused but its teacher students come from schools all over the world – as an extensive list on its website indicates – and its content is applicable worldwide. It is also the only non-university pathway to gaining the IB Certificate in Teaching and Learning. The Certificate comprises several components, including:

- a three-day workshop at a range of locations (the present advertised sites are in Cambridge in the UK, Istanbul in Turkey, Atlanta in the US and Kuwait);
- individual research and school-based practice supported by the ITC VLE;
- a portfolio requiring around 220 hours of work over 12–14 months.

The special benefits of the ITC include its applicability to teaching in all types of international schools and its focus on working with the range of students to be found in those schools. It is one of the few generally available professional development opportunities that places the needs of globally mobile emergent bilingual students at the heart of the programme. This feature is clear from the headings that describe the five modules making up the ITC:

(1) Education in an intercultural context (develop a greater understanding of intercultural perspectives).
(2) Teaching competencies for the international teacher (demonstrate competencies in international-mindedness; enhance knowledge of global themes, issues and perspectives; promote active learning and collaboration among diverse learners).
(3) The language dimension (create a positive learning environment for students of different language backgrounds).
(4) Student transition and mobility (improve practice and establish better transitions procedures within the school).
(5) Continuing professional development as an international educator.

10.4.2 Programmes designed to deliver training in integrated language and content-area learning instruction

The Sheltered Instruction Observation Protocol (SIOP) model

The SIOP model training programme is widely available in the form of live sessions and online. This programme is specifically designed to train teachers in creating an integrated language and content-based classroom. Teachers are able to sign up to SIOP institutes, conferences, virtual workshops and district trainings and to buy a range of books and resources. A typical text is entitled: *The SIOP Model for Teaching Mathematics to English Learners*.

The SIOP Model is sponsored by the Center for Applied Linguistics in Washington, DC: www.cal.org/siop/about/index.html.

Information for SIOP training and texts can be found on the website of the provider, Pearson Education: http://siop.pearson.com/.

ESL in the Mainstream

The programmes offered under the banner of 'ESL in the Mainstream' were created by the Department for Education and Child Development of the State of South Australia (www.unlockingtheworld.com/programs/teaching-esl-students-in-mainstream). Several programmes are offered, but the most widely taken up by international schools is the course entitled 'Teaching ESL students in mainstream classrooms: Language in learning across the curriculum'. As can been see from the schedule set out on the website, these programmes are offered across the world, often with international schools acting as hosts. At the time of writing, teachers may attend ESL in the Mainstream courses in China, Indonesia, Hong Kong, Qatar, and at various international schools in Europe.

The aims of the course given on its website spell out its commitment to integrated content and language learning.

The program:

• identifies the language-related needs of ESL students and develops teaching practices that address their needs in a holistic and explicit manner

- develops teachers' awareness of how to accommodate the cultural and linguistic diversity and experiences of ESL students
- provides a positive context for teachers to trial suggested strategies and reflect critically and openly on their teaching

Take-up of ESL in the Mainstream training in international schools

ESL in the Mainstream is especially effective for teachers in international schools, since the providers have to some extent tailored their offering to fit the profile of these schools. Teachers who have had access to ESL in the Mainstream find that it contributes greatly to their professional understanding and practice in the classroom. For this reason, some enlightened international schools consistently offer their teachers the opportunity of travelling to a training centre, or make the decision to host a course themselves.

Key Points in This Chapter

Integrated language and content instruction

- Integrated language and content instruction enables emergent bilingual students to acquire the language needed to participate in content-area learning.
- CBI is the form of integrated language and content instruction on which much of the integrated teaching in international schools is based.
- Curriculum content is used as a vehicle for providing authentic language-learning opportunities.
- Integrated classrooms are places where students are offered meaningful and engaging learning experiences.
- Embedded technology offers students independence in structuring their own path through a learning task.

Instructional scaffolding

- Instructional scaffolding provides a practical means of enabling emergent bilingual students to engage with CBI.
- Instructional scaffolding leads students step by step through learning tasks.
- Ongoing assessment of an individual student's present level of language-learning development is a key element in supplying instructional scaffolding at an appropriate level.

Differentiation and emergent bilingual students

- Teachers arriving new in international schools may be familiar with the concept of differentiated instruction.
- It is an approach that sits well with integrated language and content instruction.
- Differentiation, when used effectively, builds on students' present level of learning to take them forward.

Opportunities for teachers in international schools that offer focused professional development

- Opportunities for focused professional development include in-school provision by programme coordinators, conferences organised by regional international school associations and courses sponsored by universities.
- The SIOP model training programme, ESL in the Mainstream courses and the International Teacher Certificate offer targeted training appropriate to teachers in international schools.

Resources

Accreditation agencies
Council of International Schools: www.cois.org.
National Association of New England Schools and Colleges: www.neasc.org.

Integrated content and language instruction sites
Sherris, A. (2008) *Integrated Content and Language Instruction.* CAL Digest. Washington, DC: Center for Applied Linguistics: www.cal.org.

Content-based instruction
The website of the Center for Advanced Research and Language Acquisition (CARLA) gives useful background to the development and rationale for CBI on a link entitled: 'Content-based second language instruction: What is it?': www.carla.umn.edu/cobaltt/cbi.html.

Content and language integrated learning
CILT webpage on the National Centre for Language site: www.cilt.org.uk/secondary/14-19/intensive_ and_immersion/clil.aspx.

Sheltered instruction
Website of the Center for Applied Linguistics, Washington, DC: CAL topics, 'English language learners: Sheltered content instruction': www.cal.org/topics/ell/sheltered.html.

Language across the curriculum
Straight, H.S. (1998) *Languages Across the Curriculum.* CAL Digest, October. Washington, DC: Center for Applied Linguistics: www.cal.org/resources/digest/lacdigest/html.

Professional development links
Cambridge International Education training opportunities: www.training.cie.org.uk/courses.
Center for International Education, George Mason University, Washington, DC: http://cehd/gmu.edu/centers/cie/.
Centre for Education in an International Context, University of Bath: www.bath.ac.uk/ceic/.
ECIS International Teacher Certificate: www.internationalteachercertificate.com.
Endicott College, Beverley, MA: www.endicott.edu/internationalmasters.
IBO site setting out information regarding its IB Educator Certificates and other PD opportunities: http://www.ibo.org/programmes/pd/award/.
'Sheltered instruction observation protocol' (SIOP) model training programme sponsored by the Center for Applied Linguistics in Washington, DC: www.cal.org/siop/about/index.html. SIOP text, 'The SIOP model for teaching mathematics to English learners' information for SIOP

training and texts can be found on the website of the provider, Pearson Education: http://siop. pearson.com/.

'Teaching ESL students in mainstream classrooms: Language in learning across the curriculum', training course sponsored by the Department of Education and Child Development of the State of South Australia: www.unlockingtheworld.com/programs/teaching-esl-students-in-mainstream.

Publications relating to instructional scaffolding

Gibbons, P. (2002) *Scaffolding Language, Scaffolding Learning* (with a Foreword by J. Cummins). Portsmouth, NH: Heinemann.

The document by Yelland, N. and Masters, J. (2007) *Instructional Scaffolding to Improve Learning,* on the website of the University of Northern Illinois, is useful further reading in this area: www.niu.edu/facdev.

Differentiation resources

For further information visit the website of Alberta Education: www.education.alberta.ca. This site contains a resource called 'Making a difference: Meeting diverse learning needs with differentiated instruction'. Separate chapters can be uploaded on to PCs or tablets.

An article entitled 'A teacher's guide to differentiating instruction' can be found at: www.education. com.

Tomlinson, C.A. (2000) Differentiation of instruction in the elementary grades. *ERIC Digest*, available at: http://ecap.crc.illinois.edu/eecearchive/digests/2000/tomlin00.pdf.

References

Bransford, J., Brown, A. and Cocking, R. (2000) *How People Learn: Brain, Mind, and Experience and School.* Washington, DC: National Academy Press.

Gardner, H. (1983) *Frames of Mind: The Theory of Multiple Intelligences*. New York: Basic Books.

Ninio, A. and Bruner, J. (1978) The achievements and antecedents of labelling. *Journal of Child Language* 5, 1–15.

Sherris, A. (2008) *Integrated Content and Language Instruction.* CAL Digest. Washington, DC: Center for Applied Linguistics.

Straight, H.S. (1998) *Languages Across the Curriculum*. CAL Digest, October. Washington, DC: Center for Applied Linguistics.

Thomas, W.P. and Collier, V.P. (2002) *A National Study of School Effectiveness for Language Minority Students' Long-term Academic Achievement.* Santa Cruz, CA: Center for Research on Education, Diversity and Excellence.

Vygotsky, L.S. (1987 [1934, 1960]) Thinking and speech. In R. Rieber and A. Carton (eds) *L.S. Vygotsky, Collected Works*, Vol. 1 (trans. N. Minick) (pp. 39–285). New York: Plenum.

Wood, D.J., Bruner, J.S. and Ross, G. (1976) The role of tutoring in problem-solving. *Journal of Psychiatry and Psychology* 17 (2), 89–100.

11 Planning for the Language and Content-area Learning of Emergent Bilingual Students

Chapter 11 sets out suggestions for planning new content-area topics in classrooms that contain emergent bilingual students. The aim of planning in this way is to ensure a strategic approach to promoting the language and content-area learning of students at all levels of English language proficiency.

The sequence of Chapter 11 is as follows:

- Introduction: Planning to promote the language and content-area learning of emergent bilingual students.
- Planning the introductory phase of a new unit of study.
- Planning assessment approaches for a new unit of study.
- Planning different kinds of support for students' learning.

Introduction: Planning to Promote the Language and Content-area Learning of Emergent Bilingual Students

Ensuring that emergent bilingual students have access to language and content-area learning in mainstream classrooms is a major part of a teacher's responsibility in international school classrooms. The aim of the planning outline offered in this chapter is to help teachers in carrying out this responsibility. By incorporating a range of consistent strategic approaches at the planning stage, teachers can make a real difference to the learning experiences of this group of students.

A further advantage of using a planning framework is that it serves continually to remind teachers of the needs of emergent bilingual students. This can be necessary in the face of the many new pedagogic initiatives that tend to flow through international schools and which sometimes threaten to overwhelm basic classroom practice.

Applicability to all types of classrooms and programmes

The suggestions for planning contained in this chapter are designed for use alongside the pedagogical frameworks found in international schools. They can be applied in classrooms that offer enquiry-based programmes such as those of the International Baccalaureate Organisation (IBO; www.ibo.org/general/what.cfm) and in schools that have adopted curriculum frameworks derived from schooling systems in Australia, Canada, the UK and the USA. They are valid for use in collaborative planning sessions with teacher colleagues and on the planning documents that the IBO and other providers supply.

Building up expertise in delivering an effective learning experience to emergent bilingual students

To make the process of incorporating these approaches seem less daunting, it is a good plan for teachers unused to the degree of diversity in international school classrooms to start by including only one or two of the suggested modifications. As teachers become practised in implementing these new approaches and perceive the real difference they make to students' learning, they can add new strategies.

Explaining the sequence of the chapter

The planning suggestions below are divided into phases representing the key elements in teaching a new content-area topic or unit of study. Within that framework, the content of the chapter is divided into items that teachers working with emergent bilingual students need to consider and plan for.

The impact of effective planning on the learning and wellbeing of emergent bilingual students is discussed in the case of each item. This is followed by practical suggestions for implementing effective practice. Lastly, in each case, a real-life example of an effective strategic approach that benefits emergent bilingual students is provided. The examples are taken from an actual extended multidisciplinary unit of work on the Renaissance designed for students aged from 11 to 12 years. This unit culminates in a week-long field trip to Florence, Italy and takes place on an annual basis.

11.1 Planning the Introductory Phase of a New Unit of Study

The introductory phase of a new content-area unit is a key element in promoting the learning of emergent bilingual students. Table 11.1 sets out the elements that provide emergent bilingual students with an effective foundation for language and content-area learning. These are offered as guidelines to planning a unit in whatever form the planning cycle takes in a school.

Text Box 11.1 Key elements of a classroom designed to support emergent bilinguals

The following list sets out once more the key elements of a classroom designed to support the language and content-area learning of emergent bilinguals.

- consistent procedures;
- visual supports and real-life examples for the introduction of new material;
- activating prior knowledge;
- supportive questioning techniques;
- awareness of the need for the teaching of new specific language skills;
- modelling of outcomes;
- shared learning activity followed by group and/or individual learning activity;
- scaffolding supplied to individual students at appropriate levels;
- incorporation of specialist English support into the ongoing work of the class;
- differentiated ways of assessing and measuring students' understandings;
- an overall encouraging and positive approach to the sharing of learning in the classroom.

These are the basic approaches, to be recast in age-appropriate forms for different age levels. The chief difference between the age groups lies in the prior life and educational experiences of the students at later year levels. When their prior knowledge is activated effectively, older students tend to have a greater ability to research new material independently in their own languages or in the school language, online or from informational texts.

11.1.1 Introduction to a new content area of study

An effective introductory phase to a new unit of work lays a solid foundation for the classroom activities that follow. It is helpful always to present the new unit within a wider context so that the new material relates to something near at hand or current in the lives of the students. Teachers can choose from a variety of resources to offer visual links to the new topic which allow for discussion and the sharing of information. With a basic understanding of the essentials of a topic, students can then move on to investigate more deeply in English or their home language.

Questions to guide teachers in the planning of the introductory phase

- Could you use real-life events to introduce this unit of study?
- What connections can you make with school and community themes?
- Could you introduce this topic via an already completed unit of study?
- Could you use video or audio material in introducing the topic?

Table 11.1 Items in the introductory phase of a new unit of study that have the potential to provide an effective foundation for the learning of emergent bilingual students

Item	Teacher action	Provision of contextual and foundational material via print, audio, video or technological means	Collaborative input from professional colleagues and classroom helpers	Use of students' mother tongues to promote learning in the new unit of study
(a) Introduction of a new unit of content-area study	Use a variety of media to introduce the topic as well as talk. Provide a framework for the content and sequencing of the new unit.	See (b) below.	Parallel activity from specialist English language teachers via in-class or in pull-out classes to introduce essential key word vocabulary for initial understanding of the topic.	Post the framework for the unit of study online via the parent portal or the school's VLE. This approach allows students to make an initial investigation in their home languages.
(b) Introduction to the resources available in school and classroom to support students throughout the unit of study	Introduce students to the resources that are available in the classroom. Demonstrate the uses of these resources by example.	Introduce students to texts, audio and video equipment, apps and programs available on mobile devices and computers. Liaise with librarian colleagues to plan sessions in the library to explain and demonstrate the resources available there.	Enlist teaching assistants, in-class specialist teachers and CAS[a] students in helping emergent bilinguals to make use of the available resources.	Indicate to students and parents how home language resources available online and in the library can be used to support students' learning at home and in the English-medium classroom.

(continued)

Table 11.1 Items in the introductory phase of a new unit of study that have the potential to provide an effective foundation for the learning of emergent bilingual students

Item	Teacher action	Provision of contextual and foundational material via print, audio, video or technological means	Collaborative input from professional colleagues and classroom helpers	Use of students' mother tongues to promote learning in the new unit of study
(c) **Activating and building on students' prior knowledge and experience**	Draw out what students already know about a topic via guided questioning and here-and-now examples.	Source visual, textual, audio and online material that allows students to make connections with what they already know or are familiar with.		Encourage students to activate prior knowledge based on their own cultural, geographical and linguistic experience.
(d) **Supplying key word graphics to support the learning of knowledge and concepts**	Be aware of the key words and phrases that are essential to understanding the topic and participating in the learning. Incorporate key words consistently throughout the unit of work.	Source or create visuals and make use of online opportunities to give students access to essential vocabulary and to concept building.	Supply opportunities for practising key word vocabulary in authentic learning activities.	Suggest that students create bilingual key word dictionaries in English and their home languages in hard copy or online to provide support throughout the unit.

Note: [a]Creativity, Action, Service (CAS) is a compulsory component of the IB Diploma programme. Some CAS students opt to help out in the classrooms of younger students.

- Could you use art, music or dance?
- Could you find an app or other online material to introduce the topic?
- Could you go on a visit or make a longer field trip?
- Could you bring someone into the classroom to talk about the topic from another perspective?
- How can you tap into students' preferred learning styles? (See Section 10.3 for more on students' learning styles.)

Explicitly setting out the components of a new unit of study

The point of explicitly setting out the intended sequence for the study of a content-area topic is to give emergent bilingual students a sense of control and an understanding of what is going to happen next. It is helpful if the procedures for moving through a topic of work essentially follow the same pattern each time. Giving the information in advance in writing (in hard copy or online for the information of both students and parents) is an essential part of the process.

Reducing student anxiety

Teachers can reduce the level of anxiety among emergent bilingual students by making clear from the outset that they will be helped to carry out the assignments and activities that are part of the new unit of study. As students consistently mentioned in the research enquiry described in Appendix A, they appreciated and recognised the value of explicit statements about future activity and of constant offers of help. Above all, they clearly gained confidence in their ability to carry out tasks independently when the teachers made good on their promises to provide support.

Example 1 From the Renaissance in Florence unit of study: Introducing a new content area

Step 1: Introduce the topic of the Renaissance by showing the online presentation with a voice-over made by a technology teacher and a group of students on their return from the previous year's Florence trip. (It was customary for the accompanying technology teacher to send back a photo-montage of the trip while in Florence to keep parents up to date with their children's experiences.) This showing is used to introduce a number of key themes associated with the topic in a user-friendly manner.

Step 2: Introduce the concept of rebirth behind the use of the term 'the Renaissance'. Show an image of a pre-Renaissance painting (the Duccio Madonna that they will later see in the Uffizi, for instance) side by side with a painting of the Madonna made during the Renaissance (the Botticelli *Madonna of the Pomegranate*, also in the Uffizi). Begin the investigative process by asking students to talk about the differences between the two paintings.

Step 3: List words that recur or are critical to an understanding of the topic. These can be displayed on a SmartBoard or conventional whiteboard. These form the basis for student-created dictionaries and key word visuals.

Step 4: In classrooms where mobile devices such as tablets are embedded, provide students with access to information relating to Florence in a variety of interactive ways.

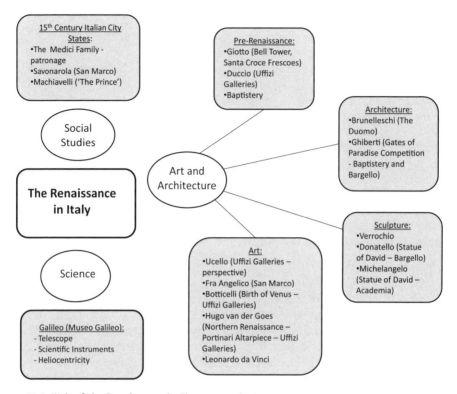

Figure 11.1 Web of the Renaissance in Florence project

An example of available apps is *Firenze – Virtual History*, produced by Anoldo Mondatori Editore S.p.A. This app presents students with images of architectural structures, paintings, biographies of famous Renaissance figures and maps, all of which offer users interactive ways of gaining further detailed information about the highlighted area. Most of the museums, galleries and other state-owned buildings in Florence provide online access via virtual tours, timelines, etc.

Example 2 Webbing the Renaissance in Florence project

Webs of this type can be created using PowerPoint as here, apps such as Popplet lite (https://itunes.apple.com/gb/app/popplet-lite/; see Figure 11.1).

11.1.2 Introduction to available resources

At the start of a new unit of study, teachers need to introduce students to the resources that are available to support work on the new topic. Students coming from different education systems and perhaps from less well-resourced schools may be unfamiliar with the range of resources available in many international schools.

Two elements may be unfamiliar to new arrivals. The first is the ways in which the resources themselves are used. This may involve the need to learn new technological applications and for students to be introduced to the functioning of a large library or media centre. The second unfamiliar element may be the degree of learner independence that is encouraged in most international schools. In general, after an initial introductory phase, class learning is structured in a way that involves students making choices about the resources they will draw upon in carrying out a learning activity.

Supportive means of introducing students to resources include:

- Walking students around the classroom showing what resources are available during class time: these may include audio material, reference texts, class libraries, computers, and mobile technological devices such as tablets or laptops. Their peers, teaching assistants and CAS (Creativity, Action, Service – a component element in the IB Diploma course) students can be asked to show emergent bilingual students how these resources are used.
- Arranging practical orientation sessions in the library with librarian colleagues to ensure that students are familiar with:
  - the workings of the library;
  - how to find information texts at different reading levels;
  - the location of the home language sections (to find guidebooks and other texts relating to study in their home languages);
  - the guidelines for making use of online facilities.
- Introducing students to specific programs and applications on the internet via PCs and on mobile devices, if available. New students may need guidance in making full use of these opportunities.

Example 3 From the Renaissance in Florence unit of study: The range of resources supplied to underpin work on the unit

- Lists of online material and links such as:
  - ItalyGuides site that offers virtual tours with notes on 14 key sites in Florence associated with the Renaissance: www.italyguides.it/us/florence/florence_italy.htm;
  - 'Renaissance: Focus on Florence' on the Interactives link on the Annenberg Learner site: www.learner.org/interactives/renaissance/florence.html;
  - The website of the Museo Galileo, which offers translations in multiple languages of the opening page as well as virtual tours of different rooms of the gallery: www.museogalileo.it.
- Highly illustrated topic books.
- Guidebooks in different languages (during the annual trip each year teachers search out guidebooks to Florence and other texts in students' home languages to serve as resources for emergent bilingual students).
- Maps and plans.
- Related fiction texts at a range of reading levels.

- Model kits (teachers are given sufficient funds while in Florence to purchase model kits from museum shops and other sources for use with the following year's students).
- Art materials.
- Liaise with librarian about displays/book collections associated with the topic.

11.1.3 Activating/building on students' prior knowledge and experience

Activating students' prior knowledge and then building on that knowledge is a key part of the introductory phase of a new unit of study. Teachers can only offer effective instructional scaffolding when they understand the present level of students' mastery of the concepts and language skills related to the study. Effective questioning (a topic in Section 13.1) is a core strategy in establishing students' prior knowledge and experience.

Example 4 From the Renaissance in Florence unit of study: Questioning to activate prior knowledge relating to the unit

- What do students know about Italy? Geographical location? Famous Italians? Food? Soccer teams? Cars? Language?
- Have they been to art galleries with their parents/former school? Has any student visited countries/cities/museums, etc. where Renaissance works are to be seen?
- Have they studied other periods of art history associated with their home cultures or the previous places where they have lived?
- Show students images via SmartBoard or on screen of well-known Renaissance paintings, sculptures and buildings (the Mona Lisa, the Duomo group of buildings, the statue of David). Do they recognise them?
- Refer to the different forms of artefacts that are covered by the term 'art history': paintings, frescoes, sculpture, buildings, town planning, etc.

11.1.4 Supplying key word graphics to support the learning of content-area knowledge and concepts

Highlighting the key words related to a new unit of study gives emergent bilingual students a framework on which to build. Key word visuals are most effective when used explicitly from the start in the introductory phase. It is also an effective policy to involve students in constructing their own key word formats as the unit of study progresses. This is a manageable and enjoyable task when carried out collaboratively in pairs or by small groups of students.

Formats for graphically representing underlying concepts related to a unit of study include flowcharts, outlines, graphs, Venn diagrams, action strips, timelines, webs and trees (Figure 11.2). They can be created using the Shapes, SmartArt or Chart applications on the computer or via educational apps such as Popplet and Popplet Lite, or professional apps such TouchDraw and Flowpad Lite. Formats such as flowcharts, webs and diagrams linked by directional arrows allow quite complex conceptual material to be

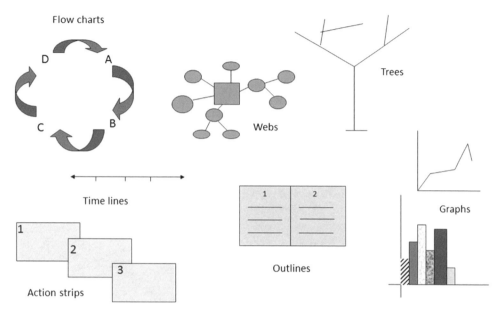

Figure 11.2 Formats that help to give emergent bilingual students access to content-area material

illustrated visually. An effective key word visual offers a visible framework of the shape of the content.

Note: Websites and apps useful for creating key word visuals are included in the Resources section at the end of the chapter.

Supplying students with the tools that will help them to learn more independently

The purpose of key word visuals is to supply students with tools that will help them to make discoveries for themselves rather than to present them with a comprehensive account of the topic. This point applies to the learning approaches found in most class-rooms but is critical in the case of programmes of study such as the Primary Years Programme (PYP) of the IBO (www.ibo.org/general/what.cfm), which is centred on enquiry-based learning. In an enquiry-based classroom the emphasis is on students researching and carrying out activities that answer questions that have been established early in the unit. Key word support in general should lead students towards discovering concepts for themselves rather than presenting them with the answers.

Make the best use of key words lists and visuals by:

- including essential words for understanding the unit of study;
- emphasising these words in class talk;
- including concept words as well as words that name things;
- explicitly depicting relationships between items of information;
- supplying (or liaising with parents about) a home language translation;

- repeating the key words in spoken and written instructions;
- using the key words in all the supportive grids, frames and graphic organisers;
- getting students to create a personalised dictionary relating to the unit of study using an app such as the *Oxford Primary Dictionary* created by EducationApps Limited.

Example 5 From the Renaissance in Florence unit of study: Figure 11.3 shows a key word graphic setting out in brief Galileo's contribution to the study of astronomy

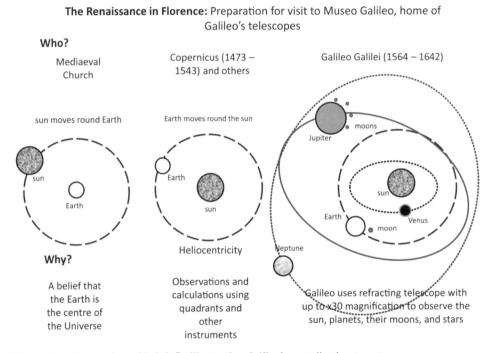

The Renaissance in Florence: Preparation for visit to Museo Galileo, home of Galileo's telescopes

Figure 11.3 Key word graphic briefly illustrating Galileo's contribution to astronomy

11.2 Planning Assessment Approaches for a New Unit of Study

Effective planning of a new unit of work builds in opportunities for teachers to assess emergent bilinguals' development in language and content-area understanding. This includes assessment that provides evidence to teachers about an individual student's ongoing development as well as the final assessment of students' overall knowledge and understanding. Effective assessment of emergent bilinguals offers teachers a clear picture of what students know about a content area. It concentrates on finding ways for students to show what they know and understand regardless of their level of English.

Note: The topic of assessing emergent bilingual students in international schools is the focus of Section 7.1. Some of the same material is presented here in the context of planning assessment within a new unit of study.

11.2.1 Assessment to inform instruction (formative assessment)

Effective scaffolding of emergent bilinguals' language and content-area learning is based on a clear understanding of a student's present level of knowledge and grasp of concepts. When all the professionals who work with a student share a common view of her or his place on the learning continuum, they are then in a position to provide instructional scaffolding at an appropriate level of challenge to take the student forward.

11.2.2 Assessing a student's overall knowledge and understanding related to a unit of study (summative assessment)

It is standard practice in many curricula and programmes to round off a unit of study with an activity designed to display students' knowledge and understandings. In the areas of literacy and numeracy, for instance, it is common practice to use pieces of writing and number or word-based problems for this purpose. Over the years, however, the range of pieces of work that students are asked to produce as a means of displaying their learning has broadened. Many schools – international schools among them – have embraced a wider view of how learning can be assessed.

In some classrooms, students are encouraged to choose the format that they feel best suits the nature of the content they have been working on. In some schools it is now customary for students to create their work in collaboration with other students rather than individually. Value is placed on a student's ability to work cooperatively and part of the assessment process is to understand the ways in which an individual student has contributed to a group enterprise.

Ways of assessing the degree to which students have met the learning targets built into the design of the new topic include:

- talking about their learning by engaging in teacher-guided reporting; for example, see Section 13.1;
- writing about their learning;
- creating handmade posters or online interactive storyboards via Kidspiration (www.inspiration.com/kidspiration) and VoiceThread (www.VoiceThread.com), for example;
- using puppets to recount a story or retell information;
- using tablets to create movies – animation and movie making apps include iStopMotion for iPad (http://boinx.com/istopmotion/ipad/) and Avid Studio for iPad (renamed as Pinnacle Studio for iPad: http://www.pinnaclesys.com/publicsite/us/products/studio/ipad/);
- online presentations;
- using drama and music to illustrate their understanding of the topic.

Programmes that use sets of criteria to assess students' work

Some programmes of study offered in international schools use sets of criteria as the measure to assess summative pieces of work. Among these programmes are the Primary and Middle Years programmes of the IBO (see Section 4.3). Sometimes students themselves are asked to contribute to the process of drawing up the criteria which typically consist of several lines which describe the elements of increasingly effective pieces of work. Criteria can be a powerful tool for raising the level of student achievement when they are referred to by teachers and students during the course of the unit of study.

Criterion-referenced assessment and emergent bilingual students

Assessment that is based on sets of criteria that are shared with students during the unit of study may present some challenges in a classroom that contains newly arrived emergent bilingual students. For students and parents who come from different educational systems the idea of assessing work against criteria may be unfamiliar. Teachers will need to take the time to explain how assessment via criteria functions and to provide examples of student work that has been assessed in this way. (For more on this issue, see Section 4.4 and Section 8.2.)

Teachers also need to be ready to explain the meaning of the language in which they are couched. The wording of criteria tends to be quite abstract and to contain words that beginning emergent bilingual students rarely meet. Teachers will need to break up the criteria descriptions into short sentences expressing the same meaning in more concrete terms. In many schools, emergent bilingual students are assessed by other means until they are able to participate in discussion about criteria.

11.2.3 Assessing content-area learning in early and intermediate level emergent bilingual students

The aim of effective assessment for emergent bilingual student is to find methods that test their knowledge of content rather than their use of English.

The following approaches provide ways for emergent bilingual students to display their content-area learning:

- Give emergent bilingual students more time to carry out standard assessment procedures.
  - *Sometimes the English of emergent bilingual students is far enough advanced for them to complete mainstream classroom assessment activities if they are given more time. Asking specialist teachers and teaching assistants to help out with the language required to complete assessment tasks is also a useful approach.*
- Provide tables and frames to help students explain what they know about a topic.
  - *Hard copy or online tables and frames can be used to guide students through assessment tasks and to show their understanding of a content area. Quite complex material can be made manageable in this manner.*

- Ask students to carry out sorting and sequencing tasks in place of written tests.
  - *Providing illustrations or short sentences that students are required to place in an order that shows their understanding of the topic can be an effective means of finding out what beginning learners of English understand.*
- Ask students to fill in various forms of cloze tests.
  - *Cloze tests take the form of pieces of text with words omitted. Students must fill in the gaps with appropriate words. For early learners of English, the words can be given at the bottom of the page. Developing learners can be asked to supply the words themselves. Cloze tests offer a useful way to find out whether emergent bilingual students have understood key aspects of a content area.*
- Ask students to create a graphic account of their conceptual understanding via flow-charts, timelines, webs and diagrams.
  - *Using graphic means to display learning is an effective way for students to set out both the facts and conceptual underpinning of a content-area topic. Students can make use of the computer programs and apps mentioned earlier to create these graphics.*
- Ask students to create an online presentation with a partner.
  - *Students who would find it difficult to produce extended pieces of writing are frequently able to display their understanding of a topic by creating an online presentation in collaboration with a partner.*

Example 6 From the Renaissance in Florence unit of study: Supplying a supportive context for emergent bilinguals to display their knowledge and understanding

Provide emergent bilingual students with named images of key buildings/paintings/portraits relating to their study of Florence. Ask students, in pairs, to construct a poster or other graphic means of conveying information about one of the sets of images. The information can include the foundation of the building, the life story of the architect, the way the building was constructed, the role of the building in the history of Florence.

This can be done with paper and art materials or online via an application such as VoiceThread (www.voicethread.com) which comes in app or program form. VoiceThread also allows students to provide a commentary or to invite teachers and others to contribute their own thoughts and comments.

11.3 Planning Different Kinds of Support for Students' Learning

The aim of this section is to suggest practical approaches on the part of the teacher that enable students at different levels of English language development to engage and learn in content-area classes. The strategies are designed to help teachers to adopt an integrated approach to content and language learning in their classrooms. Table 11.2 sets out strategies that have been found to be effective in classrooms that integrate language and content-area learning.

Table 11.2 Effective strategies for classrooms that integrate language and content-area learning

Strategy	The strategy in practice	Collaborative input from professional colleagues and classroom helpers	Use of students' home languages to promote learning
(A) **Teaching the specific language skills that students need to participate in content-area learning**	Explicitly teach the language skills needed in a content area by practical illustration and example.[a]	Collaborate with colleagues and helpers in sourcing models, frames and online material that enable students step by step to master the necessary language skills.	Explain the validity to students and parents of encouraging emergent bilinguals to practise a new language skill in their home language. This approach supplies a basis for subsequent work in English in the classroom.
(B) **Scaffolding students' learning with visual organisers and graphic supports**	Find or create hard copy, online and app-based materials that take students step by step through a topic or new way of working.	Collaborate with specialist teachers and classroom helpers in resourcing frames, grids, webs, flowcharts, etc. that scaffold the learning of new material.	Ascertain whether emergent bilinguals' prior knowledge in their home language can be used as a support for learning in an English-medium classroom.
(C) **Considering appropriate differentiation approaches**	Decide whether the learning of students will benefit from differentiation: of outcomes, of level of support, of degree of challenge, etc.	Decide upon the role of in-class professionals and helpers in supporting differentiation, by working with levelled reading groups, for example.	Make use of classroom helpers and CAS students who speak the same languages as emergent bilingual students to explain content in their home language and to negotiate meaning in English.
(D) **Investigating the possibilities of incorporating technology into classroom activity**	Make effective use of technological resources available in the classroom and across the school. Embed the effective use of high-quality technological resources in ongoing classroom learning.	Liaise with technology teachers/ assistants and librarians to ensure that available resources are used across the board to promote classroom content-area learning.	Draw on technological resources to enable students to activate prior knowledge and to investigate the topic in their home languages.

(E) Planning various ways of grouping students to support learning	Use groups to provide supportive environments for learning and to give emergent bilinguals opportunities to engage in the language used for higher level activity.	Work collaboratively with in-class colleagues to ensure that time spent by emergent bilingual students in groups is used to the greatest advantage.	Try out various grouping strategies for emergent bilinguals. On occasion, group students together who speak the same language; at other times group students with different languages: the aim in each case is to produce work in English.
(F) Building in possibilities for multilingual and multicultural connections and references	Draw on multiple cultures, languages, habitats and experiences to illustrate and exemplify content-area material.	Plan with colleagues who teach other disciplines to incorporate content that offers a multi-perspectival and multicultural approach to the unit of study.	Explicitly encourage students to draw on their prior experiences and cultural and linguistic affiliations in order to make connections and to provide fresh examples related to a unit of study.
(G) Considering input from parents and other visitors	Consider whether parents or other visitors might offer illuminating input and variety into the study of content-area material.	Build up an inventory of colleagues, parents and school 'friends' who are effective communicators to diverse classes about a content-area topic.	When adults come to speak to a class, ask them to include words from their own language and references from their own cultures. Bring the world into the classroom.
(H) Planning a field trip to provide real-life experience and understanding of content-area material	Plan a field trip that provides real-life examples and information in a context outside the classroom.	Ask class helpers and accompanying adults to talk about the field trip experience in comprehensible language.	The host country in which the school is situated may be new to many students in a class. Use the opportunity of a field trip to introduce students to the language and culture of the locality in a way that ties in with the topic being studied.

Note: ᵃChapters 12 and 13 include practical suggestions towards achieving this aim.

11.3.1 Planning to teach the specific language skills needed in the unit

Explicit teaching of the language skills needed for participation in content areas is a core feature of a classroom where language and content learning are integrated. All the professionals who work together in a classroom need to be aware of their role in teaching the necessary skills and to ensure that they follow the same pedagogic approaches. In the light of increasingly collaborative approaches to planning and teaching, many schools now include specialist language teachers, teachers of special educational needs and teaching assistants in their mainstream literacy and numeracy training sessions. Teachers have found Table 11.3 useful for keeping track of the specific language skills needed in separate content areas and across the curriculum.

Table 11.3 Keeping track of the specific language skills needed in separate content areas and across the curriculum

Language skills	Language arts/English	Mathematics	Science	Social studies	Art/music
Asking and answering questions					
Contributing to a class discussion					
Reading for information					
Note-taking (in various formats)					
Summarising					
Writing in different formats and genres					
Drafting a piece of writing					
Editing and making changes					
Describing a process as in a lab report					
Report writing: oral and written					
Carrying out focused research					
Contributing to collaborative learning					
Working with a partner					
Problem solving in a small group					
Making hypotheses					

Note: See Text Box 12.1 for a discussion of an overall view of teaching literacy in classrooms that contain emergent bilingual students.

Effective teaching of specific language skills includes the following approaches:

- signposting when students need to learn how to use language in a new way;
- using authentic material to illustrate the sort of language that is used for an activity;
- leading students step by step through the different stages of practising the skill in authentic situations;
- when teaching different writing formats, providing models of what the finished product looks like and explaining the different elements;
- breaking down the learning task into bite-sized pieces so that the language component is visible;
- using available resources on PCs and mobile devices to give students supported opportunities to practise reading and writing in a new way;
- making effective use of specialist teachers, teaching assistants and other helpers to lead individual students through speaking, reading and writing activities.

Note: Chapters 12 and 13 are devoted to ways of scaffolding students' learning of the language needed for full participation in mainstream classrooms. The areas covered include the following:

- guided questioning;
- how to contribute to a class discussion;
- writing in various formats and genres;
- reading a text for information or enjoyment;
- note taking;
- writing science reports and descriptive accounts of group activity;
- solving word-based problems in mathematics;
- how to carry out research;
- how to create written reports;
- how to create an oral presentation;
- how to contribute in small-group situations.

Example 7 From the Renaissance in Florence unit of study: Specific language skills needed for participation in the unit

- Reading for information and understanding of ideas: historical fiction – informational texts – authentic material (guidebooks).
- Contributing orally when working collaboratively in a small group to research aspects of a topic.
- Writing: monographs – report writing – keeping a diary (required in Florence) – constructing a written report (online or in hard copy).

- Speaking to convey information and ideas effectively.
- Preparing an oral presentation (to be given in Florence in front of the feature being described).

11.3.2 Scaffolding students' learning with visual organisers and graphic supports

A key component of supporting the language and content-area learning of students whose English is at different levels of development is to provide visual organisers and graphic supports. The degree of support provided by scaffolding needs to offer students a manageable degree of challenge based on their existing level of competence. Scaffolding students' learning in this way allows them to acquire the necessary language to partici-pate in the ongoing content-area activity of the classroom. Technology offers ready-made opportunities to provide these supports.

Note: A discussion of scaffolding is included in Section 11.4. Ways of scaffolding students' language learning in the content areas are included in Chapters 12 and 13.

Example 8 From the Renaissance in Florence unit of study: Outline to lead students through a discussion about the impact of Savonarola's teaching

Students received prior input via a teacher-made Topic 7 sheet containing an outline of the life of Savonarola and relevant key words (Figure 11.4). Students were also given the opportunity to research the topic via the Firenze Virtual History app and illustrated information texts.

11.3.3 Applying appropriate differentiation approaches

The planning phase prior to a new unit of study is the time for teachers to consider whether differentiation offers an effective approach for individual students in their class. Certain content-area teaching sessions may consistently include a differentiated approach such as happens when students are grouped for reading or for mathematics. The school may have a consistent policy with regard to differentiating the assessment of emergent bilingual students that includes some of the approaches mentioned in Section 12.2 above.

With new units of study, teachers may also choose to differentiate by:

- providing hard copy or online information materials at different levels of graphic support and reading challenge;
- offering assignments with varying language demands;
- assigning tasks at different levels of complexity;
- adjusting the degree of scaffolding that is provided;
- moderating the level of challenge in a project;
- varying the amount of teacher support offered to individual students;
- using different means to assess the work of emergent bilingual students.

Note: A general discussion of differentiation approaches is included in Section 11.5.

Title: The Renaissance in Florence
Topic 7: What were the reasons behind Savonarola's *Bonfires of the Vanities*?

What information do you need in order to prepare for this topic?

(1) A brief outline of Savonarola's life history and career:

(2) ....

(3) ....

Savanorola's ideas: 'He thought that ...'

(1) Florentines had lost sight of God. They were too interested in making money and buying beautiful things

(2) ....

(3) ....

Describe what happened during Savonarola's *Bonfires of the Vanities*.

....

In your opinion was he right about life in Florence? Give examples:

(1) It is true that ....

(2) ....

(3) ....

Why do you think the **Florentine Signoria** put Savonarola to death? They put him to death because:

(1) The **Pope**..

(2) ....

(3) ....

(4) ....

Figure 11.4 Example of a teacher-made topic sheet

Example 9 From the Renaissance in Florence unit of study: Differentiation possibilities for the unit

Differentiation can be applied in a number of ways to enhance students' access to the language and content learning associated with the Renaissance in Florence unit of study. Differentiation needs to be designed with the individual student's level of English language proficiency in mind. Approaches might include:

- providing more readily accessible information about the topic beforehand so that students have a basic understanding of the key elements of the unit;
- instructional scaffolding offering a higher level of support;
- providing more extensive in-class and pull-out class English language support in specific activities from specialist English teachers, including the final oral presentation and written report;
- offering more extensive frames and graphic supports for large-scale projects such as the individual written and oral reports;

- allowing students to work in pairs with teacher input in order to present a joint oral report in Florence;
- providing emergent bilingual students with more focused support from accompanying teachers during the time in Florence.

11.3.4 Investigating the possibilities of embedding technology into classroom activity

The purpose of introducing embedded technology into the classroom is to provide teachers and students with new ways of enhancing learning. The programs and apps that are used in the classroom need to be of high quality so that they engage students in meaningful and relevant tasks which move them forward in their learning.

In practice, teachers may be bound by the programs and apps that the school has uploaded onto mobile devices and computers. The contribution of the teacher is to insert the available technological resources seamlessly and effectively into content-area and language learning. (The use of technology in international school classrooms is the topic of Section 7.2.)

Use of specific programs and apps

Programs and apps exist to offer built-in scaffolding of students' learning that allows them to work at ascending levels of challenge. Many come with instant feedback which most students find motivating and fun. Effective technological applications offer students a sense of control over their learning by providing new information in manageable chunks and by introducing material that builds on previous learning.

Programs and apps provide innovative ways of carrying out standard classroom tasks such as solving mathematics problems, creating word banks and constructing timelines and flowcharts. They also offer new possibilities in the form of restricted-access blogs, interactive posters and interschool communication. Most teachers will find that students at all levels of English proficiency will adapt quickly to incorporating technology in this way.

Embedded technology is effective in the following instances.

- The use of technology is meaningful and intrinsic to the study of a content area or learning a new language skill.
- Technological applications offer students a high-quality learning experience. (Some programs and apps offer only limited and repetitive tasks.)
- Technology provides a focus for shared talk about a learning task.
- Technology allows emergent bilingual students to incorporate their home languages and cultural references into interactive newsletters, posters and classroom blogs.
- Teachers have a key role in guiding and motivating the learning of emergent bilingual students even in a classroom with high-quality technological provision.
- Teachers adopt assessment approaches that include work carried out via technological means.

- Emergent bilingual students continue to be exposed to stimulating and engaging spoken and written input from teachers and peers (i.e. that technology is not used to keep beginning and emergent bilingual students occupied while proficient users of English carry out complex tasks).

Example 10 From the Renaissance in Florence unit of study: Technology allows emergent bilingual students to display their cumulative learning

Students are asked to use a program or app to give an account of what they have learnt about one of the topic sheets that are used every year to supply a framework for the unit of study. Programs such as Glogster Edu (www.edu.glogster.com), Easel.ly (www.easel.ly/) and Kidspiration (www.inspiration.com/kidspiration, for younger children) offer emergent bilingual students effective means to display their learning in visual and interactive ways. These programs provide ways of creating posters and graphics which allow the importation of images, audio clips and video. The process allows students to recount what they have learnt and to discuss information and concepts with peers and teachers. This is an effective parallel learning activity to be monitored and supported by specialist English language teachers either in-class or in a pull-out class setting.

11.3.5 Using different ways of grouping students to support learning

Different sorts of instructional groupings have the power to provide emergent bilingual students with positive and supportive learning experiences, if managed appropriately. Working with a partner or in a multilingual group is a way of introducing emergent bilingual students to collaborative learning. Working together in a group to achieve a task enables students to hear and practise the language used in this type of classroom activity.

These are some of the advantages to be gained from effective grouping:

- Working in a group that includes proficient English speakers exposes emergent bilinguals to the authentic language needed for carrying out cooperative learning activities.
- Working with students who speak the same language allows emergent bilinguals to use their own language to negotiate meaning in English.
- Working with a partner or small group around the computer or with individual mobile devices offers an environment where students focus on content rather than language.
- When effectively managed, groups are fun.
- They allow students to make verbal contributions in a less exposed context than whole-class discussions.
- When asked to carry out a task at a conceptual level, groups serve to model the language of higher level thinking and problem solving.
- They provide opportunities for emergent bilingual students to experience the steps needed to complete a higher level activity.

For groups to be effective, teachers need to ensure the following:

- Students should be grouped in different ways for different learning purposes. Grouping can cease to be a positive experience if students are always grouped by overall ability, level of English or on some other basis.
- If a group appears to be dysfunctional in the way the students work together, then teachers should reconstitute the groups in a class.
- Teachers need to articulate and explain the behaviours that lead to groups working effectively. Each student should be assigned a meaningful role in completing the task; proficient users of English should be expected to give time for emergent bilinguals to express themselves.
- The process of assigning the individual contributions required to complete a task within a group should be closely monitored by the adults working in the classroom. These roles typically include students acting as scribes, taking the role of presenter of material to the class, creating artwork, working on an online presentation, making a model, researching specific content-area material and interviewing knowledgeable people.
- The teacher needs to ensure that different roles are assigned to different students when the group tackles the next task. In particular, emergent bilingual students should not always find themselves with the less visible or less demanding roles.
- Teachers need to monitor the interactions in a group constantly to ensure that each student is allowed to contribute in a meaningful manner and that each student's voice is heard.
- Teachers need to have an assessment structure in place that enables the contribution of each student to be evaluated. Parents sometimes worry that group work does not allow individual contributions to be assessed satisfactorily. Teachers need to be ready to supply evidence that indicates that they are keeping track of individual work.

Example 11 From the Renaissance in Florence unit of study: Creating 'expert' groups to research one of the topics associated with the unit, e.g. the competition for making the panels for the Gates of Paradise in the Baptistery in Florence

- Based on previous topic sheet and key word input, small groups of students carry out further research together via the web and through texts at different reading levels. Different groups focus on individual topics.
- Each group creates a poster either in hard copy form or in an online presentation to deliver the information to the other students. If online, students can include voiced comments and images via a program such as VoiceThread (www.voicethread.com). (See Section 11.3.4 'Investigating the possibilities of embedding technology into class learning', above.)

- Each 'expert' group in turn delivers its presentation to the rest of the class.
- They mention the places in Florence that relate to the topic and which the students will visit.
- Other students are encouraged to ask questions and to become masters of the new information, perhaps by filling in a frame of key points.

11.3.6 Building in possibilities for multilingual and multicultural connections and references

Throughout this Handbook, the value of making multilingual and multicultural connections has been emphasised. In international school classrooms, this approach benefits all the students in a class in the following ways:

- The culture and language of the surrounding community and host country offer opportunities for all sorts of near-at-hand learning.
- All students benefit from being exposed to a wide range of cultural, linguistic, historic and geographic references as well as being made aware of a range of viewpoints.
- Emergent bilingual students in English-medium classrooms gain when their own experiences and linguistic and cultural heritages are incorporated into mainstream teaching and learning.

These are some of the ways in which teachers can plan to include meaningful multilingual and multicultural connections:

- When introducing a new content-area topic, use a range of geographical and cultural contexts as examples.
- Call upon students to refer to their own experiences when establishing prior knowledge in a whole-class discussion.
- Offer informational texts that draw on a range of references rather than referring only to the English-speaking countries in which they may have been published.
- Ensure when referring to famous people living and dead that they represent a range of cultural, political and religious ways of thinking.
- Draw on the local community and host country for examples and experiences that bring reality to a topic.
- Use technology to enrich the classroom by making use of programs, apps, cultural links, current affairs offerings and interpersonal connections via Skype in both English and students' home languages.

Note: The value and practice of using students' home languages to promote learning in an English-medium mainstream classroom is discussed in Section 10.2.

Example 12 From the Renaissance in Florence unit of study: Introducing students to modern Italy

Learning about the Italian language and elements of Italian culture can be an illuminating and enjoyable experience and provides a context for the days in Florence. Possible approaches include:

- Drawing on resources in the classroom: Italian students (if they are willing to contribute), or students who have lived in or who have previously visited Italy.
- Ending each day in the classroom in the run-up to the trip with a 20-minute session on the Italian language. These sessions should be lively and entertaining, with the targeted language items being obviously applicable to the visit and with role play and games.
- Including sessions on Italian food, aspects of Florentine life and an introduction to sketching. (Sketching and worked-up drawings are an integral part of the time in Florence; the students are encouraged to illustrate an understanding of perspective as exemplified in the work of Ucello.)

11.3.7 Considering the possibilities of input from parents and other visitors

Parents, knowledgeable adults and other visitors offer ways of bringing fresh insights and new points of view into the classroom. Some of the contributors such as professional storytellers or visiting authors may be arranged in conjunction with librarians. Other valuable input can be gained from parents or other adults known to the school who may be able to offer illustrated accounts or provide examples of musicianship or another cultural activity. It is helpful for planning if teachers across a year level build up a list of possible speakers that relate to the planned topics of work for the year.

For visiting contributors to be effective, it is useful to apply the following criteria:

- Might the contributor provide an illuminating introduction to a new unit of work?
- Might the contributor be able to bring to life an aspect of the unit of work that would otherwise only be described verbally or viewed via video (e.g. playing an instrument or carrying out a craft activity, describing what it is like to live in an area that has been affected by the building of a dam, or working with one of the aid organisations)?
- Might contributors be able to offer students personal accounts from their own experience that bring to life major historical and present events (e.g. accounts of exploration or a meeting with a famous person, perhaps)?
- Does the contributor bring a new cultural or other viewpoint into the classroom?

And practically:

- Does the contributor have the presentation skills necessary to keep a class of students, of whatever age, engaged and appreciative?

Text Box 11.2 Field trips

Field trips relating to an extended area of study offer the possibility of meaningful and enriching insights. When, as in the case of the Renaissance in Florence study, they precede an extended residential trip, they are an opportunity to set out the ways in which students are expected to behave in public places. They also provide an opportunity for teachers to observe the interaction between individual students outside school so that they can make informed choices about room sharing and the creation of learning groups.

In the case of the Renaissance in Florence study, the class was able to visit a major exhibition being held locally, devoted to the Northern Renaissance. There they were introduced to the work of the painter Hugo van der Goes, whose great triptych in the Uffizi Galleries in Florence is a focus of study during the trip.

A later expedition was made to a local Italian restaurant where the Italian owner was accustomed each year to introducing students to some Italian foods such as mozzarella cheese, different sorts of pasta and Italian desserts. The daily gelato is a feature of the Florence trip and the evening meals are designed to be authentically Italian (bearing in mind the students' dietary requirements).

For emergent bilingual students, taking part in field trips, particularly when they are partnered by fellow speakers of the same language, is a different and relatively stress free way of engaging in learning through English. Field trips should be relevant to classroom learning but they should also be occasions for fun and the build-up of camaraderie.

- Does the contributor speak English in a way that most of the class can follow easily? Could the presentation go ahead with the help of a teacher or another adult (or student) to act as an interpreter where necessary?
- Will the presentation involve the students in practical or other activities in order to make the content meaningful and memorable?
- Will the contributor be ready to accept student questions and to answer them in an age-appropriate manner?
- Have the students been trained in listening attentively and showing appreciation in a positive manner?

Example 13 From the Renaissance in Florence unit of study: Visit by a parent with an interest in amateur astronomy

The teacher arranged for the students who were investigating the topic of Galileo and his impact on the scientific investigation of astronomical phenomena to stay in school after dark. The parent involved brought in two telescopes which were set up on the far side of the sports field where there was the least amount of environmental light. The parent explained the way in which reflecting telescopes work. Students took it in turns to observe and to take photos of the surface of the moon, the planet Venus and the rings of Saturn.

The students found the experience very absorbing and enjoyed the interaction with a non-teaching adult who treated them as colleagues. They subsequently spoke and wrote about Galileo's theories with a greater respect and understanding.

11.3.8 Using field trips to provide real-life experience and understanding of content-area material

Field trips, either day visits or taking place over several days, are valuable ways of making learning come to life and of building up shared experiences among the students in a class. Planning to include a field trip in a unit of study provides a focus for learning before and after the visit. The most effective field trips are closely allied with the learning targets of the unit of work and make contributions to students' factual knowledge and conceptual understanding. Field trips do not have to be complex affairs to be effective and memorable.

A trip that connects closely with what students are studying provides a source of interest and stimulation that teachers can build on. Field trips provide variety and hands-on experiences that cannot be replicated in the classroom. They also have social benefits since field trips are times when students can build friendships and talk informally to teachers and other accompanying adults.

Field trips are effective and enjoyable when they:

- relate in a meaningful way to work in the classroom;
- offer insights into an area of study that can be built upon later;
- give hands-on experience of topics that can otherwise only be viewed on-screen in the classroom;
- build upon language that students have already met in the classroom;
- supply emergent bilingual students with stress-free learning environments;
- provide opportunities for emergent bilingual students to engage in small groups with an adult acting as mentor.

Key Points in This Chapter

Planning for the needs of emergent bilingual students in a new unit of study

- Teachers in international school classrooms are responsible for the language and content-area learning of their emergent bilingual students.
- Consistent planning for the full inclusion of emergent bilingual students at the beginning of a new unit of study serves to remind teachers of the needs of these students.
- The introductory phase of a new unit of study is a key element in providing an effective foundation for language and content-area learning.

- Building on students' prior knowledge enables teachers to offer a level of instructional scaffolding that is manageable for students and yet builds in an appropriate degree of challenge.
- Supplying key words associated with the new unit of study in a visual form such as a web or flowchart provides an effective foundation for future work.
- Planning a new unit of study should include assessment approaches that enable emergent bilingual students to express their understanding of content whatever their level of English language development.
- Explicit teaching of the specific language skills needed for participation in the new unit of study is a core aspect of the planning stage.
- Effective visual supports and graphic organisers scaffold the learning of students in the different phases of the unit of study.
- Decisions about the use of differentiation approaches are part of the planning process.
- Technology brings the world into the classroom. It allows students to research topics in their home language and allows them to draw on a wider frame of reference.
- Groups offer emergent bilingual students access to the language used to solve problems and to carry out collaborative projects.
- All the students in the classroom benefit from being exposed to differing points of view and to examples and references that relate to different habitats, histories, cultures and social systems.
- Parents, visitors and professional speakers are potential resources in bringing to life the content of a unit of study.
- A day trip or more extended residential field trip is a means of providing near-at-hand experiences connected with the topic being studied.

Resources

IBO programmes: www.ibo.org/general/what.cfm.
International Primary and Middle Years Curricula: www.greatlearning.com.

Programs and apps useful for creating key word visuals
Flowpad Lite, created by Vaibhav Valecha: https://itunes.apple.com/gb/app/flowpad-lite/.
Popplet Lite, created by Notion: https://itunes.apple.com/gb/app/popplet-lite/.
TouchDraw created by Eleven works LLC: https://itunes.apple.com/gb/apple/flowpad-lite/.

Examples of programs and apps for use in supporting the learning of emergent bilingual students
Animation and movie-making apps: iStopMotion for iPad: bit.ly/istopidpadapp; Avid Studio for iPad (renamed as Pinnacle Studio for iPad: http://www.pinnaclesys.com/publicsite/us/products/studio/ipad/).
Easel.ly: www.easel.ly/.
Glogster Edu: www.edu.glogster.com.
Kidspiration: www.inspiration.com/kidspiration.
Oxford Primary Dictionary created by EducationApps Limited.
VoiceThread: www.voicethread.com.

Links to Renaissance in Florence websites

'Firenze – Virtual History', produced by Anoldo Mondatori Editore S.p.A.

ItalyGuides site which offers virtual tours with notes on 14 key sites in Florence associated with the Renaissance: www.italyguides.it/us/florence/florence_italy.htm.

The website of the Museo Galileo offers translations in multiple languages of the opening page as well as virtual tours of different rooms in the gallery: www.museogalileo.it.

'Renaissance: Focus on Florence', on the Interactives link on the Annenberg Learner site: www.learner.org/interactives/renaissance/florence.html.

12 Teaching the Skills of Class Talk and Literacy to Emergent Bilingual Students

The topic of Chapter 12 is the teaching of literacy to emergent bilingual students in English-medium classrooms. The focus of the chapter is on the areas of teaching and learning that present challenges to emergent bilingual students who are new to the language of the classroom. A distinction is made between the needs of young emergent bilinguals who are learning to read and write for the first time in any language and older students who have already learnt to read and write in their home or other languages.

The sequence of Chapter 12 is as follows:

- Introduction: Learning to read and write in a new language.
- The early teaching of reading to young emergent bilinguals.
- Teaching young students to write.
- Teaching reading to older emergent bilingual students.
- Teaching writing to older students.
- Multiliteracies – learning to communicate via technological media.

Introduction: Learning to Read and Write in a New Language

The topic of this chapter is the teaching of language arts/English to emergent bilingual students. The focus is on the areas in these programmes that present a challenge to students who are new to the language in which they are expected to become literate. In the case of many of the youngest students, their first experience of reading and writing is likely to take place in the international school classroom. For older students the challenge is to transfer existing skills to learning in the new language. In both cases, teachers need to adopt a systematic approach to planning for the needs of emergent

Text Box 12.1 Teaching literacy is not just about language skills

The focus in this chapter is on the practical aspects that face teachers who are given the task of teaching literacy to classrooms containing students at all levels of English language development. This concentration on specific aspects of literacy learning does not indicate a lack of awareness of the wider issues that relate to emergent bilingual students learning to become members of a new literacy community. As was pointed out in Section 5.2 of this Handbook, language does not exist in a vacuum. Its uses and status in a given social setting reflect the way power is distributed in the cultural and political context. Within a sociocultural approach, literacy is viewed in a similar way. According to Warschauer (1997), literacy, rather than involving a set of 'context neutral, value free skills' (de Castell & Luke, 1986: 87), is in fact a means of 'apprenticing students into the discourse and social practice of literacy communities'. In other words, when children engage in literacy, they encounter the perspectives and ways of viewing the world that are embedded in what they read. Texts reflect the author's viewpoint in relation to issues such as ethnicity, class and identity – usually the views that derive from her or his own discourse community. Literacy programmes that adopt a sociocultural approach set out to validate and include the experiences of all the students in a class, not just those who share the background of the author.

A practical example of what literacy learning within a sociocultural framework looks like is given in a journal article written by a New Zealand teacher educator. Hamer's (2005) focus is an early childhood curriculum called *Te Whāriki* (Ministry of Education, 1996), which adopts a sociocultural, inclusive approach to education in New Zealand, with special reference to the Maori community. The thrust of the article is that the literacy experiences that derive from each child's experience of family and community should be brought into the classroom and given equal value and prominence.

Another approach to literacy teaching and learning that similarly recognises the need for learners to be active participators in the literacy process rather than passive recipients is critical literacy. The aim of critical literacy, according to Cummins and Sayers (1996), is to bring about a shift in the way that emergent bilingual students engage with literacy learning in the new language. An effective critical literacy approach involves a move away from 'coercive relations of power to collaborative relations of power' (Cummins, 1996). For Cummins, biliteracy is a necessary element in empowering emergent bilingual students. For teachers in an English-medium classroom, such an approach seeks to involve all the students in questioning the author's viewpoint, in critically examining the text and in constructing meaning in the light of their own experiences and cultural understandings.

bilingual students in the areas of literacy teaching and learning. ('Young' or 'younger' is used to describe students from school entrance age until around seven or eight years of age; the term 'older' is used to describe students from that age upwards.)

The sequence of the chapter

The first two sections are devoted to the teaching of reading and writing to emergent bilingual students. Section 12.1 addresses the needs of young emergent bilingual students who may have different prior experiences not only of literacy learning but also of schooling itself. The section includes suggestions on how to move children on from where they are on the literacy continuum and how to build up their confidence and expertise in reading and writing. Section 12.2 addresses the teaching of reading and writing to older emergent bilinguals who arrive in school at differing levels of literacy development in their own or another language. The section is devoted to strategies that guide and support students as they make the move to talking, reading and writing in an English-medium classroom.

The topic of Section 12.3 is the concept of multiliteracies. This term refers to the multiple types of literacy that students must learn to master if they are to make full use of the communication possibilities of technological media and applications. The section contains discussion about the role of teachers in this area and the implications of a multiliteracies approach for work with emergent bilingual students.

Introduction to Sections 12.1 and 12.2

The focus of these sections is on the teaching of reading and writing in English-medium classrooms where students have different prior experiences of literacy learning and who display a range of proficiency in English. The intention overall is to concentrate on the specific issues and strategic modifications that relate to the literacy learning of this group of students rather than to cover every aspect of a literacy programme. The suggestions are designed to be applicable to current ways of teaching literacy in most international schools.

Reading and writing go hand-in-hand

The assumption that underpins the content of Sections 12.1 and 12.2 is that the teaching of reading and writing go hand in hand. Knowledge of the skills of literacy interacts at every level, with development in one area enhancing progress in another. Reading and writing are largely treated separately here for the convenience of clearly setting out targeted strategic approaches on the part of teachers.

Note: Listening and speaking, or class talk, is also closely allied with all aspects of literacy. It is central to the teaching and learning approaches to be found in international school classrooms in the content areas. The topic is addressed in Section 13.1.

12.1 Teaching Young Emergent Bilingual Students to Read and Write

A major focus for teachers in early childhood classrooms (or Key Stage 1 classrooms in British-derived systems) is early literacy. This includes pre-literacy work as well as the initial teaching of reading and writing. This task is potentially made more challenging in international school classrooms which frequently contain high numbers of emergent bilingual children who are becoming literate for the first time in any language. There are several issues that teachers in this situation frequently raise:

- *Students at different stages on the literacy continuum.* Students new to international education coming from different national and cultural backgrounds exhibit relatively large differences in their experiences of education to this point. Many may have been in playgroups and nurseries from a very young age; others may have been at home until the ages of five or six. Some students will have already started formal literacy learning at the age of four or five which is typical in British-derived schooling systems. Others may not be due to start formal literacy learning until the age of six or seven. Parents understandably tend to be anxious about this issue. (See Section 8.2(d) and Text Box 8.3 for a discussion of parental expectations relating to early literacy teaching; see also Baker, 2014.)
- *Students at different stages of reading readiness.* Young children new to international schools therefore display wide ranges of reading readiness, both from the point of view of an individual student's general level of maturity and because of the nature of their previous learning experiences.
- *The challenge of teaching students to read and write in a language they cannot yet speak.* The challenge raised most often by teachers of young children in international schools is the difficulty of teaching students to read and write for the first time in a language that they cannot yet speak fluently. The situation is made more challenging in classrooms where there are very low numbers of first language speakers of English. This is a common feature of early childhood classrooms in international schools and means that the teacher may have few English language speakers to call upon and to act as language models in shared reading and writing sessions.

12.1.1 The early teaching of literacy in international schools

The principle employed in most international school classrooms where students have different prior literacy experiences is to 'take students on from where they are'. (Vygotsky's 'zone of proximal development' which is the theoretical underpinning for this practice is discussed in Text Box 10.2.) Within this approach, teachers make an initial assessment of a student's present level of progress in reading and writing using the assessment methods that are current in the school. Future literacy instruction is informed by the results of this assessment. The class numbers in most international school classrooms tend to be small for this age group, being generally around 18. This allows the professionals who work with the class, including the teacher, teaching assistant, specialist English language teacher and teacher librarians, to follow through on this approach. In many classrooms, these beginning-of-the-year assessments are also used to place students in levelled reading groups.

In general this approach is an effective way of targeting instruction appropriately when students are working independently or in small groups. The areas of challenge for teachers are more often the occasions such as shared reading and writing sessions when, typically, teachers work with the whole class grouped together. These are the times when teachers must consistently employ all their class management and professional skills in order to include emergent bilingual students in the work of the class.

12.1.2 'More of everything': supporting the literacy learning of young emergent bilingual students

The overall approach to working with emergent bilingual students is to practise a similar type of pedagogy to that which is generally used to teach reading and writing to young literacy learners, but in greater quantity and variety and with some additions. In other words, teachers should provide 'more of everything'. The reason for this need to provide emergent bilinguals with multiple occasions to engage with literacy activities is that they rarely begin their literacy learning with a strong foundation in the language in which the learning (i.e. English) takes place. They need more opportunities to experience language in use and more chances to practise the foundational tasks that are typically given to young readers and writers.

This is an area where technology has a valuable part to play, when it is available. (See Section 7.2 for an account of technology provision in international schools.) It offers ready-made, engaging and motivational opportunities for students to work through activities and exercises that support early literacy learning. It injects variety and fun into what might otherwise seem repetitive and potentially boring activities. It offers students a feeling of independence and control in their learning, both as individuals and when they work with a partner or in small groups.

12.1.3 Teaching reading to young emergent bilingual students

The following paragraphs set out some of the strategic approaches that enable young emergent bilingual students to make progress in their reading. They are given alongside some sentences taken from the reading programme of one international school, in order to set the suggestions in a real-life context.

Extract: Children usually start learning to read by relying on:

- *Prior knowledge of the material in the text.*
- *Words remembered from hearing texts read aloud.*
- *An increasing personal vocabulary of memorable words recognised on sight.*

In the case of young emergent bilingual students who are beginning learners of English it is likely that none of the three strategies mentioned above will be available to help them to make sense of a text. As English language beginners, these students can make little use of any prior knowledge they may have of the material presented in the text. They are unlikely to understand the meaning of or be able to retain words from the text. Lastly, they may have no existing store of basic vocabulary to bring to deciphering the text.

The following approaches are helpful in classrooms where there are learners with this profile:

Prior knowledge of the material in the text

- Stories and texts that are introduced to children in the early months of the school year should relate to universally recognisable themes such as the family, transport, common animals, the weather, school, and so on. Ideally, new units of study in any programme should relate to near-at-hand topics that are familiar to young children.
- When sharing the reading of fiction and non-fiction texts connected to a new topic it is always an effective strategy first to introduce the high-frequency vocabulary and structures that underpin the new material. The introduction can be based on real-life objects, or on photographs or uploaded audio and visual material. Picture dictionaries, online vocabulary-based games, role-play, songs and raps, among other activities, can also be used to give students a basic understanding of the topic in question.
- Allowing parents to borrow copies of shared reading texts prior to their use in class gives them the chance to talk over the content with their children in their home language. In this way, emergent bilingual children are more easily able to make sense of what they hear and to use their prior understanding of the content to enhance their take up of new vocabulary in English.

Words remembered from hearing texts read aloud

- Teachers can access print or e-books on standard topics via apps or publishers' web-sites. Hearing a number of books read aloud that deal with the same content-area material enables young bilingual students to become familiar with words and phrases and to recognise them again when they recur in new reading books.
- Educational publishers now offer sets of texts or e-books on standard topics that provide games and interactive activities connected to levelled texts. These allow students to work through attractive material at their own pace and to build up familiarity with core vocabularies that relate to standard topics. (Oxford Owl is the site of a well-known educational publisher that offers texts in these formats; see also Sesame Street e-books. See the Resources section at the end of the chapter for links.)

An increasing personal vocabulary of memorable words recognised on sight

- Certain features in books intended for young students help early readers to build up their sight vocabulary. The features that contribute to this process include texts where basic sentences are repeated on each page with the substitution of one or two words that introduce a slight change of focus. This type of story is even more helpful if the illustrations closely follow the changes in the text. *Brown Bear, Brown Bear, What do you See?* By Bill Martin Jnr. and illustrated by Eric Carle is a well-known example of this sort of text. Here the colour of the animal and the animal itself changes on every two-page spread. This text is admittedly an old favourite, but it retains its place in early childhood classrooms because of its charm and value for young readers.

Extract: Children are given direction in developing key strategies in reading by:

- *Use of contextual cues: Does that make sense? Does that sound right?*
- *Use of phonic cues: How does the word begin? How does the word end? Does it sound and look right?*
- *Use of syntactic cues: Does the word seem to make sense grammatically? Is that what you would expect within the context of the sentence?*
- *Use of self-correction: Does what I have read make sense?*

Again, with young emergent bilingual students, the key strategies may not be immediately accessible to young students who do not speak the language that they are reading. Effective use of contextual clues requires readers to be able to guess what might be coming next, in line with the meaning of an individual sentence or a longer passage. Beginning learners of English find it more difficult than proficient speakers to make good guesses. They simply do not have the experience of the spoken language in order to call upon their prior knowledge to inform their reading.

Teachers need also to be aware that the use of phonic cues (where students sound out single letters and clusters of letters to decode the word and to construct meaning) relies on students being already familiar with the word itself as well as the meaning. The same is true for syntactic cues, where students use their existing knowledge of how phrases and sentences are made up to 'feel' whether a word makes sense in the context. Finally, self-correction is obviously more difficult for students who may not have the necessary familiarity with everyday spoken English nor an overall grasp of the meaning and content of a sentence or longer piece of writing.

Some approaches that support emergent bilingual students in developing their use of the key strategies

- It is helpful to introduce students to the content that they are about to meet in a text. Teachers can use talk or online material in order to emphasise central aspects of the topic. When students feel at home with the overall content of a text they can learn to apply the key strategies.
- Teachers help students when they explicitly model the use of the key strategies. This can be done at shared reading time or in smaller groups when the steps of each strategy can be consistently spelt out.

- Prior to reading a new text, students benefit from being introduced to the written forms of the key words that are new to them and from being shown how the initial and final letters are guides to recognising the word. At the same time, students need to read the words aloud in context so that they have a chance to practise the pronunciation.
- Most emergent bilingual students need more practice in recognising and learning how to pronounce individual elements of words. Phonics work is more effective in the case of emergent bilinguals if it takes place within a framework of overall meaning at sentence level.
- Giving students more time to make sense of what they are reading during small-group and individual guided reading sessions is a helpful approach. Bilingual students need time in order to process what they have read if they are to learn to self-correct.
- Emergent bilingual students need to read and re-read a text in order to become familiar with the application of the key strategies. Teachers and other adults who listen to children read should concentrate on helping students to develop a strategic approach to working out how a word sounds and what a word in the context of the sentence means. This is a more effective approach than discussing individual words in isolation.

Further strategies that support young emergent bilingual students in learning to read

- Choral reading.
  - *Choral reading, where small groups or the whole class read passages of a story together under the guidance of a teacher, is a way of taking the pressure off individual students and of reinforcing aspects of effective reading such as intonation, highlighting the way in which punctuation informs meaning and reading expressively.*
- Creating word walls, personalised dictionaries and word banks around a new topic.
  - *As students meet new words in the course of fresh units of study, they should be encouraged to write these down in clusters as aide memoires for future reading and writing activities associated with the topic. (See the Resources section at the end of the chapter for links to websites giving suggestions for building up personal dictionaries and word walls.)*
- The value of bilingual texts.
  - *Bilingual texts or translations of classic young children's books such as* The Hungry Caterpillar *by Eric Carle or* Rosie's Walk *by Pat Hutchins provide a powerful reinforcement of a young child's learning in both languages. Many schools offer parents guidance in how to support their children's reading at home.*
- The use of quality apps and online material.
  - *Quality apps and online material offer engaging and effective reading experiences and provide user-friendly ways for emergent bilingual students to practise their reading skills. The websites of quality children's educational publishers are good places to start, as are the websites of teacher organisations and texts that review educational apps and online material.*

12.1.4 Teaching young emergent bilingual students to write

Young emergent students learning to write need the same levels of individualised support as when they are learning to read, and for similar reasons. These reasons include different experiences of formal education and different levels of literacy readiness as well as the overarching issue of learning to write in a language that is new. There are also a number of aspects to the teaching of writing as it is generally practised in international schools that parents may find unfamiliar and teachers will need to be ready to articulate the rationale for the way that they teach students to write.

Strategies that support young emergent bilinguals in learning to write:

- Teachers should be sure that young emergent bilingual students are familiar with the topic in the spoken form of the language before being asked to write about it.
  - *Young emergent bilingual students cannot be expected to write in a language which is not part of their existing vocabulary. The adults working with a child need to have talked through the topic extensively with the student individually or in a larger group first. This is an occasion where a word bank with illustrations is helpful.*
- Young writers should be invited to write about things that are near-at-hand and familiar to them.
  - *Very young students should only be asked to write about things they have experienced themselves or have learnt about in school. In the case of young bilinguals this also includes being familiar with the vocabulary and basic structures needed to talk about the topic. In all cases where young students are engaged in writing, they should be encouraged to add their own drawings in order to convey their meaning better and to express their thoughts and feelings more fully.*
- Where young emergent students have already received literacy instruction in their own language, they should be encouraged to create pieces of writing in both their languages.
  - *Such approaches, where students create roughly equivalent bilingual texts, have the effect of enhancing their overall language development. The support of an older student who is a fellow speaker of the same language, or of a parent, is helpful to the student and provides a valuable resource for the teacher. See Section 9.2 for an extended discussion about the positive uses of children's home languages to enhance classroom learning.*
- It is helpful to young writers if they are asked to write in a format that they recognise from a story they have heard read aloud or have read themselves.
  - *Replicating a familiar format either at sentence level or in longer passages is supportive of emergent bilinguals who are learning to write. The activity is made more enjoyable when writing of this type is made into a small book with illustrations and details about the student author.*
- Shared writing sessions with the whole class or small groups, where teachers act as scribes in response to students' suggestions and comments, provide an effective means of modelling how a piece of writing is constructed.
  - *SmartBoards (interactive whiteboards), pocket charts and other large-scale visual means are helpful for bringing to life the possibilities of sentence-building.*

- Practising the recognition and formation of letters can take place on paper or via one of a number of useful apps where tablets are available.
  - *Multiple ways of practising the recognition and formation of the upper and lower case letter shapes used in English are available. These include using apps such as Blobble Write, making ABC books, creating the letters in modelling clay or by drawing and cutting out, as well as traditional pencil-and-paper approaches.*
- Schools have varying approaches to the teaching of handwriting. Cursive/print, style of writing, etc.
  - *Some international schools systematically teach one style of handwriting. They may start with the print form and move on to cursive writing, although many now start with a modified cursive variety. In some cases, new emergent bilingual students may already have started to learn a different style of Roman script. In French schools, for instance, students are taught a distinctive script which is almost part of the French identity. Where this is the case, teachers need to be sensitive to students' prior experiences and accept writing that is legible.*
- An effective technique for teaching young writers is to supply supportive frames and graphic outlines which lead students step by step through the stages of a writing task. These can be teacher-made or sourced online. (For downloadable templates of graphic organisers see http://www.netrover.com/~kingskid/graphic/graphic.htm. For 25 reusable graphic organisers that guide students in writing in a range of formats see the app *Tools 4 Learning* by Mobile Learning Services.)
  - *There are many apps that supply story starters and frames to help students construct narratives. Among these are Story Ideas (bit.ly/storyidapp) and Story Builder for iPad (bit.ly/storybuilder). These technological applications are very attractive to all ages of student and involve the manipulation of illustrations as well as different quantities of writing. Teachers need to ensure, however, that the time taken to work through the material is in line with the value of what the students are being asked to do. The apps vary greatly in quality and teachers are wise to consult trusted publications that review what is available in the way of educational software.*
- Students should be encouraged to read and re-read their own writing aloud in the presence of an adult.
  - *Reading their own writing is a way of increasing students' spoken and reading fluency. It also allows teachers and students to discuss the writing in detail sentence by sentence and to agree on how the piece of writing could be made more effective.*
- In many schools, advancing young writers are encouraged to regard their first attempt at a piece of writing as a draft. They are then encouraged to read through and reflect on their writing and to make changes.
  - *Where schools encourage the use of drafts as an integral part of the writing process, teachers may need to explain the rationale behind the approach to new parents at the first open evening and then individually thereafter if necessary. Parents from some backgrounds are uneasy with teachers who allow children not to aim immediately for correct spelling, punctuation and a grammatical use of language. It is important that parents see a correct (and corrected version) as the end product, although the widespread use of word processing on the computer makes the concept and value of drafting far more familiar than previously.*

- In many international schools, incorrect spelling is not immediately corrected in early childhood classrooms.
  - *In many early childhood classrooms it is felt that an undue emphasis on correct spelling stands in the way of students achieving writing fluency. In the case of emergent bilingual students, it is important to achieve a balance between encouraging them to write in general and to requiring them to create writing that is comprehensible and enjoyable to read. English spelling is notorious for its challenges, but is nevertheless an integral part of the meaning of words. Perhaps the answer is to draw a line between what is expected when students are drafting and what is expected from the final version.*

Further supportive approaches in teaching younger emergent bilingual students to write

Print and online dictionaries should be made available to students to check the spelling of new words they wish to use. (See the Resources section at the end of the chapter for suggestions.)

Young emergent bilingual students should be encouraged to write in a range of formats, including diary writing, personal experience, keeping a weather chart, writing a postcard to a grandparent, and so on. It is all writing!

Where possible, students should be given free time to gather round computers in small groups in order to play one of the numerous English-medium games that involve vocabulary and spelling. The groups can be made up of students who speak the same home language or different home languages.

12.2 Teaching Literacy to Older Emergent Bilingual Students

Older emergent bilingual students entering an English-medium international school for the first time generally have the advantage of being literate in their home or primary language (not always true of students who have experienced multiple disruptions in their education). Where this is the case, the process of learning to read in a new language is potentially less challenging since these students are likely already to have developed a strategic approach to reading even when they may be unfamiliar with talking about the process in this way. In some cases, students may already have begun to learn both spoken and written English in their previous school or their parents may have arranged tuition with the upcoming move in mind.

12.2.1 The importance of encouraging emergent bilingual students to continue reading in their home languages

At the first Open House or Back to School Evening of the year, in one-to-one discussions with parents and with students themselves, teachers should take the opportunity of emphasising the value to emergent bilingual students of continuing to read in their home languages. When they continue to read all sorts of material in their home languages, students not only develop a wider vocabulary and more advanced cognitive understanding in those languages but also transfer these skills to their reading in the new language. In other words, students only have to learn to read once. They are able to apply all their skills in decoding and making sense of meaning in their home language to learning to read in the new language. They know how reading works. New words and concepts learnt from reading in the home language are foundational in making sense of material that they read in English.

Continuing to read in the home language is sometimes a challenge, as parents and students will confess, because the stresses of the school day in an English-medium environment and the need to do homework makes them disinclined to do any further reading in any language. Teachers, parents and school librarians should do everything in their power to make reading in the home language attractive, by supplying accessible and up-to-date print and online material. The overall desired outcome for emergent bilingual students is that they emerge at the end of their education as bi-literate as well as bilingual.

12.2.2 Selecting reading material for older emergent bilingual students

In most schools, by the time students are aged eight or nine, they are no longer divided into levelled reading groups. This removes the possibility of differentiating by levelled texts, although it has the advantage of giving emergent bilingual students exposure to whole-class learning. Nevertheless there is a place for texts known as high-interest graded reading material in the mainstream classroom. These texts are produced by English language teaching publishers (see the McGraw Hill and Penguin Readers websites in the Resources section), and provide emergent bilingual students with reading material that is enjoyable and challenging without being beyond their reach. It is up to teachers to advise students about books at an appropriate level. In some cases standard school novels have been issued at different reading levels so that all the students in a class can share in a common experience. Recommendations to offer this type of literature to emergent bilingual students come with the proviso that teachers should move them on to mainstream texts as soon as it is feasible.

From the start, emergent bilingual students in international schools are expected to join with the whole class in carrying out research in order to create a report in paper form or online. Teachers need to ensure that they have a range of informational books available with differing amounts of text and illustration in order to cater for emergent bilingual students. The same is true for online materials, although many students appear highly motivated by quality apps and programs and stretch themselves to read quite challenging material, especially if given more time and the means to translate unfamiliar key words. (The skills involved in reading a text for information are included in Section 13.3. Scaffolding the creation of written or oral reports is addressed in Section 13.4.)

12.2.3 Guiding students in talking about reading

Talking about a text that has been shared by students either in a whole-class or smaller group is a standard strategy at the heart of teaching students to think deeply about what they read. Talking about reading gives students the chance to hear and practise the sort of language needed to engage in the exploration of meaning. Sharing a text together provides teachers with a framework to ask the questions and to institute enquiry that takes students' thinking and learning to a higher level.

Engaging with a text – an unfamiliar learning behaviour for some new emergent bilingual students

Shared discussion about reading – digging down deeply into the text and expressing their own responses to what they read – may be an unfamiliar activity for students from systems where this type of approach is not usual. This can be an issue for teachers when older students arrive at an international school from these schooling systems. In this case, students need to be introduced to the ways in which texts can be explored as well as to the language needed to engage in this type of approach. This tends not to be an issue in the case of young children who are learning to read for the first time in any language. In this case, they will learn to engage in this way with a text as an integral part of their literacy learning.

Some examples of the language that students need to share in talking about reading

Phases in exploring a written text

- *Introducing a text.*
  - Students need to learn the vocabulary required to talk about a text. The key words for analysing the narrative, the role of the characters and the plot of a story need to be explained and practised using authentic texts. Students need also to learn a range of adjectives that allow them to describe the appearance and personalities of characters: drawings with labels accompanied by short sentences and role play are ways of ensuring students are able to take on board this vocabulary.
  - Teachers introduce the text via links to familiar stories and classroom topics. They use visual means such as real-life objects and online graphics if appropriate.
  - Teachers and students talk together to establish what they can find out about the text from the title and any visual cues:
    - *What do you think the book is going to be about? What does this illustration tell us? Where is the story set? Does it look as if it is happening in modern times? How can you tell?*
    - *Words such as* author, setting, illustration *and* character *have their meaning established and are used consistently.*
- *Moving through the narrative.*
  - The main points of the narrative are emphasised as teacher and students read through the text.
  - Teachers and students establish the overall shape of the narrative by a shared structured retelling using a simple frame where appropriate.
  - Teachers encourage students to dig deeper into the text by eliciting ideas about character, causation and outcomes:
    - *What do we know about the family at the beginning of the book? What happens that changes their lives? How does the family react to these events? What action do the characters take? How do things turn out in the end?*

- ◦ Teacher and students discuss the role that each character plays in the story. How do their actions give insights about their motives and possible outcomes?
  - – *Who is the character who makes things happen? Who would you say is the hero or heroine in the story? Does a book need a hero or heroine? Why does the author spend so much time telling us about Emil? Why does Emil always stay behind?*
- ◦ Teacher and students work out any underlying aspects of the story:
  - – *Why do the children seem so worried about their father? Why does Rick keep getting himself in trouble?*
- ◦ Teachers and students discuss the way the central issue is resolved:
  - – *How did things work out in the end? Did you expect the book to end in this way? Do you believe that the characters would have acted in that way? What makes you think that?*
- *Talking about personal responses to the text.*
  - ◦ Teachers in the class model ways for emergent bilingual students to express their own feelings about the text. They should express these thoughts initially in quite simple phrases and sentences. Later, as students become more adept at explaining what they think, the teacher can introduce a wider range of vocabulary in order to allow students to express more complex thoughts.
  - ◦ Students are encouraged to reflect on the aspects of the book that engage them, and also on the reasons why some sections are less compelling. They are encouraged to give specific examples from the text to supply reasons for their views:
    - – *Which were the parts of the book did you like best? What made you interested in the story? Do you think some bits could have been missed out? Would you recommend this book to a friend? What sort of people might like this book?*

Reading genres

Reading programmes in international schools frequently include texts for whole-class reading and small-group study that offer examples of writing in a range of genres. The term 'genre' describes the different categories of writing in fiction and non-fiction. Fiction genres include folk tales, historical re-imaginings, poetry, science fiction and adventure stories, among others. Typical non-fiction genres include biography, travel writing and diaries and journals.

The term genre is usually associated with reading programmes, although reading in a range of genres is obviously a first step in learning how to write for different purposes in different formats for different audiences. When teachers introduce a new genre, they customarily point out the characteristics of the form including the layout, the type of language and the special features that distinguish it. This is an occasion when the holistic teaching of reading and writing makes perfect sense.

12.2.4 Teaching older students the skills of writing

Teaching students to write in a new language when they already know how to write in their home or another language is a different process from teaching younger students to write for the first time in any language. Teaching older emergent bilinguals to be effective writers is nevertheless a challenging task. New students are likely to have experienced different prior educational experiences, including variations in the methods and expectations surrounding literacy teaching and learning. The same students will show a range of proficiency in English, from being complete beginners to being quite advanced learners. All the emergent bilingual students in a class, along with proficient speakers of English, will show a range of motivation and aptitude in the skills of writing.

Teachers have two main objectives when teaching emergent bilingual students to write: they need to introduce students to the different modes, formats and genres which are required within the school programme and they need to model the language that is typical of writing in the different forms. These objectives go hand in hand with ensuring that students are familiar with the content-area vocabulary and structures that are a necessary foundation for writing in any form.

Text Box 12.2 Learning to read and write in a different script

Many emergent bilingual students, including speakers of Arabic, Chinese, Japanese, Korean, Hindi and Hebrew, among others, have languages that are written using scripts and writing systems that are different from English. Before they can engage in reading and writing in English they have to surmount a range of challenges that do not face students whose languages use Roman script. The challenges include the need to learn the left-to-right directionality of English in place, perhaps, of symbols that are written from right to left or up and down the page. They need to learn how to form letters and numbers in Roman script, how to recognise and pronounce words in the new script and how to spell them. Only then are they in a position to make sense of the content of written material as a whole and to engage in tasks that involve writing.

Introducing students to a new script is not necessarily the major challenge that it might seem to be. The whole process is aided when reading and writing are taught side by side so that developing skills in one area serve to reinforce skills in the other. Where students are still very young there are several ways of giving them practice in forming Roman letters and in reading back words, including some attractive online options such as Letter Quiz (http://tantrumapps.com/letter-quiz/). Providing similar opportunities for older students to practise reading and writing in Roman script is a sensitive area, since much of the printed material is aimed at young learners. Fortunately, there are apps available for older students that are designed to provide practice in forming letters. These include: Easy Penmanship (bit.ly/easypenmanship) and Smarty Cursive (bit.ly/smartycursive). Technology as a whole has a powerful contribution to make in helping students to master the left-to-right directionality of English and become familiar with a new script.

A basic rule for teachers working with students who are new to the English writing system is to allow more time – time to make sense of written text in Roman script, time to form the letters and to work out the spelling of new words when writing and time to find ways of expressing their thoughts through these unfamiliar means.

Strategies that teach emergent bilingual students to write in a range of modes, formats and genres

As with the teaching of reading to students who can already read in their own languages, students who are used to writing in their home languages arrive with a rich resource on which to build when learning to write in a new language. They are in a position to transfer their skills in sentence making and paragraph building to their writing in English. Existing knowledge of the sort of language to use in writing in different formats also transfers successfully.

The concept of learning to be independent writers who use a range of writing formats to express their own ideas may, however, be new to some emergent bilingual students from different backgrounds. In some educational systems students tend to write only in response to teacher-directed prompts such as writing the answers to comprehension questions. This type of writing takes place in international schools as well, but in general students are required to be more individual and expressive in the way they write. Teachers need to be aware of the need to teach explicitly the sort of writing that is required in the curricula and programmes of study to be found in international schools.

Modes, genres and formats

Most writing programmes in international schools include teaching students how to produce different types of writing, often expressed in terms of modes, genres and formats. The term 'mode' used in this way describes the purposes of a piece of writing, e.g. narrative, persuasive or expository. The term 'format' is used to describe the way that writing is structured within the different modes and genres (see the paragraphs above for more on genres).

An overall strategic approach to teaching emergent bilingual students to write in different formats includes the following actions on the part of the teacher:

- Emergent bilinguals cannot be expected to embark on a piece of writing without a basic knowledge and understanding of the proposed content. Building on prior learning and introducing students to the key words and basic concepts associated with a new content-area topic of study are foundational approaches for teachers in international school classrooms.
- Students should be encouraged to build up personalised word-banks or topic-related dictionaries as they move through the phases of a new unit of study. This can be done in a notebook or online. This resource provides them with a ready reference during the writing phase.
- Teachers need to prepare students for writing by providing models of the sort of format that is required. Authentic material, provided that the level of language is accessible to emergent bilinguals in the classroom, is the most engaging and useful. Where students are being asked to write an autobiographical account, for example, teachers should search out examples of work created by previous students or supply print or online texts that model the format.

- Key elements in the format that students are being asked to write in should be selected and explained.
- Teachers should talk to librarians and the parents of emergent bilingual students in order to source examples of the target format/genre in students' home languages. Material in the target format in their home language gives students an understanding of what they are expected to achieve in their own writing.
- In classrooms where translanguaging is practised, students should be encouraged to write first in their own languages before moving into English. Understanding the features of the format is equally well learnt in either language. (See Section 9.2 for a discussion of translanguaging.)
- When students are asked to write in a new format it is helpful for teachers to discuss the way the work will be assessed. What qualities are found in effective examples of writing in the format?
- Classroom and specialist English teachers can usefully collaborate in taking students step by step through the way in which language is used at the different stages of a writing format. Using SmartBoards or whiteboards to break down the phases into bite-sized elements is an effective strategy.
- It is helpful with early learners of English for adults working in the classroom to talk through with students what they would like to say and to discuss possible phrases and sentences that will enable them to get their thoughts down on paper. As students develop their English language proficiency they will become aware of the differences between spoken and written English. In the early days the aim is to build up their confidence as writers.
- Teachers can support emergent bilingual students who are learning to write in new formats by supplying templates and outlines that lead them through the process. These can be teacher-made, drawn from a textbook or found online. Technology is a valuable tool in helping students to write, with the proviso that the material is of good quality and offers a sufficient degree of challenge.
- It is helpful if a teacher reads over the writing with the student and discusses it in the light of the student's own aims and against any assessment criteria that describe effective writing in the format.
- Emergent bilingual students should be congratulated on their effort and achievement when they make a significant step forward in their writing. Learning to create a well-structured piece of writing which says something worth reading in a new language and maybe a new script tends to be one of the most testing activities for emergent bilinguals in mainstream classrooms. They need encouragement and targeted praise to help them along the path.

The 'writing process' approach to writing

An approach to writing that is found in some international schools is described as 'the writing process'. Within this approach, students are invited to make initial drafts where the focus is on constructing meaning. These drafts are then shared with the teacher and fellow students who offer suggestions and make helpful comments about improving the content. After further reflection, the author then makes appropriate changes to the content and corrects grammatical errors and mistakes in spelling and punctuation. The last step is for the piece of writing to be published and shared in its final form with a wider audience of peers and parents.

Aspects of this approach are valuable for working with emergent bilingual students. Initial drafting where the focus is on the creation of meaning frees them from labouring over grammar, spelling and punctuation (although students and parents should be kept fully informed of the reasons for not insisting on correct spelling and punctuation). The notion that writing is not once-and-for-all and can be changed is also helpful. In the early days, however, following the entire process through step by step can be cumbersome for emergent bilingual students. They find it hard to factor in comments from peers and may find it difficult to perceive where they have made technical errors. Teachers need to be flexible in their use of this approach and should feel able to sidestep some of the phases if students become bogged down and exhausted.

Text Box 12.3 Writing is writing!

Learning to write does not always need to involve extended and testing activity. Emergent bilingual students can be offered opportunities to write more informally and in short bursts rather than over a longer period. This is the type of writing that is involved in many modern media and it is useful as well as being more fun for students to know how to communicate in different spheres.

Several current practices in international school classrooms require students to write in short focused ways. Personal response journals give space for students to jot down their thoughts about their reading as they move through a text. Paper and online posters designed in partnership or in small groups require students to negotiate the most apt wording with others. Extended field trip diaries and daily journals encourage students to make concise notes on a regular basis. The skills are not the same as those required by more extended pieces of writing but arguably they replicate more closely the writing skills that today's young people use as a matter of course when communicating via social media and other messaging platforms.

12.3 Multiliteracies

The widespread introduction of technology in many international schools has led to a reassessment of what is meant by literacy. 'Multiliteracies' is a term that has been coined to describe 'the diverse forms of literacy practice required for work and leisure, citizenship and community participation, personal growth and cultural expression' (O'Rourke, 2005: 1). In the case of emergent bilingual students, the capacity to communicate in all these areas in two or more languages is a further aspect of any definition of literacy teaching and learning in international schools. Within this definition and in response to the possibilities opened up by technology, the idea of literacy has expanded to include multiple communication modes where users have the capability of interacting with diverse global audiences.

A multiliteracies approach allows teachers to tap into students' own interests and experiences and gives them opportunities to become familiar with multiple ways of communicating their thoughts and ideas. For emergent bilingual students, this approach allows them to work alongside their proficient English-speaking peers on a more equal basis since, arguably, new technological applications give them readier access to a means of communication than traditional formats. With a wider view of what constitutes literacy in today's classroom, teachers increasingly incorporate new technological applications into literacy teaching and learning in their classrooms. The following examples are only a few of the possibilities available:

- *The language of blogging.* The aim of effective blogging is distinctive and effective communication. Blogging allows more varied and informal writing including fragment sentences and a move away from the 'solid paragraph' approach. Integrating blogs effectively into discussion and evidence gathering allows students to think critically and argue well. A program such as Kidblog allows students to blog safely within a private classroom blogging space.
- *Interactive posters and graphics.* These applications are described on a website devoted to reviewing educational programs and apps (Educational Technology and Mobile Learning: see details in the Resources section at the end of the chapter) as 'great learning and teaching materials to use with your students in the classroom. From explaining difficult processes to visual brainstorming, interactive graphics are a good way to consolidate students learning and promote their comprehension'. Using an application such as Glogster, students can insert text, photos, audio clips and video. Fellow students can respond with their own comments in text boxes. The type of language needed to be effective in this medium is short, focused, punchy and personal.
- *Animations apps and programs.* Animation apps such as iStopMotion for iPad and Avid Studio for iPad (see the Resources section at the end of the chapter for details) can be used by teachers to generate discussion about plot and character. Such programs can also be used to initiate literacy activities such as scriptwriting where students learn the use of characters' speech to carry a narrative forward and to indicate character development. Animation applications are also valuable as a means for students to demonstrate their knowledge and understanding in the content areas.

12.3.1 Thoughts about the multiliteracies approach

The multiliteracies approach asks that teachers and parents change their way of viewing the uses of literacy. Both these groups understand that technology has led to an explosion in the ways in which children and young people expect to communicate with each other. Most accept that technology has the power to provide enriched learning opportunities within the classroom. At the same time, parents expect students to be proficient in traditional forms of writing and tend to express concern when writing in school seems to take the form of snippets and informal pieces of instant communication.

Enthusiastic supporters of the multiliteracies approach argue that the essence of good writing in any context is that 'it works' and that today's students need to learn how to write effectively in a wide range of media. The answer at present (although things may change in the future) is to provide a balance in literacy teaching and learning. Students from all backgrounds should be taught how to express their ideas and understandings via carefully structured pieces of writing, while at the same time learning how to make effective use of the communication opportunities provided by technology.

Key Points in This Chapter

- Emergent bilingual students arrive in international schools with differing experiences of schooling as a whole and of literacy teaching and learning in particular.
- Teachers need to be prepared to take students on from wherever they are on the literacy continuum by means of effective assessment of their existing levels of literacy readiness and development.
- The issue for young emergent bilingual students is that they are learning to read and write for the first time in any language.
- The overall approach with young learners is to provide 'more of everything' in the form of more targeted support, more practice and more individual encouragement.
- With older students the challenge for teachers is to guide them in transferring existing language skills in their home or other languages to their literacy learning in English.
- With older students the overall approach is to provide models, scaffolds and step-by-step guidance in carrying out an unfamiliar literacy activity.
- New technology applications provide rich opportunities for both younger and older students to practise their language skills, to communicate their ideas and to display their learning.

Resources

Overall guidance relating to supporting different age groups of emergent bilingual students in the content areas

Chadwick, T. (2012) *Language Awareness in Teaching: A Toolkit for Content and Language Teachers.* Cambridge: Cambridge University Press. This book is designed for teachers of students generally aged from 14 to 16 who are preparing for the Cambridge 16+ examinations known as the International General Certificate of Secondary Education (IGCSE). This examination is offered in many international schools.

Mertin, P. (2013) *Breaking Through the Language Barrier: Effective Strategies for Teaching ESL Students in Secondary School Classrooms.* Woodbridge: John Catt Educational. This book is designed for teachers working with students aged 11 and upwards.

Learning Village – Online English language learning for learners in school. An online course designed to support English language learners in the mainstream classroom, appropriate for curricula used in international schools. See introductory material and video at www.ealteaching.com/

Sears, C. (1998) *Second Language Students in Mainstream Classrooms: A Handbook for Teachers in International Schools*. Clevedon: Multilingual Matters. This earlier Handbook is aimed at emergent bilingual students from ages four to around 14.

Books in print and e-books for use with young readers

Brown Bear, Brown Bear, What Do You See? (1967) by Bill Martin Jnr, illustrated by Eric Carle: New York: Henry Holt.

Oxford Owl e-books published by Oxford University Press. Interactive e-books offering activities that support young literacy learners: www.oxfordowl.co.uk

Rosie's Walk by Pat Hutchins. A classic book available in multiple forms including bilingual versions.

Sesame Street e-books offering interactive texts, also available on apps: www.ebooks.sesamestreet.org.

The Very Hungry Caterpillar by Eric Carle. Another classic young child's text that provides an example of the features that help young children to learn to read. It is published in multiple versions including bilingual texts.

Apps that contribute to literacy learning

Apps that offer practice in forming Roman letter shapes in upper and lower case:

For young students: Letter Quiz (bit.ly/letterquizapp);

For older students learning to read and write in a new script: Easy Penmanship (bit.ly/easypenmanship) and Smarty Cursive (bit.ly/smartycursive).

Blobble Write: an app or downloadable program that helps students learn to form upper and lower case letter shapes: www.blobbleworld.com.

Oxford Dictionaries website, offering a range of children's dictionaries and describing the use of personalised dictionaries: http://www.oxforddictionaries.com/words/for-children-and-schools.

Website that offers suggestions for creating effective word walls (to offer immediate access to necessary topic-related vocabulary): www.k12reader.com/10-great-word-wall-strategies-for-classrooms/.

Technology applications that extend students' use of literacy

Downloadable templates of graphic organisers: http://www.netrover.com/~kingskid/graphic/graphic.htm.

For 25 reusable graphic organisers that guide students in writing in a range of formats, see the app: *Tools 4 Learning* by Mobile Learning Services.

Glogster is described as 'an interactive visual learning platform: this platform offers students the possibility of creating interactive posters and other graphic forms that allow them to download text, photos, audio and video clips and for their peers to post comment: www.glogster.com.

Kidblog offers the means to produce restricted access blogs that are safe for children to use: www.kidblog.org.

Multiliteracies

Educational Technology and Mobile Learning. A resource of educational web tools and mobile apps for teachers and educators: www.educatorstechnology.com.

O'Rourke, M. (2005) Multiliteracies for 21st Century Schools. Australian National Schools Network. *Snapshot* 2. http://www.darlingdeer.com.au/lcindex.html.

Animation and movie-making apps: iStopMotion for iPad: bit.ly/istopidpadapp; Avid Studio for iPad (renamed as Pinnacle Studio for iPad): http://www.pinnaclesys.com/publicsite/us/products/studio/ipad/.

References

Baker, C. (2014) *A Parents' and Teachers' Guide to Bilingualism* (4th edn). Bristol: Multilingual Matters.

Cummins, J. (1996) *Negotiating Identities: Education for Empowerment in a Diverse Society*. Ontario, CA: California Association for Bilingual Education.

Cummins, J. and Sayers, D. (1996) Multicultural education and technology: Promise and pitfalls. *Multicultural Education* 3 (3), 4–10.

de Castell, S. and Luke, A. (1986) Models of literacy in North American schools: Social and historical conditions and consequences. In S. de Castell, A. Luke and K. Egan (eds) *Literacy, Society, and Schooling*. New York: Cambridge University Press.

Hamer, J. (2005) Exploring literacy with infants from a sociocultural perspective. *New Zealand Journal of Teachers' Work* 2 (2), 70–75.

Ministry of Education (1996) *Te Whāriki: He Whāriki Matauranga mō ng ā mokopuna o Aotearoa*. Early Childhood Curriculum. Wellington: Learning Media.

Vygotsky, L.S. (1987 [1934, 1960]) Thinking and speech. In R. Rieber and A. Carton (eds) *L.S. Vygotsky, Collected Works*, Vol. 1 (trans. N. Minick) (pp. 39–285). New York: Plenum.

Warschauer, M. (1997) A sociocultural approach to literacy and its significance for CALL. In K. Murphy-Judy and R. Sanders (eds) *Nexus: The Convergence of Research & Teaching Through New Information Technologies* (pp. 88–97). Durham, NC: University of North Carolina.

13 Scaffolding the Learning of Emergent Bilingual Students in the Mainstream Classroom: Class Talk, Mathematics, Science and Social Studies

This chapter is devoted to practical suggestions for scaffolding the learning of emergent bilingual students in mainstream curriculum areas. It focuses on the spoken and written language needed for participation in these areas and on the need to teach the learning behaviours required in programmes and curricula to be found in international schools.

The sequence of Chapter 13 is as follows:

- Introduction: Scaffolding the learning of emergent bilingual students in the curriculum areas.
- Including students in class talk.
- Teaching mathematics to emergent bilingual students.
- Scaffolding the learning of science.
- Guiding emergent bilinguals through the report-writing process.

Note: As in the previous chapter, the terms 'young' and 'younger' are used to describe students between the ages of three and eight and 'older' is used to describe students between the ages of eight and 14.

Introduction

This chapter is devoted to the language and learning needs of emergent bilingual students in the areas of mathematics, science and social studies. The chapter is prefaced by suggestions for systematically including these students in class talk, an activity which is central to the pedagogic approaches found in international schools. The suggestions provided here are designed to scaffold the learning in the content areas of emergent bilinguals with a range of prior schooling experiences and who exhibit different levels of proficiency in the school language.

In order for teachers to include students with this level of diversity in the learning of the classroom, they need to adopt a consistent strategic approach that enables students to participate fully. These strategies include the modelling and explicit teaching of the language skills and learning behaviours required for successful participation in mainstream content areas.

Sequence of the chapter

Section 13.1 is devoted to class talk and ways of including emergent bilingual in whole-class and small-group discussions, activities that underpin the learning approaches in most international schools. The section sets out practical actions on the part of the teacher that enable students to make sense of what they hear and to build up the ability and confidence to contribute.

Section 13.2 is concerned with scaffolding the learning of mathematics. The section addresses the different challenges presented by younger students who are learning this subject for the first time and older students who have been learning mathematics in their previous schools for some years. Practical suggestions are set out which are designed to meet the challenges presented by students who have been taught mathematics in different ways and who have experienced variations in prior sequencing of mathematics content. Science is the focus of Section 13.3, with the emphasis on scaffolding the learning of students in programmes that may be unfamiliar to them, such as the enquiry-based approach of the Primary Years Programme (PYP) of the International Baccalaureate Organisation (IBO) (www.ibo.org/pyp/curriculum/index.cfm).

Finally, in Section 13.4, the topic of oral and written reports is addressed. Reports of this type are a feature of international school classrooms and are very challenging to emergent bilingual students unused to this sort of activity because of the amount of language processing that is required. This section sets out a set of supportive strategies alongside the different stages of creating a report based on personal investigation and evidence gathering.

13.1 Class Talk

The aim of this section is to suggest ways in which emergent bilingual students can be included in class talk of all sorts, whether in whole-class sessions or in smaller groups.

13.1.1 Including emergent bilingual students in class talk

Classrooms in international schools typically contain students at every level of English language development from complete beginners to speakers for whom English is their primary language. Learning how to manage such groups so that each student is given a chance to contribute is an essential professional requirement for teachers in this situation.

Clearly the level of students' English language proficiency is a factor in their ability to participate; however, as experienced teachers often point out, the personality of the student has a large contribution to make. Students' readiness in taking risks and their ability to make effective use of the language they have acquired may have more impact on their level of participation than the apparent level of their English. Teachers often give instances of students with very limited English who contribute effectively in discussions while proficient speakers of English prefer to remain silent.

The point of this section is to highlight the strategic approaches that make a difference to the ways in which emergent bilingual students are able to engage in class talk. Such strategies include enabling students to construct meaning out of what they hear and easing the way for students to contribute to a class conversation or focused discussion.

13.1.2 What is meant by class talk?

Class talk is used here as a term to describe the different aspects of classroom discourse. In international school classrooms, as in many schools, class talk is the medium that sustains the social and academic activity of the class. Class talk is the means of imparting practical information about the routines and events of school life and of building up a sense of community within the classroom. It is also a key element in the type of teaching and learning to be found in most international schools, where it serves as the foundation for later enquiry and investigation in the content areas.

(a) Shared conversation and discussion

The overall aim for teachers during whole-class conversations and discussions is to find the means to allow emergent bilingual students at different levels of English proficiency to make sense of the meaning of what is being said and to contribute their own thoughts. The following strategies contribute to achieving this aim:

- Introduce the sort of atmosphere for general class discussion that gives opportunities for humour, sharing and bonding.
- Slow down the dialogue: create a class atmosphere where each student is given time to process the language needed to contribute.
- Avoid leaping in to rephrase immediately.
- Allow students several attempts: avoid immediately solving students' communication problems for them.
- Ask a speaker of the same home language to explain the meaning – and then ensure that it is repeated in English.
- Help students to make the best use of the language they know by suggesting vocabulary and helpful phrases.
- Keep an ongoing visual record of basic vocabulary and grammatical structures relating to the topics that are routinely discussed in general class discussion. Display

these items in the classroom or encourage students to keep an online personal dictionary.

- Collaborate with specialist English teachers to ensure that beginning emergent bilingual students are taught basic question-and-answer formats. These should include questions that use question words such as What? Where? When? Why? and How? as in 'What did you do at the weekend?', and questions made by inverting verbs, as in 'Did you see the pictures of the flooding in Indonesia on television last night?'.
- Engage in a question-and-answer dialogue with a proficient English speaker first in order to model the language for emergent bilingual students, e.g. 'How did you get on with your homework last night?', 'It took a long time because I couldn't find the information I needed.'
- Post important announcements on the school's virtual learning environment (VLE) (if used) or website or supply a back-up in hard copy form.
- Establish a routine of students immediately writing down important information in their class diaries.

(b) Giving instructions

Emergent bilingual students need to be able to understand instructions if they are to feel a sense of control over their activity in the classroom and when carrying out homework. Instructions about the sequence of an upcoming unit of study or for individual assignments are more effective if teachers systematically follow the same routines. These include:

- Signalling with body language and by a routinely used opening phrase that an important announcement is about to be made. *'Listen carefully please: this is important!'.*
- Using consistent phrases in setting out the sequence of upcoming units of study.
- Adopting a regular pattern for setting out instructions for individual assignments.
- Posting instructions in the same place and in a similar format on the school's VLE, website or via hard copy.
- Checking to ensure that students have understood the instructions.
- Asking a student who speaks the same home language to intervene to help a student to understand.
- If it is apparent that an individual student has difficulty in following homework instructions, communicating with parents about ways to ensure that students understand what is expected of them. Check that someone at home is able to read and understand English. If that is not the case, ensure that someone in the school community is brought in to provide back-up for the family.

(c) Guided questioning

Guided questioning is a key strategy in allowing emergent bilingual students first to establish the basic information about a topic and then to move on to higher level conceptual understandings. Guided questioning using the following sequence offers an effective means of structuring and expanding the learning of emergent bilingual students.

The examples are taken from a social studies topic entitled 'How We Move Around'. This unit of study was designed for young students aged five to seven years. The pedagogical approach is of a type to be found in many international school classrooms that derive their programmes largely from national curricula. The approaches are equally valid for use with all ages of students.

- In classes that contain emergent bilingual students at every level of English language proficiency guided questions are used to establish the basic facts about a topic.
- The process is more effective if students also receive introductory input in visual, oral or experiential form.
  - *In this case the class is seated on the floor round a teacher holding a Big Book entitled* This is the Way We Go to School, *published by Scholastic News Non-Fiction Readers: Kids Like Me (Global Awareness) – a series designed for multicultural classrooms (http://listbuilders.scholastic.com).*
- Effective guided questioning should also elicit students' prior knowledge or personal experience of the topic.
  - *'Where you lived before, how did you go to school?'*
  - *'How do you come to school now?'*
  - *'What other forms of transport do you see when you come to school?'*
  - *'How do these forms of transport move along?'*
- Key vocabulary words and phrases central to an understanding of the topic should be emphasised throughout the introductory sessions and displayed in a visually meaningful manner in the classroom (a simple list is not a very effective means; see Section 12.1 for more on effective key word graphics).
  - *Types of transport are displayed on a SmartBoard or via flash cards, video, etc. Pairs of students are asked to group transport images under headings setting out the different forms of propulsion. Teachers use questions to ask why students are making their choices.*
- When students have acquired a working outline of the topic, teachers are then free to move on to questions that require students to engage at a higher level with the content of the topic. Questions of this type tend to be open ended. Such questions ask students to present their own views and to give reasons for their opinions.
  - *'Can you give me the reasons why many children don't walk to school anymore?'*
  - *'What would it be like if we didn't have transport to help us move around?'*
- Higher order questions can also be used to encourage students to:
  - Explain why something is important:
    - *'Why is it a good thing that people can move around?'*
  - Make connections between different examples of the same event or feature:
    - *'What is the difference between the ways that people get around where you lived before and here?'*
  - Give opinions:
    - *'Why do you think people like driving around in their own cars?'*

- – *'What do you think leads to traffic jams?'*
- ○ Suggest solutions to problems:
  - – *'How could we cut down on the amount of traffic on the roads?'*
- ○ Make comparisons:
  - – *'What is the quickest way of getting to school?'*
  - – *'Which way of getting children to school uses the least fuel?'*
- ○ Draw conclusions from what they have seen or experienced:
  - – *'We've talked about pollution. What was the air like where you lived before? What is the air like here? What are some of the things that make a difference to the quality of the air in a place?'*
- ○ Generalise and apply their learning:
  - – *'What other aspects in modern life lead to poor air quality?'*
  - – *'What do you think is the best way for children to get to school?' 'Why do you think that?'*
  - – *'Why would it be better if everybody came to school on bikes?'*

(d) Teacher-guided reporting

A form of class talk described as 'teacher-guided reporting' is a way for the teacher to provide a framework of questioning that allows students to display what they have learnt. The occasion can involve a student reporting back to the whole class about research undertaken in a small group or it can take the form of teacher conversations with individuals or small groups of students. The teacher's role is to guide students through a topic so that they can reveal their understandings, with oral prompts where necessary.

The following questions and comments are examples of the way in which a teacher-guided reporting session provides students with a framework to talk about their work undertaken in connection with the *How We Move Around* unit of study:

- *'What have we learnt today/this week? Let's start with the ways we move around. Tell us first of all about the way you came to school today.'*
- *'What forms of transport did your group work on?'*
- *'What did you discover about the ways that bikes and scooters move along?'*
- *'What makes different forms of transport move around?'*
- *'Why do we have different forms of transport?' 'Could you go to another country across the sea by car?' 'How do you think things get into the shops?'*
- *'What are the good things about being able to move around?'*
- *'Tell us about traffic jams. Have you ever been in one? Do you know why the cars and buses had stopped? Did all the transport stop during the traffic jam?'*
- *'What are the problems about so many people wanting to move around? Can you give me any examples of the problems caused by so many cars?'*

Asking students to report on what they know or have found out provides teachers with information about the level of a student's understanding which helps to inform future teaching. A further benefit is that the process of getting together their thoughts helps students to make sense of what they know.

For emergent bilingual students, reporting in this way without guidance can be daunting. They may not know how to structure their report or what information to include. In both cases, teachers guide students via appropriate questioning to reveal what they know without putting words into their mouths. Teachers skilled in this role help students to structure their learning in a way that leads to further understanding of the key information and concepts on the part of the speaker and listeners.

Teachers should encourage speakers of the same home language to explain the questions to early users of English. The aim is for students to produce answers in English. This is an approach that should be used with sensitivity in classrooms where there are a number of sole speakers of one home language for whom this strategy is not a possibility.

13.2 Scaffolding the Learning of Mathematics in the Mainstream Classroom

13.2.1 Younger students

Young emergent bilingual students exhibit a wide range in their prior experience of schooling as a whole and in their formal learning of mathematics in particular. New students may have already received one or two years of teaching if they come directly from school systems that begin formal education at the age of four or five. Others of the same age may not yet have started formal mathematics teaching of any sort. The same approach applies as for the teaching of literacy to this age group. The new students need to be assessed to find out where they are on the mathematics learning continuum and teachers need to be prepared to take students 'on from where they are'.

In the case of mathematics, a mix of experience in the class is potentially more challenging since mathematics knowledge is arguably built up in a relatively sequential manner. Students need to understand basic number concepts and operations in an appropriate sequence so that they have a consistent foundation for later learning.

Mathematics as a subject may seem easier for emergent bilinguals to engage in since it is numerically based. However, mathematics in international school classrooms involves students from very young ages in talking about mathematical facts and concepts and in solving word-based problems. Mathematics teaching in early childhood classrooms tends also to involve hands-on activity and practical projects which involve the use of new language and learning behaviours. Teachers in these classrooms need to incorporate strategic approaches that enable emergent bilinguals to participate in all these activities.

13.2.2 Older students

Older students arriving new at an international school are likely to have experienced a similar variety in their experiences of mathematics teaching and learning. In the case of older students the number of years of teaching they have received may vary along with the content and the approach to mathematics teaching in general. In the case of students who come from schooling systems such as those in Singapore, Korea and Japan and the major cities of China (see PISA test results, 2012), their level of mathematics is likely to be in advance of many of the students. Others will have covered less ground because they started school at a later age in their previous schooling systems. Emergent bilingual students of all backgrounds are faced with the challenge of learning the language needed to participate in all aspects of mathematics learning in an unfamiliar language.

Older emergent bilingual students have the potential advantage of being able to use their existing knowledge to inform their future learning of mathematics content as well as the language they need to engage in the subject. This is certainly true with numerical calculations although not the case with the solving of word problems where the need to understand the nature of the problem and to talk with others about its solution present challenges to early learners of English.

13.2.3 Activities to be found in mathematics classrooms in international schools

The way mathematics is approached in international school classrooms may present a further barrier for emergent bilingual students used to different educational systems. This is especially true of schools that have adopted the IB programmes which are based on enquiry-based and cross-disciplinary learning. In this case, students may be required to work in small groups on mathematics-related projects involving a different and unfamiliar use of language and a more applied approach to mathematics. In general, the approach to mathematics learning in international school classrooms tends to include experiential collaborative activity alongside more traditional individual ways of working. This may be unfamiliar to many of the new emergent bilingual students in a class and part of teacher's role in a mathematics classroom is to teach the language and learning behaviours needed to function in this type of programme.

13.2.4 Mathematics resources in mainstream classrooms

The approach to mathematics that is found in many international school classrooms involves a range of resources and materials. The aspects of these resources that relate to their effectiveness or otherwise with emergent bilingual students are set out here.

Textbooks

Most international schools rely on textbooks (or workbooks in the case of younger students) to provide the basic framework of the mathematics programme. Many of these textbook series are attractively presented with a high graphic content. In the case of workbooks designed for young learners, the activities generally involve frames and graphic guides that lead students through their learning.

In most textbooks, even for quite young children, some of the new mathematics facts and concepts are presented via word-based explanations. Often the examples given contain culturally related material such as Western-style food stuffs and other items and assume a certain lifestyle. Typically textbooks use the weights and measures systems and currencies that derive from the publishers' countries of origin. These differences can confuse young learners. In an international school, from time to time at least, students should be asked to carry out mathematics activities that involve other measurement and currency systems, including their own and that of the host country.

- Examples of use with emergent bilingual students:
  - *Where mathematics workbooks and textbooks have been chosen with a view to their high graphic content, there are benefits to be gained from using them as a foundation for teaching emergent bilinguals mathematics in English. For young children, the repetition of graphic and number-based activities found in most workbooks provides a useful experience of vocabulary and concepts. Many children enjoy the sense of achievement that comes from working their way through manageable tasks to the end of the book.*
  - *For older students, well-chosen textbook series provide a foundation for their mathematics learning that they can return to and which provides a consistency of approach in the classroom. Students from other schooling systems are likely to be used to an all-encompassing use of textbooks and find security in the continuing use of textbooks to put over and practise new material.*

Manipulatives

(Manipulatives are sets of objects that give students insights into theoretical concepts via the use of hands-on manipulation.) Although manipulatives are traditionally used for work with younger students, they are a useful addition to the tools that teachers have to hand in teaching mathematics to students of all ages. Manipulatives have the ability to provide students with the foundation to understand mathematics at a conceptual level. Commercial manipulatives that can be purchased include coloured tiles, pattern blocks, Cuisenaire rods and geoboards, among others. They can include found objects such as shells and pebbles and students can model or cut out their own versions. For older students, virtual manipulatives may be more appropriate and flexible to use and can be found on general mathematics sites such as Math Playground (www.mathplayground.com).

The value of manipulatives for work with emergent bilingual students is that they can be used not only to put across a mathematics concept but also to introduce students to the language involved in talking about mathematics via collaborative activity. Small groups or pairs of students discussing the placement of manipulatives either with real-life objects or online in order to display conceptual information is a very powerful enabling activity.

- Examples of use with emergent bilingual students:
    - *Fractions are an example of an area where manipulatives are a useful tool for helping students to understand the concepts behind the numbers. Using fraction strips or pattern blocks that can be manipulated into whole objects such as cakes or pies and then divided into component fractions is a familiar but effective strategy.*
    - *Activities that involve manipulation can be carried out online using programs such as Math Playground, an open-access site which offers a range of attractive virtual manipulatives for students to move into place on the screen. However, engaging students in real life collaborative activity potentially involves them in more talk about mathematics concepts and more overall language usage.*

Modelling and construction materials

In classrooms where students of all ages are expected to create visual and 3D means of displaying mathematical information and concepts, teachers should build up a store of useful aids to modelling and construction.

- Examples of use with emergent bilingual students:
    - *Modelling and construction materials allow students to engage in applied mathematics activities which bring to life the concept being taught and allow them to display their learning. The process of making a scale model such as a bridge or building with a partner or of making a model of the school campus to scale, for instance, embeds an understanding of what scale means and involves students in both practical and higher level language.*

Measuring tapes and beakers, scales, clipboards etc.

These items are typically found in the classrooms of young students and are used to give children practice in weighing, measuring and carrying out surveys. Often they are used in learning activities and projects that integrate mathematics and science. Activities that involve students in carrying out practical activities alongside their peers and in talking over the results and ways to display them are stress-free methods of introducing emergent bilingual students to the language involved.

- Examples of use with emergent bilingual students:
    - *Classroom equipment that enables students to measure or weigh or allows students to make lists and collect data is valuable for use where these activities are embedded in larger scale experiments and investigations. Students who are asked to measure the displacement of water, for instance, are involved in hands-on mathematical activities that involve speculation, suggesting, theorising, etc.*

Technology

Technology is a powerful aid in mathematics teaching and has the potential to support the learning of emergent bilingual students in engaging and motivational ways (see

Section 7.2, 'Technology provision in international schools', for a summary of the provision available in many international schools).

Basic applications that are in use in most classrooms at an age-appropriate level are calculators and SmartBoards (interactive whiteboards). It is worth remembering that not all new emergent bilingual students will be accustomed to their uses in school and teachers should factor in time to teach them how to engage with these items in the classroom.

Technology has the power to enhance mathematics teaching in many ways. It offers students attractive opportunities to practise basic mathematical activities in areas such as arithmetic, geometry and algebra. It has the power to engage small groups of students in making suggestions about solving number and word problems. As a plus, many of these activities come in the form of interactive games with instant feedback and scoring which motivate students to compete against themselves and others.

- Examples of use with emergent bilingual students:
  - *An area where the interactive capability of online mathematics programs is a valuable teaching tool is in the collecting of data and creating graphs which display analysis of the results in different ways. One attractive offering of this sort for young students is Graph and Tally (www.turtlediary.com). In this program students are shown how to carry out a survey, create a tally sheet to show the different objects being counted and then are led through the creation of various graphic forms of displaying the information collected. The options include Venn diagrams, picture and bar graphs and pictographs. A program that offers a similar capability for older students is Create a Graph (www.neces.ed.gov/NCESKIDS/createa-graph). In every case, the power of these programs for use with emergent bilingual students lies in students working together in pairs or in small groups to complete a task. The usefulness is enhanced if the online learning is applied to real-life mathematics activities involving further language.*

13.2.5 Overall strategic approaches

There are a number of overall strategic approaches that effectively support younger and older students when applied consistently throughout mathematics classes:

Teaching mathematics vocabulary

- Identify key phrases or new vocabulary to pre-teach.
- Provide visual cues, graphic representations, gestures, found items and images to introduce and model key items of mathematics vocabulary.
- Show students how to build up personal mathematics dictionaries with definitions in both number, word and graphic form. This can either be on paper or via an online

application such as A Maths/Math Dictionary for Kids (www.amathsdictionary-forkids.com).

- Teach vocabulary via the use of manipulatives, a word wall, etc.
- Encourage students to offer bilingual support to each other.
- Involve parents in talking over mathematical terms in their home languages. Send a limited number of terms home for family discussion each week if this seems appropriate.

Modelling and teaching the reading and understanding of written mathematics problems

- Students need to be able to read and understand the text, both the meaning of individual words in context and the overall question that is being asked.
- Students need to be able to talk over the answers and come up with solutions.
- Teachers need to show students how to move from making sense of the words to creating number sentences.
- Teachers need to place students in small groups to make diagrams, create graphics or construct graphs that illustrate ways of leading to the answers.
- Teachers and students need to work together to show how to set out the answers to written mathematics problems.

Talking and writing about mathematic learning

- Individually, in pairs or in small groups, ask students to reverse the process of solving word problems. Have students translate symbols and numbers into words and write the sentence out. This makes clear the process involved in solving the problem.
- Write out standard mathematics numerical statements in word form – leave blanks for students to fill in. Use this approach in helping them to learn mathematics theories.
- Emergent bilingual students tend to find geometry one of the most accessible aspects of mathematics because of the graphic content. Use geometry as a means to build up confidence in preparation for more abstract topics such as algebra.
- Embed mathematics in hands-on science investigations so that students have further experiences of speculative mathematics language.
- Include writing activities in mathematics classes. Model how students might describe the way they reached a solution to a problem. Ask them to write about their overall mathematics learning.
- Ask groups of students to create problems that require the use of a single mathematical concept. Ask them to provide visuals or manipulatives to help other students to solve the problem. (See Text Box 7.4 for an example of students working in this way.)

Text Box 13.1 A checklist of terms used in writing down mathematics problems

See also bilingual glossaries supplied by University of the State of New York and NY State Education Department: www.p12.nysed.gov/biling/.

- **Terms associated with addition:** add, plus, combine, and, the sum of, increased by, find the total, all together, in all. 'Two and two make four.'
- Terms associated with subtraction: subtract from, decrease by, less, take away, minus, difference, have left, How much change does he …? How much longer does it take to travel by road than to travel by …? How much greater is … than …? How much less is … than …? fewer/more than, 'Ten take away five equals five.'
- **Terms associated with multiplication:** times, multiplied by, … times as much/many …, find the product. 'Six sixes are 36.'
- **Terms associated with division:** divided into, divided by, how many in each …? How many times larger …? 'Eight divided by four makes four.'
- **Ways of asking and giving answers**: total, equals, makes, what is the result? How much is left when …? Give the total.
- **Terms involving comparison:** high, higher, highest, higher than, large, larger, Which is the larger? Which is the largest? Is the red apple heavier than the green apple? smaller than, greater than.
- **How much? How many?:** Explain the grammar behind the different forms.
- **Commands**: choose, choose between, build, find, explain, use, try, put, repeat, do, make.
- **Questions:** How far did …? Is it possible for …? What kind of …? What number did you use to …? Into how many slices did Mum divide the pizza? What day of the week did …? How long did it take the car to …? How long did it take for … to reach …?
- **Volume:** more, less, greater than, smaller than.
- **Measurement:** longer, shorter, How long is …? How far is …?
- **Weight**: How heavy is …? How much does it weigh?
- **Estimation:** What's your guess about how …? What do you think is …? What is the likely result? What do you think would be a good answer? approximately, roughly, About how much bigger would you think …?
- **Illustrated vocabulary of geometry**, with names and simple definitions of shapes, angles and forms.
- Provide vocabulary words for **weights**, **measures** and **currency**. Do not assume that emergent bilingual students will understand the weight, measurement or money terms used in international school texts.

(Continued)

Text Box 13.1 A checklist of terms used in writing down mathematics problems (*Continued*)

- Supply both **imperial** and **metric** terms if necessary in your school. Allow students to make up word problems using their own currencies.
- Do not forget to display a **list of common symbols and their definitions** for easy reference: addition, subtraction, multiplication, division, equals, per cent, greater than, smaller than, etc.

Adapted from the author's earlier Handbook (Sears, 1998).

13.3 Scaffolding the Learning of Science in the Mainstream Classroom

Science teaching in many international schools takes a form that would be familiar to teachers and students in other schooling systems. Students are introduced to a new topic via a hands-on demonstration, video or text. The teacher introduces the concept that underpins the new material and then gives students instructions about setting up an experiment that will demonstrate the concept in practice. Often the experimental phase begins with a demonstration by the teacher. Students are encouraged to generate a theory from the data they gather and to generalise their theory to other contexts. Very often in this type of programme, at some stage in the school year, students take part in a larger scale project either individually or in small groups which builds on and demonstrates a topic within the year's curriculum. Many schools enhance their science teaching with science fairs and field trips.

An approach to science of this type is found in international schools at primary (elementary) level that use programmes imported from English-speaking school systems. This approach is also typical of science teaching in most programmes delivered to older students, including the Middle Years Programme (MYP; www.ibo.org/myp/curriculum/) of the IBO (although with differences and additions).

The programmes where science teaching takes a different form are the IB PYP (www.ibo.org/pyp/curriculum/index.cfm) and to some extent the International Primary Curriculum (www.greatlearning.com/ipc/news/ipc-science-learning/). Both these programmes adopt, in different formats, an enquiry-based or investigative approach to science.

13.3.1 Teaching science to emergent bilingual students

New emergent bilingual students in international schools are faced with similar challenges in the science classroom to those in other content areas. They are faced with the need to acquire the vocabulary and structures that are involved in carrying out science activities and also to learn the spoken and written language skills that are specific to science.

The teacher's role is similarly to scaffold the learning of emergent bilingual students as they move through the phases of a science topic of study. Most of the strategies that are effective in giving emergent bilingual students access to science learning are applicable to the different programmes of study and curricula to be found in international schools.

Note: a useful approach which is effective for all types of science programmes is to provide a bank of science terms which can be on permanent display or on the school's VLE. Students themselves can also build up their own dictionaries of essential science vocabulary as they move through the content of the science programme on offer in the school.

13.3.2 Challenges for new emergent bilingual students in enquiry-based science programmes

Emergent bilingual students who enter international schools that offer the IB PYP learn science as part of the overall enquiry-based approach built round a limited number of units of study. The element that may be new to some students and their parents is that science in the PYP tends not to be treated as a separate subject. There is a requirement that a science course of study is covered, but implementation in the classroom tends to be embedded in cross-disciplinary Units of Inquiry. Emergent bilingual students in PYP schools learn their science in the same way as they learn other content-area subjects such as social studies – that is, via holistic enquiry-based learning.

Becoming accustomed to embedded science learning in enquiry-based programmes

Students (and their parents) who have come directly from national schooling systems where science is largely teacher and textbook driven may find the basic premises of enquiry-based learning difficult to comprehend. In place of structured learning involving prescribed programmes of study, they must adjust to a more open-ended style of teaching and learning. In enquiry-based learning it is students' own investigations and research which are the central means of gaining knowledge and understanding about a science topic.

In order to participate in this type of learning, students in a class must become familiar with the sort of classroom activity that involves:

- the collaborative creation of meaning (in place of teacher-supplied information);
- designing their own questions and methods of enquiry;
- joining with others in carrying out investigations (in place of independent assignments);
- speculation about outcomes (rather than knowing that there is a right answer);
- using their own results as a basis to generate theory (instead of acquiring theoretical understandings from the teacher or a text);
- being assessed on their own learning initiatives (rather than on predetermined knowledge items).

13.3.3 Phases of an enquiry-based science unit of study (the strategies set out here are also appropriate for use in curriculum-driven science classes)

A Unit of Inquiry with the title 'Light and Dark' is used to provide examples of what the strategies for scaffolding the learning of emergent bilingual students look like in practice. In the unit, a group of early learners of English are invited to focus on the ways in which nocturnal animals have adapted to their living conditions. The specialist English teacher is involved in the planning of the work with these students throughout. The unit is designed for students of 9–10 years old.

Pre-teaching, front-loading, introductory phase

Students are introduced to basic information about the topic. They are given tasks that enable them to find out key facts independently.

- *Students work in small groups to create webs that set out natural and man-made sources of light.*

Class teachers and specialist teachers agree on the pre-teaching of key words connected to the topic.

- *The specialist teacher creates key word visuals which are then given to students to research online in their home languages or in a picture dictionary. This can also be given as a homework assignment.*

Teachers introduce ways of thinking about 'Dark and Light', including cycles of darkness and light, adaptation and change, and how darkness and light affect the movement of living things.

- *Emergent bilingual students are introduced to the way the topic relates to living creatures. Teachers use online material to get information across and display vocabulary in use. They use material such as National Geographic's* Night Owls *or the BBC site* Nocturnal Animals, *to be found by Googling the titles.*

The class teacher uses guided questioning (See Section 13.1.2(d) to encourage students to engage with the topic and to contribute their own thoughts and understandings related to the unit of study as a whole.

The teacher ensures that students' prior knowledge about the topic is activated and that their own experiences are introduced into the discussion.

Teachers and students together establish key questions that illuminate the topic.

- *Class and specialist teachers work with emergent bilingual students to create questions that relate to the adaptation of nocturnal animals.*

The teacher guides students individually or in small groups in constructing meaningful experiments and investigations that relate to the key questions.

- *Class and specialist teachers support emergent bilingual students in deciding on a research topic. They agree to investigate the special features of nocturnal animals that allow them to live in the dark. A visit to the nocturnal animal house at the local zoo is to be the site for the observations.*

Teachers and students decide on the means of displaying the findings from their experiments and enquiry.

- *Students, supported by teachers, decide to make a PowerPoint presentation to display their findings, importing their own photos and diagrams to display adaptive features such as the eyes of nocturnal animals.*

The teacher sets out the means of assessing the outcomes of students' investigations.

- *The criteria for a successful investigation are explained to the emergent bilingual students separately from the whole class.*

Students carry out their experiments and investigations and make generalisations based on their findings. See Section 13.4 for further ways of carrying out an investigation and of reporting the findings.

- *They ask the librarian to help them.*
- *They visit the zoo again to conduct an interview with the keeper of the nocturnal animal house.*
- *They make notes and drawings and research further detail about the construction of the eye of a sloth.*

Students are given time to create their presentation.

- *One of the parents of the emergent bilingual students comes into school to help them put it together.*

Finally, the groups present their findings in the form of an oral report, poster, online presentation, video clip or by other means.

Teachers and students reflect together on the presentations, discuss how they measure against the assessment criteria, ask questions and make suggestions about future learning and student action.

13.4 Scaffolding Written Reports and Oral Presentations

Many of the academic programmes that are current in international schools require students at some point in their study of a content-area topic to create a written report or prepare an oral presentation based on personal research. In enquiry-based programmes, much of the learning is displayed by means of reports in various formats. Reporting on a science investigation is a standard way of expressing evidence-based theoretical conclusions.

Reporting activities of this type presents challenges to emergent bilingual students when they are in the beginning and intermediate phases of their English language development. Each stage in doing the research and creating a report requires students to process and organise large amounts of language. Many of the stages involve students in using different language skills. The whole project is expected to occupy many hours of student time in the classroom and at home and to be a key element in assessing a student's command and understanding of a content-area topic. It is not surprising that emergent bilingual students (and their teachers and parents) find written reports and oral presentations daunting.

13.4.1 Breaking down the investigation and reporting stages into manageable chunks

Many teachers adopt a policy of breaking down the investigation and reporting stages into sections under headings, usually with a date beside them. Often this schedule is posted on the school's VLE on the class link or given to the students in paper form. Students are expected to have worked through the stage by the date given and thus to have the final piece of work completed on time.

From the point of view of emergent bilingual students, this information is rarely at a basic enough level to act as a scaffold for the process of carrying out and reporting on a personal investigation. Class teachers who wish to support such students in gaining benefit from the process will need to provide an accessible, step-by-step outline of the stages involved.

A fundamental strategy is to liaise with the other adults who work with a student in order to supply support at an appropriate level at all stages of the project. This collaboration includes specialist English teachers, teaching assistants, special needs teachers (where they are involved) and, perhaps controversially, the students' parents.

With regard to parental involvement in large-scale projects, most teachers in international schools recognise that parents have a valuable part to play in supporting their children's learning. Many parents are in a position to explain what is required at each stage of the process in their shared home language and to help the student negotiate each aspect of the project in English. Some teachers might question the validity of assessing an end-product where it is understood that there has been considerable parental input. More experienced teachers recognise that parental support enables students to carry out complex tasks and gives them access to content-area learning and practice in essential language skills. Later, most parents see the value of standing back and letting their children work through the tasks in a more independent manner.

13.4.2 Setting out the stages of creating a report based on personal research

The following outline sets out the essential stages needed to create a report based on personal research. Suggestions for step-by-step support during each stage are included. The outline was created to scaffold a project entitled 'Living and Working in London'. The international school which the students attended is based in central London.

(1) Discuss students' experiences and understandings about London. Arrive at some key questions about living and working in London.
   – *Offer suggestions about topics to consider: how people get about; London is a series of villages; the arts in London; the places that visitors to London most like to visit; the meaning of the river for Londoners; London's markets; what people do on a Sunday; the communities who live in London.*
   – *Guide students in framing questions that lead to insightful and illuminating accounts of the topic.*

(2) Talk with students about what they each aim to investigate.
   – *Students can work individually, in pairs or small groups. Ask students to come up with questions about an aspect that interests them that will lead to the gathering of information and insights about living and working in London.*

(3) Brainstorm what the students need to do to find evidence that answers their questions:
   – *What sort of evidence do they need to gather? What do students need to find out? Whom do they need to speak to? Where do they need to go to gain information?*

(4) Make out a contents list for what they should include in a report.

   According to the level of English of the students involved, teachers can supply written prompts to support students in working through aspects of the report: these can take the form of guiding questions and comments that reflect students' own views about relevant content.

   Title: Covent Garden: the history of London in a building
   – *What are your research questions?*
   – *How are you going to find out the information you need?*
   Introduction: The history of Covent Garden shows how cities change.
     Write short chapters about the following topics:
   – *A brief history of Covent Garden Market.*
   – *Why did the Market move?*
   – *What is Covent Garden used for now?*
   – *How has the building changed?*
   – *What does this say about modern London?*
   – *The buildings around Covent Garden (Opera House, etc.)*
   – *Why people visit Covent Garden now.*
       ○ *Photos/graphics that illustrate the points;*

    ○ *Language seen and heard around Covent Garden;*
    – *What does the history of Covent Garden tell us about modern cities?*
    – *Are changes of this sort good for London or do they present problems?*

(5) Join with students in deciding the most effective format for presenting their final report. Provide examples of similar final reports.
    – *Options for creating the final report setting out the results of the investigation include: a version on paper in a folder; a series of posters created in hard copy or online including photos and graphics; a series of labelled models; annotated maps; creation of a detailed timeline; video account of images of Covent Garden; a history set out as a comic; a PowerPoint presentation.*

(6) Get students to create a template for the final format in which they will present their report.

(7) Brainstorm with students a list of where they can gather evidence which supports or illuminates their intended topic. Join with students in listing the sources of information:
    – *The London Tourist Board: online research or a visit to pick up brochures;*
    – *Information offices at famous sites;*
    – *London Transport websites;*
    – *Museum shops and websites;*
    – *Guidebooks and history texts;*
    – *Books from the library or other museums/cultural association libraries;*
    – *Visits arranged by the school or by parents where students can amass information on the topic with photos using tablets or notebooks and cameras. Where tablets are used, students can then import photos into interactive posters;*
    – *Interviews with knowledgeable and experienced people;*
    – *Online virtual walks;*
    – *Resources obtainable from the country/ies where the student's mother tongue is spoken.*

(8) Construct a rubric (sets of criteria) together that sets out the desired qualities of an effective report, making sure the rubric is comprehensible to students.
    – *What do students think are the key elements that should be contained in an effective report?*
    – *Use examples of former rubrics to guide the discussion.*
    – *Make sure that students understand the language.*
    – *Use the agreed rubric to guide discussion with students about the progress of their project.*

(9) Begin the investigative phase of the topic.

(10) Practise reading for information using an authentic piece of writing that relates to their reports in texts and online.
    – *Use a SmartBoard or screen attached to a projector to talk students through the ways of reading a text for information: pick out aspects such as title, paragraph headings, layout, choice of illustration and graphics, the labelling under the visual elements. Underline key sentences and the key words which keep recurring.*
    – *Carry out the same process with an information website. Note that the layout online tends to be less linear and more web-like with bite-sized chunks of material presented in boxes and via links.*

(11) Practise writing down short notes either online, on index cards, or on paper.

(12) Practise reconstituting the notes in ways that fulfil the writing requirements of the format chosen for the final report.

(13) Consider a field trip as a means of gathering information.

- *Field trips are fun; they are a means of promoting authentic language while focusing on content; they bring the world into the classroom; they empower students, particularly in groups, to construct their own knowledge; they vary the pattern of school life for fatigued beginning emergent bilingual students. Where students speak the same home languages, they gain from using this language to negotiate focused information for use in the English-medium classroom.*

(14) Encourage students to use tablets (mobile devices) and video cameras to collect visual evidence. Show students how to search for and save illustrations and diagrams or make drawings that convey the findings.

(15) Supply sufficient class and homework time for students to assemble their report in its final form with the help of supportive adults.

(16) Give students time to practise presenting their report to the rest of the class (and parents if considered appropriate).

- *Give students guidelines about preparing an oral presentation and give them time to practise giving the report before they are finally expected to deliver it.*
- *Depending on the format of the report, get students to make short notes on index cards. Point out that making an oral presentation is not the same as reading sentences aloud. Underline the value of using headings to act as prompts for what they intend to say. Encourage students working together to share the responsibility for the oral presentation. Give students time to practise their presentations alongside the visual elements they wish to introduce.*

(17) Revisit the rubric: talk over with students how their report meets the criteria; discuss with students what they now feel makes an effective investigative report:

- *Have we been successful in finding out something that gives us a better understanding of the topic?*
- *Have we produced a piece of work that shares that understanding with other people?*
- *What could we have included that would have made our report even more interesting/accurate/meaningful?*
- *How will the knowledge we have gained change our visits in London in the future?*

Key Points in This Chapter

- New emergent bilingual students arrive in international schools with a range of prior schooling experiences and with different levels of English language proficiency.
- Students need to acquire both the language needed for participation in the curriculum and the learning behaviours that the pedagogic approach requires.
- Class talk is a key element in the learning in international school classrooms. Teachers need to adopt a strategic approach to ensuring that emergent bilingual students are able to contribute.

- Younger students who are learning mathematics for the first time need to learn both the content and language of the subject.
- Older students can potentially use their existing knowledge of mathematics to inform their mathematics learning in English.
- Older students may need to learn the language of problem solving if they have not been accustomed to that approach.
- Technology offers a powerful means of scaffolding the learning of emergent bilingual students in mathematics and science.
- Teachers need to offer consistent strategic support to students asked to create an aural or written report. Activities of this type demand high levels of language processing and are challenging to emergent bilinguals.

Resources

Texts used to illustrate guided questioning

This is the Way We Go to School, published by Scholastic News Non-Fiction Readers: Kids Like Me (Global Awareness) – a series designed for multicultural classrooms: http://listbuilders.scholastic.com.

Online mathematics resources

A Maths/Math Dictionary: www.amathdictionaryforkids.com.
Create a Graph: http://nces.ed.gov/nceskids/createagraph/.
Graph and Tally: www.turtlediary.com.
Math Playground: www.mathplayground.com.
OECD Programme for International Student Assessment (PISA): www.oecd.org/pisa/.

Science resources

IB Primary Years Programme (www.ibo.org/pyp/curriculum/index.cfm).
International Primary Curriculum (www.greatlearning.com/ipc/news/ipc-science-learning/).
IB Middle Years Programme: www.ibo.org/myp/curriculum/.
Videos: BBC's *Nocturnal Animals* and National Geographic's *Night Owls:* found by Googling these titles.

Epilogue: Final Thoughts

The world of international schools is never static. During the writing of this Handbook, the trends mentioned in the Introduction continued to be present and to develop at an extraordinary pace.

Rapid Increase in the Number of Schools Describing Themselves as International

The opening up of all sorts of international schools continues. Some of these new schools are being established to meet the educational needs of children from among the ever-expanding group of globally mobile families who travel the world. Many more are being founded to provide an English-medium education leading to universally recognised qualifications for the children of aspiring families in locations worldwide. Newspapers and magazines make frequent mention of this relentless drive for an education that allows young people to take up higher education opportunities in one of the English-speaking countries or to be advantageously equipped to compete in the global employment market. Schools of this type include the clones of renowned independent schools in the USA or the UK which are set up in the countries of East Asia and the plethora of fabulously equipped schools that are constantly coming on-stream in the countries of the Gulf.

Many experienced international school educators might query the international credentials of such schools. However, teachers who work in them are faced with many of the issues that are considered in this Handbook and will need all their professional skills and personal qualities to face the challenges of these complex classrooms.

A Continuing Move Towards Promoting the Maintenance and Development of Students' Home Languages

A further trend that continues in a number of international schools is an awareness of the value and importance of the school taking upon itself the responsibility for maintaining and promoting the language(s) of its emergent bilingual students. Among these schools there is an increasing commitment to the provision of classes to teach students' home languages and a move towards the beneficial practice of meaningfully including these languages in mainstream classroom teaching and learning.

Alongside the group of schools that foster the development of all the languages in a student's repertoire, there remain schools that do not see this practice as part of their fundamental role as international educators. One trend that remains true of the international school sector as a whole is a patchy commitment to mother tongue maintenance and development. Indeed, in some schools the provision of specific language teaching and support for emergent bilingual students is also less than effective. These are areas that concern the community of international educators committed to the well-being and fulfilment of emergent bilingual students in our schools. They remain the focus of ongoing campaigning efforts to convince school leaders of the value of implementing effective language policies.

The Potential of the Effective Use of Embedded Technology

Finally, the feature which has the potential to affect positively the lives of all students in international schools and especially emergent bilingual students should be highlighted. This feature is, of course, the effective and informed used of embedded technology to offer an enhanced educational experience in the classroom. I am not talking here of the innumerable new capacities made available via the latest technological gadgetry, although that is an exciting and stimulating part of the use of technology in schools. The use that I am referring to is the potential role of technology in empowering and enriching the in-school and out-of-school experiences of individual emergent bilingual students being educated in English-medium classrooms. Technology allows emergent bilingual students to stay connected to their language, their culture and their community of family and friends, whether they be near at hand or on the other side of the world. Used effectively in the English-medium classroom, it allows them draw on the knowledge and understandings they have gained in all aspects of their lives to enrich their overall learning. Used wisely, technology has the power to validate all the life experiences of emergent bilingual students and to lead to more favourable educational outcomes.

Note: I am indebted to email and live discussions with Frances Bekhechi, Maurice Carder, Eithne Gallagher, Mary Langford and Patricia Mertin on this topic. Their publications are cited throughout this Handbook.

Appendix A

The research enquiry described here and carried out by the author was designed to gather data from three groups of participants as they reflected on the lives and experiences of globally mobile children and young people in one international school. The aim of this qualitative investigation was collaboratively to construct accounts that would allow the generation of theory based on what the participants themselves expressed about the experience of global mobility. The focus throughout the study was on the experiences of emergent bilingual students being educated in English-medium international schools. A rich seam of data led to an eventual focus on identity and the formation of the self in globally mobile international school students.

A total of 76 participants representing students, parents and teachers were interviewed during the course of the enquiry. The three groups were interviewed in order to ensure a multi-perspectival account of what it means to be a member of a community where global mobility is a shared experience. A key element of the approach to this study was the view that the participants were proactive contributors in the interview process rather than merely 'vessels of answers'. To this end, I adopted a semi-structured approach which allowed interviewees to pursue their own chains of thought.

The interviews covered the personal histories of the participants, the changes in their use of language caused by their global mobility, their views about where they thought of as home, and what sort of people they felt themselves to be. Illuminating instances from the data were used as evidence in suggesting theoretical accounts of the ways that emergent bilingual students maintain and develop their identities in an English-medium international school.

Dr Trevor Grimshaw of the University of Bath was a major contributor to the process of publishing the results of the enquiry, which were written up in the following articles:

Grimshaw, T. and Sears, C. (2008) 'Where am I from?' 'Where do I belong?': The negotiation and persistence of identity in international school students. *Journal of Research in International Education* 7 (3), 259–278.

Sears, C. (2011) Integrating multiple identities: Narrative in the formation and maintenance of the self in international school students. *Journal of Research in International Education* 10 (1), 71–86.

Sears, C. (2012) Negotiating identity in English-medium settings: Agency, resistance and appropriation among speakers of other languages in an international school. *Journal of Research in International Education* 11 (2), 117–136.

Appendix B

The small-scale research enquiry described here and carried out by the author was designed to provide data about the attitudes of parents of newly arrived young emergent bilingual students in one international school. The enquiry took the form of a survey of 25 families and a two-hour focus group session attended by 13 mothers (no fathers were available). The questions on the survey were designed to establish the reasons why parents had chosen an English-speaking international education for their children. The parents were asked to rate the priority given to their reasons on a numerical scale. The survey also included questions about the number of previous moves the families had made and the use of languages inside and outside the home. Under each question, parents were given space to make their own comments.

The focus group session comprised a series of semi-structured questions which related to the use of languages in the family's repertoire, the value parents placed on maintaining and developing these languages and the reasons why they thought this was important. The women shared many stories of the way that language use had changed in their families and the emotional and practical impact that the changes had brought about.

This small piece of focused research was used as foundational material for a chapter entitled 'Listening to parents: acknowledging the range of linguistic and cultural diversity in an early childhood classroom'. The chapter was published in:

Murphy, E. (ed.) (2011) *Welcoming Linguistic Diversity in Early Childhood Classrooms*. Bristol: Multilingual Matters.

Bibliography

Baker, C. (2011) *Foundations of Bilingual Education and Bilingualism* (5th edn). Bristol: Multilingual Matters.

Baker, C. (2014) *A Parents' and Teachers' Guide to Bilingualism* (4th edn). Bristol: Multilingual Matters.

Bekhechi, F. (2011) Meeting the needs of young second-language learners who struggle. In E. Murphy (ed.) *Welcoming Linguistic Diversity in Early Childhood Classrooms*. Bristol: Multilingual Matters.

Bialystok. E. (1991) *Language Processing in Bilingual Children*. Cambridge: Cambridge University Press.

Bourdieu, P. (1991) *Language and Symbolic Power* (trans. G. Raymond and M. Adamson). Cambridge, MA: Harvard University Press.

Bransford, J., Brown, A. and Cocking, R. (2000) *How People Learn: Brain, Mind, and Experience and School*. Washington, DC: National Academy Press.

Brewster, J. (2011) The role of the library in supporting young language learners and their families. In E. Murphy (ed.) *Welcoming Linguistic Diversity in Early Childhood Classrooms*. Bristol: Multilingual Matters.

Bruner, J.S. (1960) *The Process of Education*. Cambridge, MA: Harvard University Press.

Bruner, J.S. (1966) *Towards a Theory of Instruction*. Cambridge, MA: Harvard University Press.

Carder, M. (2007) *Bilingualism in International Schools: A Model for Enriching Language Education*. Clevedon: Multilingual Matters.

Carrillo Syrja, R. (2011) *How to Reach and Teach English Language Learners: Practical Strategies to Ensure Success*. San Francisco, CA: Wiley/Jossey-Bass.

Cenoz, J. (2009) *Multilingual Education: Basque Educational Research from an International Perspective*. Bristol: Multilingual Matters.

Chadwick, T. (2012) *Language Awareness in Teaching: A Toolkit for Content and Language Teachers*. Cambridge: Cambridge University Press.

Collier, V.P. (1989) How long? A synthesis of research on academic achievement in a second language. *TESOL Quarterly* 23 (3), 509–531.

Collier, V. and Thomas, W. (1997) *School Effectiveness for Language Minority Students*. NCBE Resource Collection 9. Washington, DC: NCBE George Washington University, Centre for the Study of Language Education.

Cummins, J. (1979) Cognitive/academic language proficiency, linguistic interdependence, the optimum age question. *Working Papers on Bilingualism* 19, 121–129.

Cummins, J. (1984) *Bilingualism and Special Education Issues in Assessment and Pedagogy*. Clevedon: Multilingual Matters.

Cummins, J. (1996) *Negotiating Identities: Education for Empowerment in a Diverse Society*. Ontario, CA: California Association for Bilingual Education.

Cummins, J. (2000a) *Language, Power and Pedagogy: Bilingual Children in the Crossfire*. Clevedon: Multilingual Matters.

Cummins, J. (2000b) Putting language proficiency in its place: Responding to critiques of the conversational/academic language distinction. In J. Cenoz and U. Jessner (eds) *English in Europe: The Acquisition of a Third Language*. Clevedon: Multilingual Matters.

Cummins, J. (2008) BICS and CALP: Empirical and theoretical status of the distinction. In B. Street and N.H. Hornberger (eds) *Encyclopedia of Language and Education, Vol. 2: Literacy* (2nd edn). New York: Springer.

Cummins, J. and Sayers, D. (1996) Multicultural education and technology: Promise and pitfalls. *Multicultural Education* 3 (3), 4–10.

de Castell, S. and Luke, A. (1986) Models of literacy in North American schools: Social and historical conditions and consequences. In S. de Castell, A. Luke and K. Egan (eds) *Literacy, Society, and Schooling.* New York: Cambridge University Press.

de Mejía, A.-M. (2002) *Power, Prestige and Bilingualism: International Perspectives on Elite Bilingual Education.* Clevedon: Multilingual Matters.

DeVries, R. (2000) Vygotsky, Piaget and education: A reciprocal assimilation of theories and educational practices. *New Ideas in Psychology* 18 (2–3), 187–213.

Dewey, J. (1916) *Democracy and Education: An Introduction to the Philosophy of Education.* New York: Macmillan.

Diaz, R. and Klinger, C. (1991) Towards an exploratory model of the interaction between bilingualism and cognitive development. In E. Bialystok (ed.) *Language Processing in Bilingual Children* (pp. 167–192). Cambridge: Cambridge University Press.

Gallagher, E. (2008) *Equal Rights to the Curriculum: Many Languages, One Message.* Clevedon: Multilingual Matters. An outline of the pedagogical approach set out in Eithne Gallagher's book from the perspective of multilingual students can viewed at: http://www.youtube.com/watch?v=-tFA0IPeSjU.

García, O. (2009) *Bilingual Education in the 21st Century: A Global Perspective.* Oxford: Blackwell.

Gardner, H. (1983) *Frames of Mind: The Theory of Multiple Intelligences.* New York: Basic Books.

Gibbons, P. (2002) *Scaffolding Language, Scaffolding Learning* (with a Foreword by Jim Cummins). Portsmouth, NH: Heinemann.

Gregg, K.R. (1984) Krashen's monitor and Occam's razor. *Applied Linguistics* 5, 79–100.

Grimshaw, T. and Sears, C. (2008) 'Where am I from?' 'Where do I belong?': The negotiation of identity by international school students. *Journal of Research in International Education* 7 (3), 259–278.

Hakuta, K., Butler, Y.G. and Witt, D. (2000) How Long Does it Take English Learners to Attain Proficiency? University of California Linguistic Minority Research Institute Policy Report No. 2000-1. Santa Barbara, CA: University of California.

Hamayan, E., Marler, B., Sanchez-Lopez, C. and Damico, J. (2013) *Special Education Considerations for English Language Learners: Delivering a Continuum of Services* (2nd edn). Philadelphia, PA: Caslon.

Hamer, J. (2005) Exploring literacy with infants from a sociocultural perspective. *New Zealand Journal of Teachers' Work* 2 (2), 70–75.

Hayden, M.C. (2006) *Introduction to International Education.* London: Sage.

Jenkins, J. (2007) *English as a Lingua Franca: Attitude and Identity.* Oxford: Oxford University Press.

Kirschner, P.A., Sweller, J. and Clark, R.E. (2006) Why minimal guidance during instruction does not work: An analysis of the failure of constructivist, discovery, problem-based, experiential, and inquiry-based teaching. *Educational Psychologist* 41 (2), 75–86.

Krashen, S.D. (1981a) *Second Language Acquisition and Second Language Learning.* Oxford: Pergamon.

Krashen, S.D. (1981b) *The Input Hypothesis: Issues and Implications.* Oxford: Pergamon.

Krashen, S.D. (1981) *Second Language Acquisition and Second Language Learning.* Oxford: Pergamon.

Krashen, S.D. (1985) *The Input Hypothesis: Issues and Implications.* Oxford: Pergamon.

Kubota, R. and Lin. A (eds) (2009) *Race, Culture, and Identities in Second Language Education: Exploring Critically Engaged Practice.* London: Routledge.

Langford, M.E. (1998) Global nomads, third culture kids and international schools. In M. Hayden and J. Thompson (eds) *International Education: Principles and Practice* (pp. 28–43). London: Kogan Page.

Lewis, G., Jones, B. and Baker, C. (2012) Translanguaging: Developing its conceptualisation and contexturalisation. *Education Research and Evaluation: An International Journal of Theory and Practice* 18 (7), 655–670.

Lightbown, P. and Spada, N. (2013) *How Languages are Learned* (4th edn). Oxford: Oxford University Press.

Locke, J. (1996 [1693]) *Some Thoughts Concerning Education and of the Conduct of Understanding* (ed. R. Grant and N. Tarcov). Indianapolis, IN: Hacket.

Luke, A. (2009) Race and language as capital in school: A sociological template for language-education reform. In R. Kubota and A. Lin (eds) *Race, Culture, and Identities in Second Language Education*. London: Routledge.

Maalouf, A. (2006) *The Crusades Through Arab Eyes* (trans. J. Rothschild). London: Saqi.

MacSwan, J. and Rolstad, K. (2003) Linguistic diversity, schooling and social class: Rethinking our conception of language proficiency in language minority education. In C.B. Paulston and G.R. Tucker (eds) *Sociolinguistics: The Essential Readings*. Oxford: Blackwell.

Mansel, P. (2010) *Levant: Splendour and Catastrophe on the Mediterranean*. London: John Murray.

Mertin, P. (2013) *Breaking Through the Language Barrier: Effective Strategies for Teaching ESL Students in Secondary School Classrooms*. Woodbridge: John Catt Educational.

Ministry of Education (1996) *Te Whāriki: He Whāriki Matauranga mō ng ā mokopuna o Aotearoa*. Early Childhood Curriculum. Wellington: Learning Media.

Montessori, M. (2008 [1912]) *Scientific Pedagogy as Applied to Child Education in 'The Children's Houses'* (trans. A.E. George). New York: B.N. Publishing.

Murphy, E. (2011) (ed.) *Welcoming Linguistic Diversity in Early Childhood Classrooms: Learning from International Schools*. Bristol: Multilingual Matters.

Ninio, A. and Bruner, J. (1978) The achievements and antecedents of labelling. *Journal of Child Language* 5, 1–15.

Pennycook, A. (1994) *The Cultural Politics of English as an International Language*. London: Longman.

Pennycook, A. (1998) *English and the Discourses of Colonialism*. London: Routledge.

Pennycook, A. (2007) The myth of English as an international language. In S. Makoni and A. Pennycook (eds) *Disinventing and Reconstituting Languages*. Clevedon: Multilingual Matters.

Phan, L.H. (2008) *Teaching English as an International Language: Identity, Resistance and Negotiation*. Clevedon: Multilingual Matters.

Phillipson, R. (1992) *Linguistic Imperialism*. Oxford: Oxford University Press.

Pollock, D.C. and Van Reken, R.E. (2009) *Third Culture Kids: The Experience of Growing Up Among Worlds*. London: Nicholas Brealey.

Rader, D. (2011) Addressing transition and mobility issues with English language learners in the early childhood years. In E. Murphy (ed.) *Welcoming Linguistic Diversity in Early Childhood Classrooms*. Bristol: Multilingual Matters.

Rousseau, J.-J. (1979 [1762]) *Emile, or On Education* (trans. with introduction by A. Bloom). New York: Basic Books.

Ruhly, S. (1976) *Orientations and Intercultural Communication*. Palo Alto, CA: Science Research Associates.

Schaetti, B.F. (2000) Global nomad identity: Hypothesizing a developmental model. Unpublished PhD dissertation, The Union Institute, Cincinnati, OH.

Schiffer-Danoff, V. (2008) *Reach & Teach English Language Learners: Levels, Strategies and Pixie Ideas*. Danbury, CT: Scholastic Inc. See www.creativeeducator.tech4learning.com.

Scott, C. (2009) *Teaching Children as an Additional Language: A Programme for 7–11 Year Olds*. London: Routledge.

Scott, J. (2011) Writing and implementing a language policy in the primary section of a linguistically diverse school. In E. Murphy (ed.) *Welcoming Linguistic Diversity in Early Childhood Classrooms*. Bristol: Multilingual Matters.

Sears, C. (1998) *Second Language Schools in Mainstream Classrooms: A Handbook for Teachers in International Schools*. Clevedon: Multilingual Matters.

Sears, C. (2011a) Integrating multiple identities: Narrative in the formation and maintenance of the self in international school students. *Journal of Research in International Education* 10 (1), 71–86.

Sears, C. (2011b) Listening to parents: Acknowledging the range of linguistic and cultural diversity in an early childhood classroom. In E. Murphy (ed.) *Welcoming Linguistic Diversity in Early Childhood Classrooms*. Bristol: Multilingual Matters.

Sears, C. (2012) Negotiating identity in English-medium settings: Agency, resistance and appropriation among speakers of other languages in an international school. *Journal of Research in International Education* 11 (2), 117–136.

Seidlhofer, B. (2001) Closing a conceptual gap: The case for a description of English as a lingua franca. *International Journal of Applied Linguistics* 11 (2), 133–158.

Sharifian, F. (ed.) (2009) *English as an International Language: Perspectives and Pedagogical Issues.* Bristol: Multilingual Matters.

Sherris, A. (2008) *Integrated Content and Language Instruction.* CAL Digest. Washington, DC: Center for Applied Linguistics.

Singleton, D. and Ryan, L. (2004) *Language Acquisition: The Age Factor* (2nd edn). Clevedon: Multilingual Matters.

Straight, H.S. (1998) *Languages Across the Curriculum.* CAL Digest, October. Washington, DC: Center for Applied Linguistics.

Thomas, W.P. and Collier, V.P. (2002) *A National Study of School Effectiveness for Language Minority Students' Long-term Academic Achievement.* Santa Cruz, CA: Center for Research on Education, Diversity and Excellence.

Thompson, J.J. (1998) Towards a model for international education. In M.C. Hayden and J.J. Thompson (eds) *International Education: Principles and Practice.* London: Kogan Page.

Useem, R.H. (1993) Third culture kids: Focus of major study. *Newslinks* 12 (3), 1–29.

Vygotsky, L.S. (1987 [1934, 1960]) Thinking and speech. In R. Rieber and A. Carton (eds) *L.S. Vygotsky, Collected Works,* Vol. 1 (trans. N. Minick) (pp. 39–285). New York: Plenum.

Warschauer, M. (1997) A sociocultural approach to literacy and its significance for CALL. In K. Murphy-Judy and R. Sanders (eds) *Nexus: The Convergence of Research & Teaching Through New Information Technologies* (pp. 88–97). Durham, NC: University of North Carolina.

Wiley, T.G. (2005) *Literacy and Language Diversity in the United States* (2nd edn). McHenry, IL: Center for Applied Linguistics and Delts Systems.

Williams, C. (2002) *Ennill iaith: Astudiaeth o sefyllfa drochi yn 11–16 oed* [*A Language Gained: A Study of Language Immersion at 11–16 Years of Age*]. Bangor: School of Education. See http://www.bangor.ac.uk/addysg/publications/Ennill_Iaith.pdf.

Wood, D.J., Bruner, J.S. and Ross, G. (1976) The role of tutoring in problem-solving. *Journal of Psychiatry and Psychology* 17 (2), 89–100.

Index